THE
SHAMAN
WITHIN

THE
SHAMAN
WITHIN

A Physicist's Guide to the Deeper Dimensions
of Your Life, the Universe, and Everything

Claude Poncelet, PhD

SOUNDS TRUE
BOULDER, COLORADO

Sounds True
Boulder, CO 80306

Published 2014

Jacket design by Jennifer Miles
Book design by Beth Skelley

Printed in the United States of America

Library of Congress Cataloging-in-Publication Data
Poncelet, Claude.
  The shaman within : a physicist's guide to the deeper dimensions of your life, the
universe, and everything / Claude Poncelet, PhD.
     pages cm
  Includes bibliographical references and index.
  ISBN 978-1-62203-197-9
  1. Shamanism. I. Title.
  BF1611.P66 2014
  201'.44—dc23
                                    2013043267

Ebook ISBN: 978-1-62203-222-8
10 9 8 7 6 5 4 3 2 1

For Noëlle

Contents

List of Journeys, Rituals, and Inquiries

Preface

The year is 1947, and I am ten years old, wandering by myself in the open country surrounding a small village in the Condroz of Belgium. It is a relief to be here, crossing a valley with a meandering stream and a great orchard filled with cherry, apple, and pear trees, instead of in Nazi-occupied Brussels, where my family and I spent five years, facing constant bombardments, killings, daily encounters with the enemy, and a perpetual lack of basic necessities. Now that World War II is finally over, my family has come to stay in the countryside sixty miles to the south of the city, something we regularly did. Being able to be in nature, especially by myself, is deeply meaningful and nourishing to me.

On the other side of the orchard, about a quarter miles across, is a huge forest called Les Bois des Fonds (the Woods of the Bottom). It is thick with big elm, oak trees, and much undergrowth, and rich in fauna and flora. This forest is mysterious and sometimes a little scary, and I love to hike and at times get lost in it.

I also love to make plaster impressions of the tracks of wild animals such as deer and boar. Today, with my plaster mix and a small ax, which I use for cutting thin hazel branches to encircle a track, I enter the woods at my favorite spot and make my way to a small pond where animals come to drink. There are usually beautiful fresh tracks in the moist soil surrounding the pond, and I am hoping there will be a distinct set of deer tracks. I want a precise mold that will reveal every detail.

Suddenly I hear an explosive noise on my right—dead branches bursting and feet stamping. Turning toward the roar, I see a large doe barreling at full speed straight at me. I gape in awe at the animal flying toward me, her eyes open wide. Feeling a mix of wonder and raw fear, I do not know what to do. At the same time, I think that she probably knows better than

I, and I realize the deer and I are engaged in a strange kind of communication that I do not understand.

Just as she seems about to crash into me, she turns, swiftly and gracefully, without reducing her breakneck speed, and vanishes into the woods.

Silence once again prevails. My heart is thumping, and yet I am strangely at peace.

I continue on my way, and as I come to the pond, I find the beautiful tracks I had wished to see and make my best deer-track impression ever. I feel connected with that deer and thankful to her.

My encounter with that deer has always stayed with me. While it was perhaps the most striking, it was just one of many, many experiences I have had in nature where I felt in communion with another entity. I am not different or special in this regard; on the contrary, I think most people in this world have similar experiences. We just do not often share them with one another.

Years later, in the early 1960s, I am living in Pittsburgh, Pennsylvania, with my wife, Noëlle, and our two small children, working on my doctoral thesis in physics. My research is primarily theoretical and centers on the behavior of neutrons in space and time in confined, complex geometries such as those found in nuclear-reactor fuel. I am developing elaborate sets of equations in four-dimensional space and time, and looking for solutions both analytically and by using computers.

As I become more and more deeply involved in theoretical developments, a visitor begins appearing in our bedroom during the night. A young man, perhaps in his early thirties, stands in front of the dresser against the wall directly across from our bed, with his right elbow resting on the dresser top. I sit on the bed in something of a trance, and we talk. We continue for a while, until Noëlle, hearing my voice and feeling an outside presence, begins to stir. Then she sits up with a jolt, I come out of my trance, and the man vanishes.

The man comes back on several occasions over the course of a few months. I somehow know that our conversations are about my research, yet when I awake the next morning, I cannot remember what we have discussed. The encounters with the visitor are not frightening and are so vivid and real that even though I do not understand them, I do not reject them. I accept these conversations with my nighttime visitor as they are, just as I have accepted all the unusual, magical, and unexplained experiences I have been having since childhood. And because of my scientific training, I do not want to ignore or reject the recurring experiences just because they do not fit the concepts of reality I have learned.

I do not, however, share these experiences with my thesis advisor.

Several months later, after defending my thesis and receiving my doctoral degree, I have begun doing applied research for a major energy corporation and am very interested in Soviet nuclear physics, which differs in many fundamental ways from the concepts and approaches used by physicists in the United States and Europe. I spend many hours in the research library, poring over English translations of major Soviet physics journals.

One day I come across a Soviet article that astounds me. In an appendix to my own thesis, I had included an analytic solution to my equations for a simple, though unrealistic, geometry; the more realistic geometries required computer solutions. As PhD students are wont to do, I had introduced a number of new variables as well as their definitions and symbols, usually a capital letter along with multiple subscripts and superscripts using ancient Greek letters. Now I am looking at an article that replicates my mathematical solution for the simplified geometry with amazing similarity, including the exact same definitions of variables and use of symbols, subscripts, and superscripts!

A look at the publication date when the article first appeared in Russian in a Soviet journal tells me there is no way the author could have had access to my own research; my thesis had not yet been made available to anyone else. I have a strong feeling that this otherwise inexplicable coincidence is related to the bedroom visits and conversations, but I do not understand how. Had the Soviet author of the article somehow come to visit me at night to discuss our mutual research? Or was the visitor a messenger between us? I do not know. Again, I simply accept this experience as part of my reality.

It was not until about twenty years later, in 1984, that I found a framework with which I could make sense of the strange occurrences that had happened throughout my life. I was introduced to shamanism at a workshop in Berkeley, California, taught by Michael Harner. Before then I had run across the word *shamanism* in various articles and books, but it did not mean much to me. Michael, an anthropologist and founder of the Foundation for Shamanic Studies, has played an immense role in reintroducing shamanic practice and knowledge to people in the Western world. He helped me establish my practice on this path.

What I lived and experienced during my first formal encounter with shamanism—and in the many shamanic journeys, rituals, and other practices in the years that followed—confirmed what I had sensed since childhood: there is *another reality* in addition to the ordinary reality of space, time, matter, and energy that is accessible to me through my physical senses.

A core principle of shamanism, a worldwide spiritual tradition that goes back thousands of years, is that this other reality is as real as ordinary reality, and together they form a bigger Reality in which we live our lives as human beings on this planet. I later came to call this other reality the spiritual dimension of Reality, and here I use *spiritual* not in the sense of religious but in the sense of transcendental or metaphysical, sacred or hallowed. Others may have a different name for this dimension, such as *nonordinary reality,* but whatever it may be called, shamanic practice gave me tools to access it.

When I was introduced to shamanism, I was working for a large energy corporation and my professional focus was on energy and environmental policy. I had left a full professorship and tenure at a major American university, convinced that mainstream industrial and technological society was where work needed to be done to help bring about urgently needed policies and practices that were based on good science and respected both the natural environment and social justice. My evolving shamanic practice reinforced that conviction and expanded it through a deep realization that spirit, the sense of the sacred, needed to be brought back into the mainstream of modern society.

o   **◖**   o

It is summer 2005, and I am sitting on a bench in a dimly lit, windowless room in a small village in the Andes of Ecuador. Noëlle and I and two friends are about to participate in a cleansing and divination ceremony with don Estaban, a Quechua shaman. The room is empty of furniture except for the bench and a table filled with power objects and paraphernalia, which serves as don Estaban's altar. A few paintings and photographs of nature scenes and religious motifs adorn the wall behind the altar. Don Estaban is accompanied by his son and grandson, who will assist him in the ceremony, and by other members of his family, male and female.

Don Estaban has given each of the four of us a candle and asked us to rub it carefully around our entire naked body. He stands before the altar, lights the candles there one by one, and gazes at them in silence for a few minutes. He then speaks to an individual whose candle he has "read," providing information about the person's current life situation as well as advice and counsel. He uses the Quechua language, which is translated first into Spanish and then English.

Don Estaban knows absolutely nothing about us, yet what he says is astonishingly accurate and relevant. When it is my turn, the first thing he tells me is that I have done important spiritual work in the past—I think of my shamanic practice and my extensive teaching of the past fifteen years—and that in the future it is important to share my thoughts with lots of people, many more than I have in the past. The workshops I teach, which cover many of the topics in this book, are usually limited to twenty to thirty people. I think about the need to write a book, an outline of which I laid out several years ago.

In May of the following year, Noëlle and I are sitting in another windowless room with a richly adorned altar. Pictures of saints and ecstatic landscapes fill the walls around the room. We are visiting Teresa Santiago, a *curandera*, or spiritual healer, in the pueblo Teotitlan del Valle, near Oaxaca, Mexico. Teresa uses cards to do her divination work. She tells me almost exactly the same thing as don Estaban—that I must soon reach many more people with what I have learned.

I am thankful to don Estaban and Teresa Santiago—and, of course, to the spirits—for giving me a push. As a scientist and shamanic practitioner, with a foot firmly in each world and a developed ability to cross the boundaries, I am sharing the insights and perspectives I have gained over the last thirty years. I hope you will discover that the ancient practice and worldview of shamanism can be adapted to the modern Western world. With this book, I am inviting you to turn inward and call forth *the shaman within*.

Introduction

The aim of *The Shaman Within* is simple: to show how the principles and practices of shamanism can be adapted for use in the twenty-first-century Western world—and how doing so benefits both individuals and the world as a whole.

Shamanism is a very ancient spiritual tradition whose roots plunge deep into the prehistoric past. Evidence of ancient shamanic practices is found all over the planet, and shamanism, in various forms, is still practiced today by indigenous people on all continents. When I speak of reintroducing shamanism into our modern world, you might think I'm trying to persuade you to return to practices of thousands of years ago, or that I'm talking about repeating, stealing, or copying indigenous practices. I'm not. Nor am I proposing inventing an entirely new type of practice out of whole cloth. Instead, I mean integrating a shamanic perspective and the fundamental principles of shamanism—that everything is sacred and interconnected, that there is a spiritual dimension to reality, and that we have the capacity to intentionally enter this dimension—into every aspect of our modern lives, and developing and adapting shamanic practices for the needs of today. (For clarity, I use the word *modern* to signify the current industrial and technological world characterized by the Western world and culture and adopted by other societies on the planet.)

Why would we want to do this? What value could shamanism, a spiritual practice, and an ancient one at that, possibly offer us and our world as it is today? As both a modern-day shamanic practitioner and a scientist, I have found that the shamanic worldview is, in fact, timeless and that living with it enriches our lives in many ways.

WHY SHAMANISM NOW?

Shamanism is a way to empower and bring to fruition the spiritual quest for meaning. In today's world of materialistic pursuits, separateness, and pervasive lack of meaning, shamanism gives us the opportunity to reclaim the sense of the sacred we have all too often lost, yet long for. This profound sense of the sacred is present at the moment we are born—though, as babies without language, we cannot communicate our recognition of this presence in a way most adults can recognize. For most of us, the sense of the sacred is rendered dormant with the passage of time, pushed into the background by the relentless conditioning of a culture that values and relies on the rational to the exclusion of all else. Shamanism retriggers the deep knowing of the sacredness in everything, of the interconnectedness of everything visible and invisible, animate and inanimate, that is inherent within each of us.

Along with bringing us back to the sacred, shamanism can bring us back to who we truly are—our essence, the divine in us, our true nature, which I refer to as *authentic being*. This authentic being is the permanent part of who we are, in contrast to our impermanent body, mind, and ego. When we identify with our mental self and our ego, we forget our true identity, authentic being; the result is a feeling of separateness, which is what leads to disharmony and violence. Modern shamanic practice is a path to reawakening to authentic being. We recover our connection to authentic being, and mind and ego move back to their natural role of serving authentic being, rather than staying in their unnatural role as defining our identity.

For me, shamanism has been a deep spiritual practice, one that completely involves body, emotions, mind, and authentic being and that leads me back to the Oneness that is and that I am. In shamanic practice, it is authentic being that enters the spiritual dimension, and the mind and the ego are in service to authentic being, just as they need to be in the physical dimension.

Another meaningful aspect of shamanic practice is that it provides us with direct access to the spiritual realm. We need not go through an intermediary—a priest or guru. In fact, bringing that realm into our daily lives is our sole responsibility. Our teachers are *inner* guides, spirit helpers and spiritual teachers whom we contact and communicate with through shamanic practice. Consistent with the shamanic tradition, the best living, human teachers of shamanism will encourage us to pursue our own personal connection with the spiritual dimension; they will not control us or try to be spiritual authorities.

A very important characteristic of shamanism as it is practiced today is an equality of women and men that is sorely absent in many parts of our world. Shamanism is also open to young and old and to people of all social, ethnic, and cultural backgrounds. I have taught shamanic practice to individuals who follow other spiritual traditions, and I have found that shamanism can complement other spiritual practices, providing an additional approach to living with the awareness of the sacred and interconnectedness of everything.

Because shamanism is among the most ancient human spiritual practices and is found on all continents, practicing shamanism creates a bond between ourselves and all of our fellow human beings around the planet and throughout time. In my particular case, I have been able to reconnect with my ancient ancestors in Western Europe and their shamanic traditions, which they practiced long before foreign invasions imported the Greco-Roman culture and the new Christian religion from the Middle East, uprooting native culture and traditions. In a sense, shamanism allowed me to find my roots again—across a gaping chasm of nearly two thousand years.

Shamanic practice can also bring us into a unique relationship to nature, the world, and the cosmos, in which we know that everything is sacred and that we are connected to everything, including both the physical and spiritual dimensions. Shamanism offers a powerful way to remember and live our interconnectedness, to live in harmony with the world and all its inhabitants.

Finally, living in accordance with shamanic traditions and a shamanic worldview is a key way to address and heal the multifaceted crises we face in the twenty-first-century: violence, injustice, environmental degradation, and hyper-materialism among them. A shamanic perspective can restore the balance between the spiritual and the ordinary, the sacred and the secular, humans and nature, and humans and one another. This, I am convinced, is the only real solution to problems that can seem intractable. By reintroducing the sacred into the everyday world from which we have heedlessly removed it, we may heal ourselves, our human communities, and the earth.

Shamanism can help bring together the wisdom of both indigenous and modern cultures in the search for common resolutions to planetary problems. And shamanic practices and explorations, which are based on collaboration with the spiritual dimension, are models for the multifaceted collaboration necessary among human beings to bring back peace and harmony on the planet, between humans and nature, and among ourselves.

For all these reasons, shamanic consciousness and practices naturally belong in our modern world.

THE CONSISTENCY BETWEEN SCIENTIFIC AND SHAMANIC KNOWLEDGE

Over the years, I have often been asked by shamanic practitioners, workshop participants, friends, and acquaintances how, as a scientist, I can embrace shamanism as I do. Is this not a contradiction? Aren't shamanic practices and knowledge incompatible with scientific practices and knowledge?

As both scientist and shamanic practitioner, I see no inconsistency between science and shamanic knowledge or, for that matter, between science and spiritual knowledge. In fact, I have found my scientific training and practice to be a great asset in my pursuit of shamanic practice.

Science instilled in me an enthusiasm for learning about the world. My high school and university physics and mathematics teachers encouraged me to use my own capabilities and the knowledge accumulated by others over the centuries to probe the mysteries of the natural world. The enthusiasm for learning they instilled in me also led me to study the spiritual dimension of reality, to probe the mysteries of the shamanic world in my quest for shamanic knowledge.

My direct experience of what I have called the spiritual dimension of reality has always been an experience of the world. While I could not explain this experience using standard scientific knowledge, and while my shamanic experience did not fit ordinary-reality scientific models, I could not deny or reject it or call it merely imagination without violating what is for me the basic approach of science: *science does not reject the experience of reality*, whether or not such experience fits scientific models.

The scientific method, which I was taught from a young age, uses concepts, the language of mathematics, observation, and experimental data to construct models and theories of reality. The validity and acceptance of any model depend upon its agreement and consistency with our direct experience of the physical world. The final word is what the world tells us about itself, not what we think the world is like. This scientific method has led to continual improvements and refinements of our scientific models and theories.

The same principles that inform my quest for knowledge of physical reality have informed my quest for knowledge of the spiritual dimension of reality as well. Science tells us what it sees of reality through one window, and shamanism reveals what it observes through another one. It is not inconsistent for science to be open to the possibility of a dimension or aspect of reality that is not accessible to traditional scientific methods, yet is still part and parcel of the reality that science studies.

There is another aspect of my scientific training that has served me well in my shamanic practice. I learned the importance of skepticism: to keep searching, to confirm and reconfirm, to question even my own direct experience. Skepticism is an important tool to use in striving for *impeccability* in shamanic practice, especially where it concerns the shamanic journey and communication and cooperation with spirits. Skepticism can help us ensure that our shamanic practice comes from an authentic place, from authentic being, and is not contaminated or controlled by our shamanic ego or other aspects of our personal ego.

WHAT THIS BOOK OFFERS

The Shaman Within shows how the shamanic perspective and values can be applied with intention to life in the twenty-first century—to our natural environment, both planetary and cosmic; to our social and cultural environments; and to our socioeconomic structures. The book encompasses my experience and knowledge acquired over decades of practicing and teaching shamanism. For most of that time I also worked as a scientist, so it is natural that the book contains an unusual array of information and perspectives, including historical context, recent scientific findings that corroborate shamanic principles, and practical instruction in shamanic journeys and rituals. The information I share here comes from my own experience, from what others have taught me, and from my connection with the spiritual dimension. I include personal stories to illustrate what shamanic practice has looked and felt like to me, and the impact it has had on my life.

The book is divided into two parts. Part I concerns many fundamentals of shamanism and shamanic practice. In chapter 1, you will find a brief history and description of the principles of shamanism and basic instructions for shamanic journeying. In chapter 2, "Shamanism as a Spiritual Path," you will read about the spiritual aspects inherent in shamanic practice. Chapter 3 covers a range of important issues, including impeccability and the roles of the ego, the mind, boundaries, and relationships in shamanic practice and everyday life. Chapter 4 covers the shamanic view of death and dying, including practices to prepare for your own death and dying to "who you are not." In chapter 5, we explore one of the primary functions of shamanic practitioners working in their communities: helping others heal. Part I concludes with a chapter on shapeshifting, an advanced shamanic practice that has long been my primary spiritual path. Not much has been written about it, but it has been key to my many understandings of shamanism, and in chapter 6, I share with you what I have learned about shapeshifting and what it has taught me.

Part II chiefly concerns the integration of shamanism into modern life. It begins with applying shamanism to the family and daily life in chapter 7 and moves into professional life in chapter 8. These chapters include instructions for journeys, practices, and rituals designed to reconsecrate our busy lives and imbue them with spiritual meaning. Chapter 9 jumps into scientific discovery with both feet, showing the parallels between the seemingly disparate worlds of shamanism and science. I will show you how what scientists theorize and have learned in the lab dovetails with the ancient shamanic truths woven throughout the book. Chapter 10, "Journeys to the Spirits of the Cosmos," extends the traditional shamanic worldview to encompass our total cosmic environment. You will read of journeys chronicled nowhere else—visits to cosmic entities, including some only recently discovered—and you will find instructions for such journeys. In chapter 11, "The Big Bang: Cosmic Background Radiation and the Creation Myth," we journey to the core vibration of the very creation of our universe and explore the frequent themes found in myths of creation.

With chapter 12, we come back to Earth to explore another broad facet of shamanic community service: *world work,* or using shamanic practices to aid places and communities around the globe that are sorely in need of healing, such as those beset by disaster, conflict, and even war. Finally, in chapter 13, you will read about the complex relationship between modern peoples and nature and what is really required to heal it. This chapter brings the book full circle by showing how shamanism and science can work in reciprocity and how shamanism offers solutions to modern-world problems, even the biggest, most overwhelming ones.

o **◗** o

For me, *the shaman within* is not a learned state, a role, or an identity. It is a way of being, a process that leads to actions kindled by inner wisdom and intuition. It is a deep knowing of the sacredness in everything and of the interconnectedness of everything, visible and invisible, animate and inanimate.

If you are drawn to more formally enter the shamanic experience, I hope this book will engage your interest in shamanic practice and what it can offer you. For the experienced shamanic practitioner, I hope it provides new insights and practices to help deepen your shamanic practice. And whether you practice shamanism or not, I hope the book will inspire you to see that a shamanic worldview can help us respond to the most critical challenges of the twenty-first century.

I invite you to accompany me on this quest to transform the ways we humans relate to the world by calling forth *the shaman within.*

PART I

The Shaman Within

1

What Is Shamanism?

○ ◐ ○

Shamanism, as noted in the introduction, is a very ancient spiritual tradition practiced all over the planet, and it is still practiced today by indigenous people on all continents, exhibiting remarkable similarities across space, time, and cultures. Shamanic practices probably began in ancient hunter-gatherer communities;[1] cave paintings in France and Spain dating back about twenty thousand years have been linked to an early shamanic tradition.[2]

Fundamental to shamanism are the principle of wholeness or unity and the realization that everything in the universe is connected. Also fundamental is the understanding that reality has a spiritual dimension. For the shaman, everything that has form or substance has a spirit, including trees, rocks, people, mountains, places, plants, animals, and the natural elements. The term *spirit,* as used in the shamanic tradition, denotes the manifestation of this spiritual dimension, or *essence,* of a given entity. In our modern world, the word *spirit* can evoke prejudices and unease. Nonetheless, because it is a traditional terminology in shamanic practice and is used by indigenous communities, I will use it throughout the book. I urge you not to get stuck on any images or connotations the word may evoke, but to consider it part of the tradition.

A great appeal of shamanism is its universality of principles and functions around the planet and through time. While different cultures have introduced a variety of rituals, practices, initiations, costumes, and power objects, the internal essence of the shamanic journey, the work with spirits, and basic healing principles are strikingly similar worldwide. Practicing indigenous shamans are found today in North and South America, Siberia, Australia, Asia, Africa, and the Arctic.

Evidence of powerful ancient shamanic traditions is also found in Western Europe—for example, in the Celtic and Saxon cultures—as well as in more ancient Western European civilizations.[3] These traditions, however, were largely eradicated by the Roman invasion and subsequent Christianization, although nascent efforts are underway to recover them.[4] Over the past thirty years or so, a resurgence of shamanism has occurred in modern societies, particularly the United States and Western Europe.

SHAMANIC TRANCE AND NONORDINARY REALITY

The shaman works in the spiritual dimension of reality, sometimes called *nonordinary reality.* What distinguishes the shaman from other spiritual practitioners is the use of a nonordinary or *altered state of consciousness* that allows him or her to journey to this spiritual dimension. In his classic book *Shamanism,* Mircea Eliade defines this distinguishing state as an ecstatic trance, and he defines shamanism as a "technique of ecstasy."[5] Michael Harner, author of *The Way of the Shaman* and founder of the Foundation for Shamanic Studies, has coined the term *shamanic state of consciousness* to denote this ecstatic trance.[6]

The shamanic trance is a focused shift in consciousness that allows the soul of the shaman to journey in the spirit world, journey to and among spirits, and communicate and interact with spirits. In this nonordinary state of consciousness, the shaman obtains from the spirits information, knowledge, assistance, power, and other resources to help him- or herself, other human beings, the community, and the planet, as well as to further his or her own spiritual development. The experienced shaman moves back and forth between realities in a disciplined and impeccable way that contributes to the harmony and wellbeing of the world we live in. In a way, the essential work of the shaman is to *bring forth, maintain, and restore balance and congruity between the spiritual and the ordinary, everyday dimensions of reality.*

WHO IS A SHAMAN?

The word *shaman* comes to us from the word *saman* of the Tungus tribe in Siberia. It was chosen by early Russian anthropologists to denote individuals who carried out specific spiritual practices and fulfilled certain functions in their communities.[7] Shamanic practices need to be differentiated from those of priests, ceremonial leaders, medicine men, and other spiritual practitioners; today the term *shamanism* is often loosely used or misused to denote various practices, from nature rituals to magic. The shaman is distinguished from the medium, channel, and possession dancer, who typically receive spirits rather than intentionally going to meet them, although the shaman may do both.

In nearly all cultures, both men and women are shamans, and there is little differentiation between the shamanic functions they perform. It is much more a matter of individual orientation. The shaman usually has another, additional profession and conducts a normal life in ordinary reality.

Shamanism is not a religion, and the shaman is not a priest or a guru, although a priest or priestess could also be a shaman if he or she so desired. Shamanism is an experiential and individual endeavor whereby the shaman communicates directly with spirits and journeys in the spiritual realms. Hence, shamanism is fully compatible with other spiritual traditions and religions, and an individual's shamanic practice can enrich his or her participation in other spiritual systems. As Eliade shows throughout his book, historically shamanism has coexisted with other forms of religion and spirituality. Yet sadly, it is exactly the avowed individual, direct relationship with spirit that has been the basis for the brutal persecution of shamans by official state religions and state governments throughout history. Among many examples are the Christian church's persecution of shamanic traditions as its influence spread throughout Western Europe and into regions colonized around the world, the Protestant church's persecution of Sami shamans in northern Scandinavia, and the Soviet Communists' persecution of Siberian shamans.

THE SHAMANIC JOURNEY AND STATE OF CONSCIOUSNESS

As I mentioned earlier, what distinguishes the shaman is a nonordinary state of consciousness or ecstatic trance. A primary and central aspect of this state of consciousness is the shamanic journey in the spiritual realms. Shamanic practice requires discipline, concentration, and purpose. The shift into and maintenance of the nonordinary state of consciousness is essentially a matter of *attention, intention,* and *trust:* attention to being fully in the here and now, intention to bring about the shift in consciousness, and trust in the spirits and the help they provide as well as in one's own inner power.

Over the millennia, different cultures have evolved various methods that assist with moving into this state of consciousness. The large majority rely on percussion sound, with the most widespread being the monotonous sound of the drumbeat. An important gathering where shamanic work can be carried out is a *drumming circle.* A drumming circle creates a sacred space and time where a group of shamanic practitioners drum together, journey, and perform rituals and other shamanic practices for the purposes of spiritual growth, divination, healing, world work, or other personal or group work.

In some cultures, shamans use hallucinogenic plants and mushrooms to facilitate a shift in consciousness. In addition to the physiological impact of a regular percussion sound or a hallucinogenic substance, the connection with the spirit of the drum (or other percussion instrument) or the spirit of the sacred plant is important to the shamanic experience.

In shifting into an altered state of consciousness, the shaman undergoes a classic journey into nonordinary worlds outside of the physical dimensions of space and time and "sees" and experiences with the heart, the third eye, and all the senses of the energy body.

JOURNEYING IN THE UPPER, MIDDLE, AND LOWER WORLDS

Consistent with many mythological and spiritual traditions, the nonordinary realm the shaman journeys into is visualized as three worlds: an Upper World to which the shaman ascends, a Lower World to which the shaman descends, and a Middle World. The Middle World is essentially the nonordinary aspect of our daily reality. The shaman typically experiences multiple levels in the Upper and Lower worlds, and after many years of practice, he or she comes to learn the geography of the nonordinary realms and how to effectively and productively journey into the vastness of these worlds. The shaman also learns how to quickly and impeccably move from ordinary reality into the nonordinary Middle World and back.

Though I will give you basic instructions for shamanic journeying, this book is not intended as a comprehensive introduction to the practice. For that, you can consult Michael Harner's *The Way of the Shaman* and Sandra Ingerman's *Shamanic Journeying: A Beginner's Guide*—both excellent books. Better still, I encourage you to take the so-called Basic Workshop offered by the Foundation for Shamanic Studies, as well as by others around the world. Developed by Harner, this workshop provides an excellent initiation for Western-world individuals into the shamanic journey and working with spirits.

If you are new to shamanism, here are instructions for journeying into the Lower, Upper, and Middle worlds: Do the journey in a room that is quiet, not overly lit, and where you will not be disturbed. Turn off telephones, including your cell phone. Lie down or sit. It is important that you be comfortable and that your body not need attention during the journey. Use a bandana or other blindfold to cover your eyes.

A shamanic journey typically lasts ten to fifteen minutes, but can be shorter or longer depending on the shamanic practitioner's intention.

The regular beat of a drum will help you to journey. You can ask a family member or a friend to drum for you, or you can use a drumming recording. The drumming ends with four sets of seven beats, followed by thirty seconds or so of fast beats, and again four sets of seven beats. This change in rhythm indicates that it is time to end the journey and helps you to return harmoniously to ordinary reality.

An Exploratory Journey to the Lower World

Imagine yourself near a hole or entrance into the earth, a place that exists in ordinary reality and has heart and power for you. This could be a spring, an animal hole, a cave, a hollow tree, a crack in a rock, or the like. With the intention to go into the Lower World, allow yourself to enter the hole. Look for, feel, hear, smell, or taste a tunnel going down.

If you encounter obstacles or difficulties, repeating your intention will help you continue your descent.

When you come to an exit out of the tunnel, enter the Lower World. If this is your first journey, start moving about and explore.

When it is time to return, go back to the place where you exited the tunnel, move up the tunnel and out of the hole, and come back into ordinary reality. Be sure to write about your journey; when you reread it later, you may be amazed at what you discovered.

An Exploratory Journey to the Upper World

Imagine yourself near something that rises up, again a place that has heart and power for you and exists on this earth. It could be a tree, a mountain, the smoke of a fire, or a rainbow. With the intention of journeying into the Upper World, allow yourself to climb and look for, feel, hear, smell, or taste a membrane-like barrier. Cross it and enter the Upper World.

Move about and explore. You may want to move to an even higher level; if so, find a way up, climb, and cross another membrane into the second level. You may explore several levels if you like.

When it is time to return, go down the same way you came up, back into ordinary reality. Again, it is good to write about your journey and revisit it another time.

In both the Upper and Lower World journeys, using an actual feature on Earth as the place to start and end the journey helps ground the connection between ordinary and nonordinary reality and spark the shift in consciousness.

Journeying in the Middle World

Before you begin, select a place that you enjoy—a forest, a lake, a meadow, or a city square. For your first journey into the Middle World, it is best to select a destination that you are familiar with and that is relatively close to you.

Now close your eyes, and with the intention to journey and the power of your imagination, allow yourself to enter the nonordinary-reality aspect of the ordinary place you're in right now.

Then, with your intention, move from your physical location to the destination you have selected. In the Middle World you can travel faster than you could in ordinary physical reality and yet recognize features of this ordinary world. When you reach your destination, just sit or look around for a while, recognizing features of the ordinary world. When it is time to return, come back and, along the way, notice the ordinary-world features of the route back to your current place. When you are back, open your eyes and write your impressions of your journey.

With experience, you can learn to drum for yourself as you undertake a journey. The experienced shamanic practitioner can also learn to journey without the help of a drumbeat.

The shamanic journey is a deep, beautiful, and profound spiritual experience. No matter how often a shamanic practitioner has journeyed, each journey is fresh, novel, and mysterious. It is often accompanied by strong emotions—tears, joy, sadness—often all together. This is shamanic ecstasy.

The first shamanic journey I formally undertook was back in 1984 at a workshop in Berkeley, California, taught by Michael Harner. Especially for those new to shamanism, my experience may offer a helpful orientation.

I am in a tunnel, going down. It is dark. The sides of the tunnel are smooth and feel like black mud. I get stuck, look up, and see some blue sky through the hole I came down. I look for a way down, and suddenly I sneak through a gaping crack, go down very fast, and emerge from the tunnel into a vague, misty place.

I start walking and come to a pond. There I meet a swan. At first she stretches her neck and hisses fiercely. Then I walk slowly toward her, and she invites me to ride on her back. Now we are floating on the water—fast. I can see water splashing at the sides and on the bottom of the pond. I see brown algae and small fish.

We come to a small river that empties out of the pond, and the swan drops me off in front of a very tall tree, a redwood. The tree seems old and wise, and it speaks to me, but I do not understand. I walk around the tree and see a beautiful, very tall twin tree, its thick double trunks rising high like two arms of a chandelier. As I watch in wonder, a crack like thunder tears through the air, the tree breaks in the middle, and the two trunks fall, one to each side. In the center is a very large stone ball with small, blunt spikes on its surface. Suddenly a large white bear comes running down a small hill before me, and with his big front paw hits the stone and breaks it open into two hemispheric pieces. The bear runs away into the surrounding forest.

I approach the stone and see that both hemispheres have flat surfaces, like the pages of a book. There are writing and images interspersed on the surfaces. The writing is in a script that I do not understand and is slightly etched into the stone. Among the images I recognize are the shapes of people and houses. There are other shapes I cannot recognize. I stare at the unknown script, wondering what it means. I walk back from the split twin tree toward the tall redwood tree. It speaks to me again, and this time I understand.

The tree tells me that the stone contains the history, past and future, of mankind, linked to all else. At some point in my life I will be able to understand the script. The tree says that the stone also contains a message to teach me what free will really means and how it relates to the other forces that move the world. It is a challenge, and it requires a vision that is not restricted to the ordinary world, I am told.

Then the swan calls to me and says it is time to go back. I float on her back over the pond, return to the tunnel, and swiftly ascend to the surface.

This first journey, my introduction to shamanism, brought me powerfully home. It was as if I was tapping into memories, feelings, and knowledge that had been deeply buried within me for a very long time. I felt connected to the world in a fresh and dynamic way. My body was alive, my mind was alive and free, and I was awakening to my soul, to my inner spirit. I had returned to my spirit home, not accidentally or spontaneously, but with intention and while remaining connected to the ordinary world. I knew from then on that I would inhabit both worlds.

THE SHAMAN'S RELATIONSHIP WITH SPIRITS

The shaman has traditionally been viewed as the intermediary between ordinary and nonordinary reality, between the everyday world and the spiritual realms, the world of spirits. The shaman is a master at shifting from one reality to the other.

While in the altered state of consciousness of the shamanic journey, the shaman meets, interacts with, and communicates with spirits in their infinite variety: spirits of nature, of the various other forms and substances of ordinary reality, of the souls of ancestors and other departed individuals, of beings that have not yet incarnated on this planet, and many others. It is this direct connection with the spiritual dimension of our universe that makes the shamanic practice sacred work.

The shaman establishes strong, lasting relationships with a number of individual spirits who assume a major role in the shaman's development and practice. These spirits counsel, guide, protect, and instruct the shaman and help with his or her practices for healing, divination, or other purposes. In anthropological and general literature, the language denoting these spirits is diverse and not always consistent. Among the terms used are *spirit guides, helping spirits, guardian spirits*—also called *tutelary spirits*—*familiar spirits, allies, and power animals*. The choice of words does not matter.

A type of spirit guide that works closely, regularly, and in intimate relationship with the shaman usually takes the form of an animal. Shamanic practitioners in the Western world and general literature on shamanism often call them *power animals*. I realize some readers may be uncomfortable with this term, perhaps because the word *power* can have negative connotations, or because the word *animal* seems contradictory to the sacredness of the spiritual realm, or because we who dwell in the modern world have largely lost contact with nature. It is striking, however, that in practically all shamanic traditions—ancient and modern—one kind of spirit guide always appears in animal form. This may be because in the shamanic tradition all life is both equal and sacred, we are all interconnected, and we are one with nature. And as humans, we are animals ourselves. In any case, because the term *power animal* can evoke discomfort, I will use the term *ally* whenever I speak of spirit guides in animal form in this book.

When you have an animal for an ally, for example bear, it is not a specific individual, a specific bear that is your ally. Your ally is the spirit or essence of bear—you could say the spirit or essence of the species. Spirits in nonordinary reality have no forms. When you encounter and work with your ally, the ally will show itself in a certain form: say a male bear or female bear, a young bear or an old bear. This form may vary from journey to journey, and is often part of the message or teaching the ally is conveying to you.

The shaman also usually acquires one or more of what I will call *spiritual teachers*, spirits that often appear in human or symbolic form and provide spiritual instructions, guidance, and assistance. The shaman may acquire several spirit guides, allies, or spiritual teachers, each tending to have a specialized role and function. Working in relationship with such spirits is fundamental to the practice of shamanism. They are the essential source of the shaman's power and knowledge, and they are the entities who, through the shaman's intercession, perform the healings and other works the shaman undertakes.

A Journey to Meet an Ally

While you can meet and work with your allies anywhere in the Lower, Upper, or Middle worlds, I invite you to meet your ally in the Lower World. Use the earlier instructions for the exploratory journey to the Lower World. With your intention to meet your ally, allow yourself to start moving about there.

You will likely meet an animal. If that animal seems to want to be with you or play with you, that is a good sign that it is your ally. But ask it directly to be sure. The answer may come in words or some other way, such as a sign or an invitation to ride on its back. If the animal signals that it is not your ally, keep moving and calling your ally with your intention.

After you have met your ally, just be with it for a while, becoming acquainted with it.

In your first exploratory journey, you may have met an animal and spent time with it. The animal could have been an ally, and you can confirm this in your present journey.

When it is time to return, thank your ally, ask its permission to visit it again, and go back up to ordinary reality.

A Journey to Meet a Spiritual Teacher

Just as for allies, you can meet your spiritual teachers in any of the three worlds. For this journey I invite you to meet a spiritual teacher in the Upper World.

Use the instructions presented earlier for the exploratory journey to the Upper World. Your intention is to meet a spiritual teacher. Allow yourself to move about the first level of the Upper World, seeking your spiritual teacher. If you cannot find him or her, move to the second level, and so on.

When you meet a spiritual teacher, ask if he or she is indeed your teacher. Ask for permission to know his or her name. Spend some time getting acquainted.

When it is time to return, thank your teacher, ask permission to visit again, and come back down to ordinary reality.

Here is a description of the journey I undertook to meet my first spiritual teacher.

I am climbing a tree, a large pine I encountered years before while backpacking in the California Sierras. I get to the top and wonder what to do. Then I see a kind of invisible thread that rises up from the top of the tree. I follow the thread up and find myself below a cloudlike gray ceiling. I move through it and, as I emerge on the other side, see a vast plain dotted with low ridges and hills. Everything is white. I start walking, calling my teacher by using my intention.

I come upon a large grayish-blue structure, like an immense cathedral dome. On top is a long spike, rising up vertically. I climb on the dome and up the spike, go through a thin membrane, and find myself on the second level. There are colors and vegetation here, and I see nearby what looks like an entrance to a small temple.

I go to it; there are columns on each side of the entrance. I step inside and vaguely see a small rotunda in front of me. Next I see a tall figure slowly approach and stop a few feet in front of me. Even though there is light, it is difficult to make out the features of the figure. He is an older man, tall and thin, with a long robe and some form of a hat. I feel my heart beating faster and am awed. I ask if he is my spiritual teacher. He nods yes and welcomes me. I tell him my name and ask if he would tell me his name. My teacher says it is too early for that; he adds that a long time ago he was a shaman in Central Asia. He asks me to come forward, stand next to him, and look back out of the front entrance. I do, and we stay that way for what seems to me a very long time. Nothing is happening, yet I feel a great sense of wellbeing, aliveness, and connection with my teacher.

After a long silence, my teacher tells me it is time for me to return. He says I am welcome to visit him again and that he will teach and guide me as the need arises. I thank him, bow respectfully, say good-bye, and return the same way I came up.

To maintain powerful relationships with his or her spirits, the shaman frequently visits with them and honors them by manifesting their essence or energies through dance, songs, poetry, and various forms of shamanic art such as painting, drawing, and sculpting.

Your allies and teachers can also join you on journeys you undertake in any of the three worlds. The following are instructions for a Middle World journey with one of your allies as a guide. This is the foundational practice for many of the journeying instructions later in the book.

A Journey in the Middle World to a Place You Have Never Gone

Select a place on this earth that you have never seen and that you would like to visit. Enter the Middle World, right where you are, and call your ally to be there with you. You may see, hear, feel, smell, or taste it next to you.

With your intention and the guidance of your ally, start moving in the Middle World toward the place you wish to visit. You will travel very fast. Still, be aware of the features of the ordinary world you pass by; this will help you maintain your altered state of consciousness. When you reach your destination, look and walk around, observing details of the place.

When it is time to return, journey back with your ally to where you started from, thank your ally, and return to ordinary reality.

WAYS TO CONTACT SPIRITS OTHER THAN THE CLASSIC SHAMANIC JOURNEY

The classic shamanic journey is a foundation of shamanic practice. It is an excellent way for anyone to learn the nature of nonordinary reality, to communicate with spirits, and to be a link between the spiritual and physical dimensions of reality. There are, however, other ways to contact spirits, and in my own practice I regularly communicate with spirits in ways that are not the traditional journey. These ways also use intention to contact spirits and to shift our state of consciousness into nonordinary reality. They typically involve a shift into the Middle World, often at the place where we are in ordinary reality; tend to be quick; and can occur in almost any situation.

These brief, direct contacts with spirits in the Middle World could be described as brief journeys, and they can be very useful in shamanic practice. I will describe later several such contacts, particularly in chapters 7 and 8, in discussing shamanism in daily and professional life.

You may already be contacting spirits in nontraditional ways, such as some form of meditation, even though you do not formally practice shamanism. In this case, you have found your unique way of communicating with spirit guides, which is wonderful. I recommend that you additionally learn the traditional shamanic journey to expand your range of practice.

SHAMANISM IS EXPERIENTIAL

As we have seen, shamanism involves entering and working in nonordinary reality, outside of ordinary space-time, and interacting with spirits that exist outside of the dimension where our physical senses operate. Hence, the shamanic practice is fully an experiential one, and you learn to become a shamanic practitioner through individual experience and practice, typically over many years of training and development.

There are many ways to be called to the shamanic path, to be initiated, and to acquire shamanic power and knowledge. Differing ways are found in various indigenous cultures, although some are universal and also found in modern shamanic experiences. You may start on this path through a near-death experience or illness, apprenticeship with a master shaman, or a workshop. Once you have learned to journey and have acquired allies and spiritual teachers in the spirit world, you can continue to learn and acquire shamanic knowledge directly from the spirits themselves.

Whichever pathway you travel, it has always been the case that you cannot become a shaman by simply saying you are. Others must recognize you as such because of the effectiveness of your shamanic work.

WHAT DOES THE SHAMAN DO?

You have now learned something about how the shaman works: by journeying in the Lower, Middle, and Upper worlds and by working in relationship with spirits. But what does the shaman *do?* What is the point of this work?

The shaman acquires information, knowledge, and power in nonordinary reality and uses these to *help others, restore and maintain harmony on our planet,* and in the process, *grow internally and spiritually.* Among major shamanic practices are healing, working with the dying and the dead, divination, counseling, and in general seeking to align events in ordinary reality with the greater divine harmony of the universe.

Working in the spiritual dimension of nature has always been a fundamental task of the shaman, one that is fairly distinct among spiritual traditions. One especially important task for modern shamanic practitioners is helping us regain a sense of belonging, familiarity, and ease with the natural world. There is much to learn from nature, and the shaman seeks guidance from nature spirits to access nature's many teachings. The shamanic practitioner enters into contact with the spirits of animals, plants, rocks, bodies of water, geological features, the four elements—fire, water, air, and earth—and the visible celestial objects. In doing so the shaman honors nature's many components; expresses gratitude; acquires knowledge; seeks guidance, healing, and other kinds of assistance; and works to bring forth harmony.

There are many ways to communicate with spirits of nature. One is the classic shamanic journey in the Lower, Upper, or Middle worlds. Nature can also communicate directly with us, in ordinary reality and in the Middle World, through images, sound, and thought. It is possible to merge with entities such as trees, rocks, animals, and water. It is also common to perform rituals, particularly working with the four elements. Traditional ways to honor the spirits of nature and bring forth harmony include learning and singing their songs and manifesting the spirits in art, poetry, and dance.

Healing is a very important aspect of the shamanic practice, and performing healing work with others is a way shamans serve their communities. For the shaman, an illness or injury has a physical, emotional, mental, and spiritual dimension, and it is the spiritual aspect with which the shaman is concerned. A shaman works with spirits to heal the spiritual aspect of the illness or injury, which opens the way for the physical or emotional body of the patient to heal itself. It is important to understand that shamanic healing is a complement to traditional Western healing, not a replacement for it.

Shamans can do healing work in an infinite number of ways, depending on the instructions they receive from their spirit teachers or allies. A number of powerful classic shamanic healing methods have come down from the distant past and are still practiced today, including *ally retrieval, shamanic extraction,* and *soul retrieval;* all of these methods will be explored in chapter 5.

In his or her work, the shaman often uses various power or sacred objects, such as drums, rattles, blankets, stones, and wood artifacts. Objects acquire power for the shaman through the shaman's connection with the spirit integral to the object. In this sense, the objects themselves are forms of spirit helpers.

An essential aspect of the shaman's relationship with spirits is that of collaboration. The shaman does not use the spirits as objects or tools in order to carry out his or her work; nor does the shaman become subservient to the spirits, abnegating his or her own power and authority and taking action only because "the spirits told me to." The shaman connects his or her own divine self, or authentic being, to the divine nature of the spirits, thus manifesting the oneness and interconnectedness of all.

THE DIVERSITY OF SHAMANIC TRADITIONS AND CORE SHAMANISM

Shamanic traditions throughout the world vary a great deal, at least in terms of the ways in which they manifest externally.[8] Shamanic rituals, healing ceremonies, power objects, paraphernalia, and the focus on specific spirits—what one might call the "liturgy" of a shamanic tradition—will vary depending on whether they are found in the Arctic North, the Amazonian rain forest, the Himalayas of Nepal and Tibet, Australia,

Siberia, or in the many other places where shamanism has been and is still practiced. In his pioneering work to reintroduce shamanism to the Western world, Michael Harner culled from ancient and living indigenous shamanic traditions what he called "underlying cross-cultural principles and practices" and named those fundamentals "core shamanism";[9] this core shamanism has formed the basis for much of the teaching of shamanism in Western countries over the past thirty years.

Shamanism is not a static, rigid spiritual practice. It is a living, dynamic practice across space and time. Over the centuries, people have adapted their shamanic ways to changing local and regional environmental, social, and cultural circumstances—to the needs of the time—while maintaining the basic principles of sacredness, interconnectedness, and contact with the spiritual dimension of reality. This is evident in the wide variety of the world's shamanic traditions, and it is seen in the work of the individual shaman: in personal contact, relationship, and collaboration with spirits and the spirit world that is unconstrained by dogmatic rules and creeds.

A WORD ABOUT ETHICS

My teaching reflects my belief that ethics are of utmost importance in a shamanic practice, and I believe they need to be foremost in the training of shamanic practitioners. Spiritual forces are potent, and working with them is a sacred and powerful endeavor. This is why one must work with intentions that are as clear and pure as possible, aligned with the greater good of the whole and not driven by ego-centered desires or expectations. We must always be aware of the potential for the abuse of power, psychic intrusion, inflation, narcissism, and the negative interference of one's ego, personality, mental beliefs, judgments, and other prejudices. And in doing shamanic work for another, it is essential to obtain his or her permission and permission from spirits. Shamanism is not about obtaining personal power; it is about the reconsecration of life.

Popular and some anthropological literature mention evil or malevolent spirits. Indeed, some indigenous people use terms such as "harmful spirits." This may be one reason people sometimes fear shamanic practice, and it is a concern individuals raise in introductory shamanic workshops. Are there good and evil spirits? Can one be harmed by spirits in nonordinary reality?

Good and evil are concepts that emerged from ordinary reality, from the dualistic character of the physical space-time dimension. Yet spirits exist outside of duality and are thus neutral forms of energy. My own experience and that of those I have worked with is that if one works shamanically from the heart and with pure intention directed toward harmony, spirits will align with this intention and will always act in ways that will further it. It is possible, nevertheless, to willfully and intentionally misuse spiritual forces or energy to cause harm to others, and shamanic lore includes stories and examples of "black" or evil shamans. It has also been the case since ancient times that those who intentionally misuse shamanic power to cause harm to others eventually lose their power and see the harm come back upon themselves.

2

Shamanism as a Spiritual Path

o ◖ o

ince early in my shamanic practice, it has been evident to me that
shamans have traditionally followed two simultaneous paths: an
outer practice and a deep, private inner spiritual quest. This conclu-
sion is based on my personal experience, the experiences of people I have
taught and worked with, and my contacts with indigenous shamans. Only
the public aspect of the shaman's practice is generally talked about, and it
constitutes most of what anthropologists have observed and written about
in their field studies. It is not surprising that shamans generally keep their
personal spiritual life to themselves; this is the nature of any personal
spiritual quest.

Mircea Eliade recognizes the mystical and ecstatic nature of the shaman's
path. Referring to archaic shamanism, he writes, "[S]hamanism is important not only for the place that it holds in the history of mysticism. The
shamans have played an essential role in the defense of the psychic integrity
of the community."[1] Regarding the mythology and cosmology of traditional
shamans, Eliade says, "[W]hat for the rest of the community remains a
cosmological ideogram, for the shamans (and the heroes, etc.) becomes
a mystical itinerary. . . . The shamans did not create the cosmology, the
mythology, and the theology of their respective tribes; they only interiorized
it, 'experienced' it, and used it as the itinerary for their ecstatic journeys."[2]

A modern shamanic practice also contains two aspects: what I will
call a *service path,* which is the focus of many of the chapters in this

book, and a *spiritual path,* a personal pursuit. This chapter discusses the spiritual path.

Since I was introduced to shamanism, my shamanic practice has been my spiritual practice. And while I have studied and greatly benefited from Buddhism, Zen traditions, and nondual wisdom, shamanism has been my central, daily path, and my spirit helpers have been wise guides in my exploration of other spiritual traditions. As I searched for spiritual guidance in my shamanic practice, I was led—strangely perhaps—to a very ancient path: shapeshifting. Shapeshifting is a deep expression of non-separation, of our innate connection with nature. It has become central to my spiritual path, and I will discuss it in depth in chapter 6.

Developing the spiritual aspects of a shamanic practice, adapted to today's world, addresses a fundamental need of our times: a deep and widespread yearning for a fulfilling spirituality. This yearning no doubt finds some of its roots in our increasingly materialistic and consumption-oriented lifestyles—which are often void of meaning—as well as in a growing disillusion with organized religions. And because we live in a dualistic, ordinary-reality world, this yearning expresses itself in opposite polarities: On one hand is widespread interest in Eastern spiritual and mystical traditions, the revival of what has been termed paganism, and diverse "New Age" spiritual and transpersonal movements. On the other hand, this yearning finds an outlet in dysfunctional behaviors such as drug use and other escape mechanisms.

SPIRITUAL DIMENSIONS OF SHAMANIC PRACTICE

The essential nature of the shamanic practice is contact with the spiritual dimension of reality and communication with spirits. This section highlights what I see as the principal spiritual elements of shamanism and their relationship to other spiritual traditions.

The Sacred in Everything

In becoming aware of the spiritual dimension of reality, the shamanic practitioner knows and sees the sacred in everything and experiences the direct knowledge that everything comes from the same divine source—that everything *is* the Source. In this respect, the shamanic experience is in accord with the great spiritual and mystical traditions and the great mythologies, which, as Joseph Campbell beautifully says, all "point infallibly through things and events to the ubiquity of a 'presence' or 'eternity' that is whole and entire in each."[3] It is the directness of the contact with spirits that brings the spiritual practice of shamanism close to the mystical traditions. And it is this direct contact with the divine—without the need for an intermediary such as a priest or other religious official—that likely has contributed to the persecution of shamans and shamanic practitioners by some organized religions.

In addition to external, ordinary-reality spiritual teachers with whom a shamanic practitioner may choose to study, he or she can also turn to inner teachers—spiritual teachers and allies—for spiritual knowledge and guidance. The good external shamanic teacher will always refer students to their spirit guides. I have found that this direct access to inner spirit teachers and wisdom greatly helps shamanic practitioners avoid becoming absolute followers or disciples of a teacher or guru (whether the teacher asks for it or not), thus giving away their own inner power.

Interconnectedness

In working with spirits and experiencing directly the sacred or divine aspect of reality, the shamanic practitioner becomes aware that all is interconnected in the One. When I connect with the spirit of a tree, a mountain, a rock, a building, the water, or the wind, touching it with my own authentic being, I know that we come from the same Source. This knowing of nonseparation—that there is no subject and object, no "in here" and "out there"—is fundamental to every spiritual path and inherent in every spiritual tradition around the planet. It is also a knowing that is intensely called for in a world where, for most of us, separateness is a way of life: I am *here* and others, nature, and the world are out *there*. This illusion of separateness is what leads us into violence, destruction, and exploitation. The spiritual nature of shamanic practice offers an alternative.

Modern science, as we will see in part II, is telling us that the Oneness we experience at the spiritual level—that there is no separation—is true in the ordinary-reality world of matter, energy, space, and time.

Nonduality

In the course of my shamanic practice and journeys over many years, I have had numerous intense and beautiful experiences of the Oneness, the interconnectedness of everything. It is, however, not so much those experiences but rather my daily contacts with spirits that have raised my awareness of nonseparation, nonduality, and the absence of subject-object.

There is great likeness here to the teachings of nondual wisdom, and I have learned much from two teachers: one, Adyashanti, comes from the Zen tradition; the other, Gangaji, comes from the Hindu tradition.[4] In our own Western European tradition, Meister Eckhart speaks beautifully and simply of nonduality when he says, "The ultimate leave-taking is the leaving of God for God."[5] Here I can replace the word *God* with *the Source* or *the One* or *the divine*.

To paraphrase Joseph Campbell on the same subject, beholding God, or the Source, is the final barrier to becoming God.[6] Beholding implies encountering a symbol with characteristics, having an experience. There is me, and there is the Source; there is duality; there is a subject and an object. In a shamanic journey done with impeccability, it is the Source that I am, authentic being, that journeys and communicates with spirit. There is no separation.

The evolution of our relationship with spirits over the course of a shamanic practice can lead to this greater awareness of nonduality. Over the years, as my wife, Noëlle, contacted her various spirit teachers in nonordinary reality, there were instances—increasingly frequent—when she no longer perceived her teachers; they were formless, although she knew they were present and she communicated with them. At first she felt somewhat perturbed, feeling that perhaps her journey skills were deteriorating, that she was no longer journeying "right." Yet Noëlle has been a student of nondual wisdom for many years, and ultimately she realized that in a true encounter with spirit ("the Source to the Source," if I may say it that way), there is no form—only formlessness. Form is a feature of our ordinary, dualistic world.

Duality, the presence of subject and object, has been a primary feature of our Western approach to knowledge, to understanding and analyzing reality; it has, therefore, been a feature of the Western world's attempts to understand shamanism as well. In their excellent book on shamanism as seen through the eyes of Western observers over the past five hundred years,

Shamans Through Time, Jeremy Narby and Francis Huxley document how the characterizations of indigenous shamanism evolved in the writings of missionaries, explorers, historians, and anthropologists.[7] When the new-comers began encountering, observing, and analyzing indigenous shamans in the early sixteenth century, they characterized shamans as doing the devil's work, then as impostors, and then as mentally ill. Later, as anthro-pology progressed and Westerners started to not merely observe but also participate in shamans' sessions, shamans were increasingly described as workers in the supernatural or spiritual realm. With time, observation and analysis improved, and biases diminished. Yet the Western dualistic world-view, the presence of a subject and object, continued to be the lens through which shamans were seen. The "shaman" out there was indeed *out there,* someone apart. This view has led to a tendency to define shamanism as a phenomenon restricted to indigenous cultures. And it has led in the recent past to idealizing indigenous cultures and attempting to copy their ways. Part of what we have missed in our understanding is our link with Western European shamanic traditions, largely lost for about fifteen hundred years. More importantly, we have not gone inside to find the shaman within, as opposed to the "observed" shaman without.

Authentic Being

Shamanic practice, through direct contact with *spirits*—what I have called the spiritual dimension of reality, or just the *spirit world*—and through the experience of interconnectedness and nonseparation, is a path to awakening to our true nature, the divine in us. There are many terms to denote our true nature; Noëlle and I have used the term *authentic being* in our teaching, because this awakening to who we truly are leads to an expression of authenticity. As nondual wisdom teachers such as Adyas-hanti and Gangaji continually teach, we are, have always been, and always will be our true nature, authentic being. There is no need to search out there or "become" our true nature. As Adyashanti says, with characteristic humor, "Because of an innocent misunderstanding you think you are a human being in the relative world seeking the experience of oneness, but actually you are the One expressing itself as the experience of being a human being."[8] And when we live from authentic being, we see the sacred in everything.

Joseph Campbell speaks of the hero's journey as the path to awakening to our true nature.[9] He says that when we are truly ready for the adventure to come to the Source, to be authentic being, openings will present themselves where there were no openings before, and these openings are uniquely for us. In shamanic traditions all over the world these openings are experienced as initiations. A gate or a door opens or a wall disappears; we have an insight, a vision, a major teaching. The gate remains open only briefly, and we need to pass through it quickly, with openness and intention. While their essence is always internal, these initiations can be accompanied by external rituals, or they can be lived in a shamanic journey or practice. They can also be spontaneous or intentional.

I lived one such initiation during a trip to Machu Picchu in Peru with Noëlle. While visiting ancient sites in the Sacred Valley on our way to the Inca Trail that leads to Machu Picchu, I was told by spirits in several journeys that I would receive a new spiritual teacher in the spirit world who would teach me about true power and the right use of power. We took four days to hike the trail, which we were told was the ancient, customary way. On the second day of the trek, I fell ill with a high fever and chills and felt very weak. This lasted until the last day on the trail, as I painfully dragged myself up the mountain passes and lay on the ground, curled up to sleep, whenever we stopped for a meal or to rest. After the second pass, at 13,200 feet, we descended past the ruins of Sayacmarca, an impressive, tightly contained complex built on top of a small mountain spur beside the trail.

As we explored the site, I journeyed to the spirits of place—the spirit of the site, the spirits of the land, the spirits of specific buildings or places within the overall site. I suddenly heard a voice addressing me, saying he was my new spiritual teacher and I would meet him at Machu Picchu. For the next two days, his voice regularly came to me, but I could not see him or feel him in my journeys. At one point my new teacher's voice said to me, "You are weak physically, but you have power—use it to heal yourself." After we arrived at Machu Picchu, I was told by the spirits of place to journey in the central plaza to meet my new teacher. I was to be in my heart and open.

I journeyed while sitting on the center stone, a huge, heavy stele now toppled down and lying in a shallow hole in the middle of the plaza. Noëlle sat beside me, looking out for wandering visitors, as I journeyed.

I find myself in the Middle World while sitting in the middle of the plaza. I feel the presence of my new teacher and hear his voice as he leads me in a ritual focused on heart energy. With eyes closed, I see clearly the plaza in front of me, and I see many men, women, and children dressed like native Peruvians from the mountains, carrying out an elaborate ceremony with many offerings of fruits, grass, plants, and flowers. I ask to meet my new teacher and know his name, and I hear him say "I am coming."

I then see coming from the left, about forty-five degrees from center, a man dressed in a blue sweater and other modern Western clothes, as if dressed for hiking. I am shocked, for as he approaches I see that he looks exactly like me. I feel high energy pulsing through me and fully realize that my new teacher is me. He explains that the teacher who is appropriate to teach me about true power—how to handle it, openly, strongly, and with humility, without retracting—is my own true Self. He says that I now need to make the decision to completely integrate and incarnate this me who holds that ancient wisdom and to reconnect with what I have always known. It is an overwhelming decision. I open my heart, and when I do, my own Self, my teacher, the man in the blue sweater, merges into me. The ceremony is over, and I come out of my journey.

The event lasted forty minutes, and Noëlle said afterward that not one person came to the center of the plaza even though dozens of visitors circled around it at the time.

This journey had a profound and transformational impact on me, as it helped me awaken to my true nature, authentic being. Somehow through this profound, direct experience that involved all of me, I knew in a different and deeper way who I truly was and that it was only a matter of fully incarnating authentic being. I also knew, in a new way, the meaning of true power as coming from authentic being.

The Nature of Spirit Guides

When we awaken to who we truly are, to authentic being, we are awareness; we contain all knowledge. So perhaps what we learn from spirit guides during shamanic journeys we are learning from authentic being. Spirit guides, then, may be reflections of our true nature. And at the same time, spirit guides are themselves individual manifestations or expressions of the divine, the One. This is how we experience them, and this is the mystery.

A Grounded, Embodied Path

One aspect of shamanism that has appealed to me and was an important factor in my choosing it as my spiritual path is that it is a *grounded, embodied* path. This is very useful in today's world, because if we are to face society's and the planet's many challenges, we must be fully present on the earth.

In the altered state of consciousness of the shamanic journey, our entire being participates: body, emotions, and mind. It is sometimes said that during a journey, the shaman's soul or spirit leaves the body and travels in nonordinary reality. But because we are outside of space and time in nonordinary reality, I prefer to say that the shaman's spirit or authentic being is in nonordinary reality and the body, emotions, and mind respond. Thus, we fully embody the experience and teachings from spirit, and this often leads to healing. In this sense the shamanic practice is a timely and appropriate spiritual path because it helps us in our work of fully incarnating, fully manifesting authentic being in everyday life. Because we are incarnated beings living in this world of duality, this work is most important to me.

CONNECTION WITH WESTERN EUROPEAN SHAMANIC TRADITIONS

There is an aspect of shamanism as a spiritual path that I have found particularly meaningful in my own experience, one that I believe can also be meaningful to others of European descent: a shamanic practice reconnects us with our ancestors. For those of European heritage, this includes those ancient people who, before the Roman invasions and the coming of Christian missionaries, practiced shamanism on the same lands their descendants now inhabit. We have genetic, cultural, and geographic connections to those who came before us, so it is important to be aware of and honor our ancestral spiritual practices. A spiritual path rooted in ancestral traditions has power and beauty. Indeed, shamanic traditions all over the world have always given an important place to ancestors in their practices. For those of non-European descent, I recommend connecting with your own shamanic traditions.

My interest in reconnecting with my ancestral shamanic roots and recovering my ancient Western European shamanic tradition began long ago. For a number of years I was on a kind of intense "apprenticeship" with a Native American spiritual teacher. He was from the Navajo nation, and I served as his assistant in all-night peyote ceremonies. After many such ceremonies, during which he taught me much about the Navajo tradition and the ceremony itself and I learned a great deal from the peyote cactus spirit, he asked me if I would lead ceremonies on Navajo land.

This request came as a surprise to me and brought to the surface feelings and thoughts that had been simmering in me for some time. After much consideration, I told him that I needed to respectfully decline his offer. While I had learned a great deal of value, for which I was deeply thankful to him, and had great respect for the American Indian tradition, I had come to realize that this was not my own tradition and that I needed to reconnect with the shamanic tradition of my own ancestors. He smiled and told me this was my decision to make; we hugged and parted ways. And I started a long and continuing search for the shamanic traditions of the ancient people of Western Europe, learning primarily through direct contact with spirits.

Ancient myths and legends, archeological finds, and folk traditions all point strongly to the widespread and vibrant practice of shamanism in Western Europe. We find evidence among the ancient Celts, Anglo-Saxons, and Nordic people, as well as those who preceded them.[10] The people who lived before the Roman invasion on the land where I was born, Belgium, were of Celtic origin. Classic shamanic themes and elements found all over the world permeate Celtic myths, legends, traditions, and ancient art. These include the existence and reality of an "Otherworld" peopled by spirit beings, gods and goddesses, and magical plants and animals; animal guides that help and protect; shapeshifting; magical flight; death and rebirth, dismemberment, and soul theft, loss, and retrieval; the consecration of nature, including trees, rocks, and water bodies such as springs; various forms of divination; and contacts with the ancestors.

While there are multiple hints of a strong shamanic culture and tradition in Western Europe, little is actually known about the Celtic and pre-Celtic shamanic practices of the region. Several factors have combined to erase many of the ancient traditions and practices and create a deep and dark chasm between today's descendants of these early peoples and their shamanic traditions. These factors include the purely oral tradition of these ancient cultures, waves of foreign invasions (in particular by the Romans), and the bias in late pre-Christian and early Christian-era descriptions of Celtic religion and spiritual practices by Greek and Roman authors who considered the Celts to be crude barbarians. Other causes were the spread of the Christian church through its missionaries, the distortions and Christianization of the early written transcriptions of Celtic traditions and myths by monks and Christian scholars, and the enduring repression of indigenous spiritual practices by the official church.

In my search to reconnect with my ancestral shamanic traditions, I have used the shamanic journey and other classic shamanic techniques to directly recover Celtic and pre-Celtic indigenous shamanic knowledge, practices, rituals, and healing methods from a variety of sources. I learned from spirits of ancestors, ancient shamans, places, and nature, as well as my own spirit guides. This personal work led to the development of a workshop, following my conviction that it was very important for the people I taught in Western Europe to get in touch with their shamanic past. In preparing this workshop, I received guidance from the spirit of an ancient shaman of the Ardennes region in southern Belgium, near St. Hubert. I also received much help from tree spirits, rock spirits, and my own allies and teachers.

When we receive ancient shamanic knowledge from the spirits, much power can be evoked. As we do this work, it is important that we leave behind what we have been taught about Celtic and pre-Celtic religion and spiritual beliefs and practices by ordinary-reality teachers, scholars, archeologists, and authors who have tried to interpret the scattered and confusing bits of evidence that remain. We need to be open, empty, receptive—not biased or judgmental—so we can truly learn from the spirits themselves. Familiarity with Celtic and pre-Celtic myths, legends, gods, and goddesses may help us connect what we learn and experience with spirits to what we retain from our ancient traditions. It is preferable, however, to use nonordinary knowledge acquired from the spirits as the standard, and not vice versa. And in addition to being open, we need to approach this work with much respect and integrity.

I have incorporated much of what I learned about my ancestral shamanic tradition into my shamanic practice. It has grounded me in my spiritual path. And as I have worked to help develop a shamanism adapted to modern life, it has been very helpful to feel connected with the past and my distant ancestors.

While shamanism meets the needs for a fulfilling spiritual path in the modern world, it is not everyone's path, nor should it be. There are a variety of different spiritual paths, and while they all ultimately lead in the same direction, deciding which one resonates most at this moment in time with our body, mind, and spirit is an important personal choice.

3

Impeccability and the Art of Living

⋄ ◗ ⋄

THE ART OF LIVING

In *A Joseph Campbell Companion: Reflections on the Art of Living,*
Campbell quotes the Indian sage Coomaraswamy, who said, "Art is the
making of things well."[1] Campbell uses the examples of the Japanese tea
ceremony and poetry, where "normal, secular, common-day tools"—tea
paraphernalia and words—are used to create great beauty. Referring to
the American poet Robinson Jeffers, Campbell also defines art as "divinely
superfluous beauty."[2]

Both of these quotes have great resonance for me, as they speak to
shamanic practice and the art of living; I believe the art of living is to
be found in doing things well: every single action, every single day. In a
dualistic world—one of polarities, perceived by our ego as one of separateness, filled with objects and subjects—it means using everything we
have, secular and spiritual, to do things well. In this way, we create a
life that manifests the divine, creates beauty, and does not seek achievement as its purpose. This requires full attention to everything we do: not
making things "right" or perfect, but making them consciously, based in
the authentic being we are and in harmony with the Universe, with the
Source. To do things consciously means slowing down and not allowing
ourselves to run on automatic. This is a big challenge in an age of multitasking and an age in which we lack tribal and community support, yet it
is a form of art that is much needed in our world.

We are one being, one self. Yet our culture tends to separate, to compartmentalize: we have our physical life here, our psychological and emotional life there, our mental life here, our professional life there, our family and social life here, and our spiritual and shamanic life over there. If we hope to incarnate authentic being, we cannot be compartmentalized. We cannot limit shamanic practice to particular times and places, to drumming circles or workshops. We must integrate it into all other aspects of our lives. At the same time, we cannot develop an impeccable shamanic life if we do not also seek impeccability in our ordinary, daily life. We cannot separate our shamanic practice, or indeed any spiritual practice, from the work we must do psychologically, emotionally, physically, and socially to become fuller human beings.

For me, the art of living necessitates resisting the cultural pattern of compartmentalizing. It is a central feature of *impeccability.* Shamanic practice is a portal to living impeccably in all aspects of life.

Recognizing Obstacles That Come from Ego

Authentic being is our unchanging, permanent true nature. Our physical body, our personal ego, and our mind make up our ever-changing, impermanent self. We live in a dualistic world, a world of light and shadow, obstacles and openings, polarities and separateness. Our ego, because it tends to adhere to this duality, gives us our fears, desires, beliefs, judgments, projections, attachments, and obligations, as well as the shadows we disown, and these keep us from incarnating our true nature and practicing the art of living.

This is our shared human condition: Attachment to achievement pulls us away from authentic being. Fear and desire trap us in time and keep us from the immediate experience of authentic being. They keep us in the mind, in illusions and ideas projected on the forms of the world.

Beliefs and judgments limit us. As Joseph Campbell says, "Good and evil are not absolute. They are relative to which side you are on."[3] In judgments, we take sides. Projections, positive or negative, are related to our habit of having opinions about others. More often than not, our beliefs and judgments about others are projections of what we deny inside ourselves; thus, they place us outside of ourselves, keeping us from who we truly are. Running our life according to society's or others' expectations also keeps us away from the Source.

These ego obstacles play a central role in our stress, our sense of separation, and the suffering that follows. By contrast, when we are authentic being, the ego and its relationships recede and judgments disappear. To practice shamanism impeccably, we must acknowledge and deal with these ego obstacles. In turn, the practice of shamanism can help us to do so.

Psycho-Spiritual Tools for Ego Obstacles

There are many psycho-spiritual tools that can help us work with ego obstacles. Over many years, Noëlle, who is a wise and experienced psychologist and psychotherapist, has developed a training that uses a number of such tools, adapted from the work of other professionals in the field. I have found that they can greatly enhance a shamanic practice. The goal of these tools is not to *improve* the ego, but to let go of obstacles that impede the full manifestation of authentic being.

The first tool is based on the practice of mindfulness. Originating in the Buddhist tradition, mindfulness has been used for the past twenty-five years in the treatment of chronic pain as well as in stress-management programs for heart and cancer patients.[4] This practice encourages witnessing awareness, or pure consciousness, releasing identification with the ego mind, and being present in the here and now by focusing with ease on moment-to-moment awareness.

The second tool is a practice on projections developed by Byron Katie, which she calls "The Work."[5] We start with our judgments or beliefs about other people and use them as the basis of an inquiry about ourselves. This leads to owning our beliefs and judgments, as they reveal disowned aspects of ourselves. It invites utmost honesty and a willingness to go deep inside to authentic being. As Noëlle puts it, The Work can bring us home to authentic being and to a humorous discovery and respectful and gentle welcoming of who else inhabits our inner landscape.

Another tool is an adaptation of The Work called deconstruction inquiry, developed by psychotherapist John J. Prendergast.[6] Here we focus on negative self-judgments. This leads to owning our beliefs toward ourselves, meeting our self-loathing, and accessing and integrating polarities. Here again we find the pivotal role of awareness in witnessing and bringing us back to authentic being.

The last tool I want to mention is one Noëlle calls "the inner family of self."[7] It is based on the fact that our impermanent self, our personal ego, is made up of and acts through multiple parts, each with its own strengths and weaknesses. We are multiple players, multiple voices, multiple ego states, yet all are parts of one family on one journey: our life journey. Examples of parts we all know well include the critic, the controller, the responsible one, the suspicious one, the creative one, the playful one, and the wounded child. Applying this tool starts with becoming aware of a part of us called the witness, who observes with compassion the various parts of our ego and notes which parts are at the microphone or in the driver's seat at different times. Then we can accept reality and our parts with respect and affection, which is different from agreeing with them. This is followed by action: we inquire which part is the most appropriate to have in the driver's seat here and now, or which parts can cooperate most effectively to evaluate and deal with a situation.

These tools can further and deepen a shamanic practice, and they can help us practice the art of living in our everyday lives.

The remainder of this chapter explores themes that relate to the practice of shamanism and the art of living. One is impeccability, including impeccability with regard to boundaries, relationships, and shamanic practice and the shamanic journey. We will also look at the role of the mind in shamanic practice.

IMPECCABILITY

Impeccability can be defined as the manifestation of authentic being in everything we do in our lives. To strive for impeccability is an ever-present aspect of my own shamanic practice and my daily life, even while I admit to many instances of less-than-impeccable doing and being.

Impeccability is living with integrity from the still point inside us that is authentic being. It means being in charge in the swirl of events. It is manifesting authentic being through our personal ego, our impermanent self, without care for achievement, recognition, or gain.

Impeccability is not perfection. It has a lightness and a flow that perfection often lacks. We never quite reach impeccability, but we always *strive for* it in everything we do. In this sense, excellence and mastery can be found in impeccability; we are competent in doing what authentic being calls for, instead of just being competent in reacting to fear, fulfilling desires, being faithful to beliefs, or obeying society's or another person's rules.

Impeccability does not mean we shy away from, ignore, resist, or denigrate the world of duality we live in. It is being our true nature *and* being fully engaged and in relation with the world. Perceiving authentic being and our involvement in the world as separate puts us in a dualistic position.[8] Impeccability is holding to the permanent, the still point, authentic being, and also being engaged in the impermanent field of change and time, experiencing them as one. A shamanic practice can help in this endeavor because the shamanic practitioner knows through direct experience that everything in ordinary or nonordinary reality is sacred and interconnected in the One. Therefore, to engage in temporal, dualistic, ordinary-reality matters voluntarily and not compulsively is impeccability. As Joseph Campbell says with his characteristic pointedness, "We can't rid the world of sorrow, but we can choose to live in joy."[9]

What I call the *right use of power* is a basic element of impeccability. The misuse and fear of power is a major issue in Western culture. The abuse of and the fear of owning one's power are the same thing, manifested differently. The *right* use is a delicate point in the center. Unfortunately, most of us in Western culture have not been taught the difference between power over and power within, and we fear or refuse to be in our true original power—to know what true power is, and to assume responsibility for it. True power comes from authentic being, not from our ego, and impeccability means owning our true power and manifesting it in our lives. The modern world cries out for this kind of impeccability, and a shamanic practice can help us own and manifest true power.

Impeccability is also related to freedom—the freedom to be and manifest authentic being, as opposed to acting for ourselves regardless of the impact on others. Impeccability defines for us our responsibility as incarnated beings. Impeccability means being aware of the interconnectedness of all things and acting from this awareness; it is an awesome responsibility.

Impeccability applies to love in the forms of self-love, unconditional love, and compassion. It also means self-care: physical, emotional, mental, and spiritual. Self-care, in turn, relates to freedom, responsibility, and love. We cannot manifest authentic being if we do not take care of ourselves with impeccability. Impeccability means communicating with authenticity, compassion, and competence. And impeccability means being aware of ethical considerations and paying attention to them—*no* exceptions.

I consider impeccability of utmost importance in a shamanic practice; it is the foundation of all my shamanic teaching. Later in this chapter, I will explore what impeccability means in the context of shamanic practice and journeying. But first, let's explore what impeccability means to two other fundamental concepts related to shamanism and the art of living: boundaries and relationships.

Impeccability and Boundaries

As a dualistic world marked by separation, ours is a world of boundaries. The question is, how do we handle them, and how do we cross them? What do we bring across, and what do we bring back? What is impeccability when it comes to boundaries?

Sean Kane has written about boundaries in the way that mythtellers from all times and cultures have described them, and he provides much lucid insight into their nature and purpose.[10] In our world of matter and spirit, there are boundaries that delineate or demarcate the different aspects of what we experience as reality. The material world is full of discrete, differentiated beings. As discrete entities, we have boundaries that demarcate us from everything else and define us as individuals. I am *here,* and the rest of the world is *there.* There are boundaries between you, me, and another human being with whom you are relating; between humans and other species upon which we depend for food and sustenance; between wisdom or truth and the concepts that express both; between shamanic practice and psychological practice. I could cite many other examples. In shamanic work we spend a great deal of time crossing the boundary between ordinary and nonordinary reality.

A boundary makes possible the manifestation of individual beings and entities within the One. *Boundaries are important because they help maintain the autonomy and integrity of what is on either side.* Referring to the boundary between nonordinary and ordinary reality, Kane says that "this separation of the mysterious and the familiar has a practical advantage.

It segregates the world of the mysterious others from the world human beings have some control over."[11]

These boundaries are permeable; they can be crossed, and exchanges can be made across them. In speaking about biological boundaries—in particular our need for food, habitat, and survival and the boundaries that separate us from other species—Kane says "a living thing acquires its energy by means of exchanges across a boundary, so that the living thing remains distinct from its environment, yet interacts continuously with it. . . . Creatures consume each other and nourish each other. Life is bounded; life is in continuous exchange with other life."[12]

Boundaries can be crossed by physical matter or by energy; they can also be crossed "by words, by thoughts, and by spirits."[13] Crossing the biological boundary between living species allows nourishment and sustenance to come from the natural environment. Crossing the boundary between two human beings by using words allows an exchange between the two. Crossing the boundary between ordinary and nonordinary reality allows an exchange of spiritual energy. And in all instances of boundary crossing and exchange, the potential for contributing to harmony or disharmony requires "a sense of respect for the bounded otherness of someone or something, which we call courtesy"[14]—a sense of responsibility for one's thoughts and actions.

The essential role of the shaman is to be the boundary crosser between the ordinary- and nonordinary-reality worlds. And because shamanic practice is rooted in knowing the sacredness and interconnectedness of everything, it can help us cross other boundaries in a respectful, responsible, and balanced way.

Kane writes, "Wherever there is an exchange, there is the crossing of a boundary."[15] Boundaries are where different entities can interact; the boundary is about the integrity of each individual entity, and the exchange is about transformation. Impeccability means respecting the presence of a boundary and crossing it only when it is appropriate to do so. It also means avoiding making the boundary into an impassable barrier. The exchange goes both ways, is balanced, and is an *act of collaboration*. Respect for and impeccability in crossing boundaries is part and parcel of the art of living and is sorely needed today.

The boundaries in the natural environment that we must cross to sustain our own lives—the exchanges we need to make with other species and entities on this earth—are a major issue today. The lack of respect for these boundaries and the lack of impeccability in crossing them have led to the vast ecological destruction we are witnessing. Our species also exhibits a lack of respect and impeccability in crossing the boundaries between people, and conflicts, wars, discrimination, injustice, and violence of all kinds result. But the exchange across the boundary that delineates two individual human beings can instead be the basis for communication, cooperation, collaboration, courtesy, the balance of the feminine and the masculine, love, and compassion.

I suggested earlier the importance of combining shamanic and psycho-spiritual work in order to manifest authentic being. It is important to respect the boundary between shamanism and psychology while combining the two. How can we use psycho-spiritual tools to become more impeccable in our shamanic work? And how can we use our shamanic practice to manage our psychological issues and become more impeccable in ordinary reality?

Mythtellers, as Kane points out, speak of a transformation that occurs when one crosses a boundary between two worlds. This transformation can be subtle or intense. It is evident on the physical and biological level when we nourish ourselves with other species, plant or animal. A spiritual transformation, accompanied at times by a physical, mental, or emotional one, occurs when a shamanic practitioner crosses the boundary between ordinary and nonordinary reality. Yet, as Kane says, "transformation implies not an existence in one world and then in another; rather it implies existence in both realms simultaneously."[16] In the context of shamanic practice and the art of living, it is useful to examine further this simultaneous existence as it relates to nonordinary and ordinary reality, to the sacred and the secular realms.

Impeccability was earlier defined as being our true nature, being authentic being, while fully engaged and relating to the world. This occurs in nonordinary reality and ordinary reality simultaneously; these are just two facets of the same reality. Consciously being the One and separate simultaneously is a lifelong quest. And as Joseph Campbell says, it is not easy, pointing to "the difficulty of holding in the mind the two conscious planes simultaneously, of the multiple and the transcendent."[17]

My spirit guides led me into a shamanic journey that allowed me to experience being simultaneously One, one with the Source, and a separate entity, so that I could understand the boundary that makes us separate and learn about responsibility and courtesy. The journey uses the concept of Wyrd, or the web of life, that was central to the ancient Anglo-Saxon shamanic tradition in Western Europe.[18] According to Wyrd, the world is interconnected relationships and patterns; everything, including spiritual entities and events, is connected by an enormous system of fibers rather like a three-dimensional spider's web. Any event anywhere on the web results in reverberations and repercussions throughout it. And it has no center; any point on the web is the center.

A Shamanic Journey through Wyrd

Shift to nonordinary reality in the Middle World and, with your intention, feel, sense, hear, or see the web that connects everything. Also feel, sense, or see yourself as a separate entity as well as the boundary that makes you a separate individual. Slowly start moving on the web, across that boundary, becoming the web, experiencing the oneness with everything on the web. To complete the journey, slowly return to the separate self and again feel or see the boundary that makes you a separate entity.

Here is what happened when I made this journey for the first time.

As Noëlle and I start drumming in a room overlooking the Pacific Ocean and I shift to nonordinary reality, I can see, and almost hear and feel, a web of fibers connecting me to Noëlle, to my drum, to other entities such as the candle, the room, the house, the trees and bushes around the house, the world around me, and my own spirit helpers. I can see that everything is interconnected through this web. I also see, perhaps even more so feel, my boundary: what makes me an individual, a separate entity.

I move across this boundary and onto the web, becoming the web, becoming all. I become my drum, Noëlle, the room, the trees, the beach, the ocean, my spirits, people across the planet, people I know and people I do not know. I become landforms, other species. I become the planet itself. I feel peaceful, powerful, "planet full," sacred. I understand, in a deep and new way, that I bear responsibility for my thoughts and actions because anything I do outside of my individual self, I do to myself and everything else.

I go beyond the earth, becoming everything in the cosmos. I feel a deep sense of the sacred, of wholeness, and know that courtesy is linked to the fact that everything is sacred; naturally the sacred needs to be approached with courtesy. I become the All, I become the One, and this sensation is nearly impossible to describe, perhaps because it is not a sensation or an experience.

I slowly return toward myself. I see and feel the boundary and have a moment of hesitation, not wanting to imprison myself inside it. I move across it, feel myself as an individual, and yet also still feel the sense of Oneness, of being the Whole. I know then that nothing matters except this Oneness, this Wholeness. I come back to ordinary reality, feeling at peace, calm, nourished.

Impeccability in Relationships

Impeccability in relationships means respecting the presence of a boundary between ourselves and another, approaching it with courtesy and authenticity, and when appropriate, moving across the boundary and back, making an exchange that is balanced and harmonious. It means relating as an individual and as the One. It requires assuming full responsibility for our individual actions. These principles apply to relationships with ourselves, others, society, the rest of nature, the world, spirits, and the divine.

It is a sad but common experience for most of us that when we relate to another entity, parts of our personal ego are often in control and dictate how we approach and cross the boundary. If the part is the proud one, the arrogant one, the fearful one, the greedy one, the manipulative one, the abusive one, the spiritual one, and so on, there is often lack of respect and courtesy for the other, an inappropriate crossing of the boundary, an invasion of the other realm, a lack of balanced exchange, and taking without being offered. The outcome can be harm and disharmony. And the situation is not made any easier when the other also relates solely from his or her personal ego, which can readily evoke the wounded part, the proud part, or the self-righteous part of ourselves.

The subject of relationships is vast, and this book is not the place to treat it adequately. I wish only to touch upon it as an important issue and share tools that I have found useful in relating.

I-Thou, I-It

This tool is based on the simple yet profound concept developed by the twentieth-century philosopher Martin Buber; I call it "I-Thou, I-It."[19] Although Buber developed it in discussing relationships between human beings, it is equally useful in regard to many kinds of relationships, such as with groups, nature, and spirits. An I-Thou relationship between human beings is between two authentic beings, in the here and now—an authentic dialogue. To be authentic being, one must see the other as authentic being; and to see the other as authentic being, we must be authentic being.

Lawrence Fagg discusses the I-Thou concept in *Two Faces of Time,* his book on time as seen by modern physics and by the major religions: "Such a dialogue is a unique happening in that moment and will never happen in the same way again. All concerns about making an impression, looking good, or image building have evaporated; the two in dialogue are sharing themselves in the unplanned grace of the full living present."[20] An I-Thou relationship respects the boundary that defines each individual, so each member of the relationship can fully express authentic being through his or her individuality. The I-Thou is subject to subject, a connection.

By contrast, an I-It relationship is subject to object, a separation. The other becomes a thing; the I uses the other for his or her own advantage or purpose and tries to dominate, control, or manipulate the other.[21] It is easy to fall into the I-It mode unconsciously. I-It is often a favorite defense, or justification, for many of our personal ego parts—the proud one, the greedy one, the manipulative one, the abusive one, the arrogant one, and yes, even the spiritual one.

While I-Thou, I-It, as a tool, does not have a formal series of steps to follow, it is useful before and during a dialogue or interaction and as a basis for inquiry afterward if a conversation did not feel fully harmonious or authentic. I also find it beneficial to seek guidance and counsel from my allies and other spirit guides when I use this tool with another person.

Conscious Speech and Nonviolent Communication

There are two other tools I have found useful in relating with people. Both implicitly use the I-Thou concept. One is Conscious Speech, used by transpersonal psychologist Gay Luce in her Nine Gates Mystery School; it uses intentions to create a safe container for the topics to be addressed in the dialogue.[22] It is particularly effective when conflict, misunderstanding, or hostility is present in a relationship. The other is Nonviolent Communication (NVC), a system developed by Marshall Rosenberg.[23] The core steps of NVC are making observations rather than evaluations or judgments; expressing the feeling that an observation arouses; disclosing the need that accompanies this feeling; and making a request of the other—not a demand—related to the need. I have found NVC particularly useful in getting my personal ego parts, especially those that tend to be destructive, out of the way, and in helping me respect the other I'm in communication with, as well as myself.

It is not within the scope of this book to discuss these tools in more detail, so I invite the interested reader to explore the literature available on each. I have found that—like I-Thou, I-It—they become easier to use with practice, and that authentic communication becomes quite contagious!

IMPECCABILITY IN SHAMANIC PRACTICE, SHAMANIC JOURNEYS, AND THE RELATIONSHIP WITH SPIRITS

I mention impeccability in one's shamanic practice frequently in this book and in my teaching because, for a shamanic practitioner, impeccable shamanic practice is an essential part of the art of living.

Impeccability in shamanic practice means practicing as authentic being, manifesting authentic being through the various parts of our personal ego—which participates, as do body and mind, in shamanic work. Our ego is then at the service of authentic being, operating in the background. However, just as various parts of our ego take control of our thoughts, behaviors, and actions in our daily lives, one or more parts of our ego can take charge in our shamanic journeys, practices, and rituals, relegating authentic being to the background.

It is not easy to recognize this situation when we journey, for the ego parts that are in control are usually convinced that this is best. It is important for shamanic practitioners to regularly ask themselves, who is journeying? Which ego parts are contributing to a good journey or ritual and which hinder it? The ego parts we must be particularly aware of include the one attracted to power, the narcissist, the healer, the teacher, and the spiritual or shamanic ego, among others.

Here is a simple inquiry that can help identify those parts of our ego that may be inappropriately interfering with our shamanic practice.

An Inquiry into Ego

Start by doing a quick journey to ask your allies to help you. Returning to ordinary reality, sit down with a pen and paper or open a file on your computer. Go inside yourself, think of the times you have journeyed or perhaps enacted a ritual, and write down the parts of yourself that may have been in charge during those times. They may differ according to the type of journey—for example, healing or divination—or depending on other circumstances. Be open and let your inner witness come to the fore. Deepen the inquiry with as much honesty and self-disclosure as possible, but do not be too hard on yourself; approach this as an act of discovery, of exploration. Questions you may want to ask include: Which parts want to interfere or control or be in charge? When you are having a difficult time journeying, which part inside of you thinks he or she should be leading the journey? When specific ego parts are attempting to lead the journey, what needs are they trying to meet by doing so?

Another issue of impeccability in one's shamanic practice has to do with power and collaboration. My experience has taught me to be wary when

I hear someone say, "I did this because spirits told me so." We can misuse, abuse, or fear our power when we work with spirits.

Whether we do it to learn, heal, help others, or grow spiritually, working with spirits is a matter of *collaboration*. We who are incarnated must appreciate this fact and take responsibility for crossing boundaries. If our focus is on our ego self—specifically what we call our spiritual or shamanic ego—and authentic being and the spirits are relegated to the background, we are not collaborating. Instead, we are engaging in an abuse of power, and we can portray messages or guidance from our shamanic ego as coming from the spirits. Making spirits the focus while pushing authentic being into the background is not collaboration either; it can be fear of owning our power. Focus on the ego leads to power abuse and narcissism; focus on the spirits leads to fear of power and lack of responsibility.

For example, if a group of shamanic practitioners journeys with the intention of providing advice to a member of the group on a health problem, one of them who has the shamanic ego in charge could come up with advice based on his or her prejudices or beliefs, yet portray it as coming from spirits. Another member of the group may put spirits in the lead and authentic being in the background (which probably means a fearful ego part in the foreground); this person may be tempted to offer advice when it is not appropriate to do so publicly—because, they say, it came from spirits.

When authentic being and spirits are truly collaborating, there is ultimately no authentic being by itself or spirits by themselves; all is the One, and the issues of misuse of power do not come up. The shamanic practitioner is humble and powerful naturally.

The Spiritual or Shamanic Ego

An important and subtle part of our ego is what the nondualism teacher Adyashanti has called the *spiritual ego*.[24] In the context of this book, it can be called the *shamanic ego*. The shamanic ego is a subtle but sturdy obstacle that tries to define and control our shamanic and spiritual life, rather than letting authentic being take the lead. It is a particularly difficult part of ourselves to recognize and acknowledge because it can skillfully masquerade as authentic being. And it is very good at forming alliances with other difficult parts of our ego, such as the narcissist, the power seeker, the self-righteous, the teacher, or the healer.

An important aspect of shamanic impeccability is to become keenly aware of this common presence in our inner family of self, to become sensitive to its energy and its strategies, and to welcome it as it is without attempting to fix it. Our task is to differentiate this shamanic ego from our innate longing to return home to the Source, to relate to the shamanic ego rather than identify with it.

What is this shamanic ego, what does it do, and how does it manifest itself in our shamanic practice and our daily lives? It is a mental form of self. It thinks and speaks in spiritual and shamanic terms and concepts, such as *soul, awakening, enlightenment, spirit, energy,* and *initiation.* It comes from outside ourselves, from our cultural and spiritual conditioning and the shamanic and spiritual circles we frequent. It is based not on the here and now, but on the past, emerging from what we have read, heard, and seen, and on the future, our plans for what we will do and how we will be seen.

The shamanic ego evaluates whether we are superior, different, or have arrived and are part of the spiritual or shamanic elite. Narcissism, arrogance, and power trips reside with this form of ego, as does the fear that we might be narcissistic, arrogant, or worthless.

Another manifestation of the shamanic ego is addiction to peak experiences—the exotic, the powerful journey, the highs that one seeks to maintain. The shamanic ego is dedicated to judging and controlling the rest of our ego—and not just ours, but others' as well. It aims to run our shamanic practice and is convinced it is doing the right kind of shamanic work. Most shamanic practitioners who are willing to look inside are familiar with it.

There is nothing wrong with having a shamanic ego; it has a role to play in the theater of human consciousness. The problems arise when it is in control, commanding most of our attention and life force with its relentless evaluation—"Am I powerful enough? Too powerful? Am I seen as a powerful and wise shaman?"—and with its desire to be a shaman and seek enlightenment.

How can the shamanic ego be so strong and have such an influence on our shamanic practice? Because it mimics authentic being very well, with its avowed focus on our shamanic and spiritual practice, and because it is in direct relationship to our fear of embodying authentic being—the surrender this embodiment implies, the freedom it entails, and the consequences of assuming complete responsibility for who we are when we completely trust it.

How can we deal with this shamanic ego? Attempting to banish, imprison, or overpower it will not work, for it is part of us. It is much more effective to meet, investigate, and welcome it, to include its presence, fully experience it, and discover—to our surprise—the emptiness within it. In other words, we want to *know* it, but not *be* it.

When we run from the shamanic ego or resist it, we constrict our life force by desperately attempting to be what we *should be* while being haunted by what we think we *are*.[25] But with direct, continued, and honest inquiry into the shamanic ego, we can learn to recognize it easily. We can plainly see it as truth giver and truth judge, operating according to right and wrong and reacting with a system of judgments and blame, rewards and punishments—a figment of a dualistic world.

Gently inquire of yourself: In what ways do I judge, blame, and punish—with spite, with harsh words, by withholding love, by manipulating for the sake of perceived spiritual advancement? How do I judge and reward—with flattery, praise, treats? Who am I without the beliefs of right and wrong, judgment and blame, rewards and punishments?[26] Whatever may be going on in our dualistic world, be who you always are—authentic being—and, without judgment or blame, see the shamanic ego for what it is: a fictional overlay, an artificiality, a belief, an assumption.

We can use our shamanic practice to help us in this inquiry.

A Journey of Inquiry into the Shamanic Ego

Journey to your spirit helpers and ask if they will guide you in finding out when and under what circumstances your shamanic ego tends to take charge. Ask for advice on how you can become aware of when it does. I have found it useful to also ask spirits for an image that represents the shamanic ego. When you return from your journey, draw the picture of your shamanic ego or make a three-dimensional representation of it. You can then create a ritual, perhaps with input from your spirit helpers, in which you can show the representation of your shamanic ego to the world and declare aloud, with full attention and clear intention, "This is my shamanic ego. I honor it. I bless it. This is not who I am." As with all rituals, it is always preferable, if possible, to have other people participating and acting as witnesses.

Relationship with Spirits

How we relate with spirits is an important aspect of our practice that is often neglected or ignored. When we relate with spirits as authentic being, there is no separation; we are one with the spirits. We are them, and they are us, and the various parts of our ego are at the service of authentic being as we relate to the spirits. Our work with spirits is a work of collaboration on both sides of the boundary between nonordinary and ordinary reality.

At the same time, we know that there are parts of our ego—in particular the shamanic ego, the one attracted to power, the self-righteous one, and the narcissistic one—who shun collaboration. This is why it is important to inquire and be aware of *who* is relating with the spirits and whether any aspect of ego is playing an undue or detrimental role in the relationship.

I have found it useful to use the I-Thou, I-It concept when inquiring into my relationship with spirits. Are there times when, perhaps unconsciously, I relate to spirits from an I-It point of view? Are there times when I use my allies or spirit teachers because I need or want something, when I make demands on the spirits, when I assume spirits are there for me, or when I curtly dismiss spirits after I have gotten what I want? An I-Thou relationship with spirits, by contrast, is one imbued with courtesy, respect, love, appreciation, and gratitude. This is why I have found it useful in all my encounters with spirits to start by honoring and blessing them, asking permission to work with them, and ending my visits by expressing my gratitude.

Crossing the Boundary Back into Ordinary Reality

So far we have talked about impeccability in the shamanic practice after we have crossed into nonordinary reality—for example, during a shamanic journey. It is equally important to be impeccable when we return to ordinary reality, when we make an exchange across the boundary between realities and bring back gifts. Whether we are working alone, with a group such as a drumming circle or in a workshop setting, or with a client—and whether our journey is exploratory, for divination, for healing, or of some other kind—it is important to manifest in ordinary reality what we have received or learned from spirits. This is an essential task of the shamanic practitioner.

At a minimum, this manifestation can take the form of recalling what happened during the journey. Writing down what transpired has always been encouraged because we can easily forget the content and details of our journeys, just as we easily forget the content and details of dreams. When we are working with a client, verbally sharing the journey is usually indicated, and when we are working with a group, such sharing is also usually important and beneficial.

We also manifest what we bring back from our journeys in our everyday actions; this is another reason it is important to practice impeccability in bringing back into ordinary reality the content and information from a journey or other shamanic exercise: we will live what we have learned.

Because it takes place in nonordinary reality, a shamanic journey is an energy experience, outside of space, time, matter, or physical reality. Our mind translates these experiences into concepts, symbols, images, stories, and words, using ordinary-reality concepts and language—language developed to discuss ordinary-reality matters. Shamanic practitioners know well that this translation is imperfect and incomplete and does not fully reflect our nonordinary-reality experiences. It is only a description of our observation, of our experience. While such a description is not an interpretation, each of us uses his or her own physical-reality concepts and language to convey it.

Later, the mind interprets the experience, and such interpretation in itself is not bad as long as we can clearly differentiate between translation and interpretation. The soul—authentic being—along with the body and the mind experiences the journey, for we are one incarnate being. So while it is often useful, the mind's interpretation needs to resonate with body and soul.

So what does impeccability mean when sharing a shamanic journey with another person or with a group? It means we need authenticity and full presence when we are sharing. The ego must be at the service of authenticity. Sharing must be done appropriately and with generosity. This is a part of the art of living that we need to learn.

When sharing, it is important to convey whether we are describing or interpreting our experience. Interpretation is fine and can be useful, as long as it is labeled as such, but we must take care to avoid introducing projections, beliefs, judgments, and other stuff of the ego. It is helpful to be aware of *who* among our inner family of parts is sharing.

Impeccability in sharing also means being aware of linear time and other people's need to share, and this awareness often entails limiting our sharing to highlights of the journey. In a group, even a group of two, listening is as much a part of the sharing process as giving our own experience is. We listen with respect, openness, and courtesy, not judging or evaluating, and we refrain from interpreting. Awareness of *who* is listening is just as important as awareness of who is speaking. In both sharing and listening, just as in journeying, we need full intention, attention, and trust.

Sharing is important in shamanic practice. Sharing a journey is a form of storytelling, an art we have largely lost and one we can benefit greatly from redeveloping. For poet and essayist Robert Bringhurst, oral culture is "a key to our continued coexistence with the world. . . . Rekindling oral culture means rejoining the community of speaking beings—sandhill cranes, whitebark pines, coyotes, wood frogs, bees and thunder."[27] I could add rocks, mountains, and oceans to the list. A shamanic journey, when shared, can evoke the same response as a myth. For Joseph Campbell, the living mythological symbol is an "affect image," one that "talks directly to the feeling system and to the soul, and immediately elicits a response." When a mythical symbol is shared, he says, "there is some kind of throb of resonance within, responding to the image shown without, like the answer of a musical string to another equally tuned." The same happens when a shamanic journey is shared. In group sharing, a "sort of magical accord" can thus unite the members of the group, the manifestation of a "spiritual organism."[28] We share to manifest our connectedness with others. Journeys are not just personal; they are universal. We share to provide mutual teaching and learning. We share to clarify our own journey experience. Through sharing, group members can benefit from the experiences of others, and the wisdom of the spirits can be amplified.

When Noëlle and I journey together, at home, on a hike, or during our many travels, we always share our journeys with each other. For us, this sharing is always a special time of deep intimacy and beauty, alive with the freshness of new discoveries.

THE MIND'S ROLE IN SHAMANIC JOURNEYING

Some of the most frequently asked questions in shamanic workshops have to do with the mind's role—or interference—in the shamanic journey: "Am I making this up?" "How do I know it is not my imagination, or my mind, that is creating the journey?" "I'm in the here and now, my intention is clear, and yet it seems that my mind always wants to come along and interfere. What can I do?" "When I do my shapeshifting practice, my mind is always present. Is that right?"

Our mental capacity is part of who we are. Yet for most shamanic practitioners, and for much of the time we are practicing, the mind seems to control who we are and what we do. It tends to interfere, chatter, judge, criticize, compare, and generally mess up our shamanic work, and we have a love-hate relationship with it. Therefore, important aspects of impeccability in the shamanic practice include understanding the role of the mind and differentiating between its positive and negative contributions.

In the modern world, the mind—and in particular the intellect, our conscious mental capacities—is revered. The mind is considered the shining trait of being human. And indeed, it is a powerful faculty. It has, however, a tendency to team up with the various aspects of ego in our internal family of self. We know this all too well, having experienced the resulting judgments, criticisms, blame, projections, and denials. We could say that the mind acts as an accomplice with the inner critic or judge. The mind is also often the source of the emotions—both welcome and unwelcome—that course through our bodies.

In shamanic practice the mind can join with the narcissist in us—or the healer, the power seeker, or the part of us that is afraid to fail—and interfere with shamanic work. It can join with the teacher in us and become focused on performance. It can also team up with the shamanic ego, and their collaboration will often pass as authentic being. The outcome—a message, a healing, or a ritual—is couched in shamanic and spiritual terms, in shamanic gestures, and in shamanic expressions, but it does not have its source in authentic being and in the spirits; instead its source is the mind and the shamanic ego.

Yet the mind is a beautiful instrument. It shows its wondrous nature in the way it delves into the mystery of the physical world and crafts strategies, tools, and technologies that help and nourish others and the planet. And it can play a beautiful and supportive role in a shamanic practice.

The mind is part of the One. It is part of who we are as incarnated being. When we are authentic being, the mind is at the service of authentic being; it is not in control, with the rest of us following along, or identified with who we are. The mind needs to be seen and related to as a very useful *tool* for authentic being. We can use it without identifying with it. As Bringhurst says, "Thinking and speaking are as natural to humans as swimming is to fish."[29] The human mind does not make us any better or worse than other creatures, and it does not define who we are any more than swimming defines what a fish is. The mind is at the service of our true nature.

What is the appropriate role of the mind in ordinary and nonordinary reality? It has an important function in comprehending the world, ordinary reality—what we need to do to survive and live in harmony, joy, and beauty with the world, even if we cannot ever fully comprehend the world. The mind also serves an important role in our relationship with others, in understanding and communicating. And it stores the wisdom and truth we acquire during our lifetime.

In nonordinary reality, the mind keeps track of what is happening; it observes and takes notes. Another important role is to translate information received from spirits into symbols, images, and words and, most importantly, to help us cross impeccably back from nonordinary to ordinary reality by making the nonordinary reality's information or energy relevant to ordinary reality. The mind does this by interpreting symbols, symbolic details, events, and messages of a shamanic journey, making connections and providing a bigger context.

The mind can also fulfill a very appropriate function when it teams up with the skeptic in us. Skepticism is an essential attribute for both the scientist and the shamanic practitioner. The skeptic can inquire and verify that our shamanic ego is not in charge of our shamanic work and that the information we bring back from a journey does not come from our personal ego. It is always good to be skeptical and to honestly inquire. But we must also avoid the polarity, the inappropriate role of the skeptic. Avoiding this inappropriate role is particularly relevant when the mind and the skeptic join with the part in us that lacks confidence and rejects everything that is happening in nonordinary reality: "I'm sure I am making all of this up." "Nothing is happening."

A Journey to Remember the Role of the Mind

A useful shamanic exercise is to journey and ask spirit to indicate to you a small object that will become a power object for you and represent the true nature of the mind. This could be a stone, a piece of wood, jewelry, or any other small thing. It will remind you of the true nature and appropriate role of the mind when you need to remember it. You can also ask for a ritual to empower this object and to welcome and honor the mind in its true nature and appropriate role.

4

The Art of Dying

○ ◑ ○

I n modern societies, we tend to put a negative stamp on death and dying, and we often ignore or deny death and shy away from the topic. Death is often seen as a failure, and we spend enormous amounts of money and other resources to prevent or delay death as much as possible—at least when the death in question is that of a human being whom modern society happens to value. Death is a subject that can make us uncomfortable or afraid, particularly when facing our own death or that of friends or relatives. And yet death is an essential part of life; in fact, in many ways it defines and empowers life.

Death is a central and critical aspect of all spiritual traditions, including the shamanic tradition. It is key to the art of living. Shamanic practice can help us understand and know death, prepare for and accept our own death, and become more aware of death as an inherent part of authentic being. I cannot do justice to this vast, complex, and mysterious subject here. Yet it is such an important topic and such an integral part of shamanic practice that I will address it briefly.

When we think about death, we usually think of the death of ourselves as human beings or the death of other so-called living species, plant or animal. Death is the end of our bodies, our egos, of the form into which we incarnated as pure spirits. And it is important that we learn about this aspect of death, that we prepare for our own, and that we integrate this knowledge and preparation into our daily lives.

Yet death also has a much broader meaning, one that is equally important to attend to. There is death from moment to moment, as in the mindfulness practice of letting go of the last moment and moving into the next moment; we die to one and are born into the next. There is the dying to "who we are not," so as to be who we truly are, authentic being. Death is also the recurrent letting go of the old as we move into the new.

The body's death is inevitable. Birth, life, and death are one whole. Without incarnated life there is no death, and without death there is no incarnated life. In spiritual traditions, our individual death is viewed as a transformation in which we leave the physical form to be pure consciousness, pure spirit. We are authentic being no longer incarnated.

Death is a difficult challenge for the ego, the personal self. To the extent that we identify with the ego; that the ego and the mind are in control; and that we think of ourselves as this body, this mind, and this ego, it is terrifying to contemplate death because it means the loss of our identity as the ego perceives it. Our egos like stability and continuity. Yet nothing in the ordinary world is stable or constant. Everything changes all the time, and this fact is an invitation to see death as part of that change.

All spiritual traditions speak similarly of death and the afterlife, in meaning if not in specific images. All shamanic cultures have death and resurrection initiations to prepare us for death and life by enabling and empowering transformations that bring us closer to living as authentic being. In spiritual traditions, death is often portrayed as a beacon in life. We can use our understanding and our awareness of death as a way to come back to authentic being and remain it as much as possible as we go through life.

Much of our anxiety about our own death and death in general, as well as about impending catastrophes in our personal lives and in the world at large, results from not accepting that everything in our physical world comes and goes—everything ends. The personal ego likes to grasp, and grasping is a major source of our problems throughout life. What we grasp, in fact, cannot be held because nothing in the physical world is permanent. What is permanent is the Source.

The physical world's impermanence is central to many spiritual traditions and their teachings about death. If we are at peace with impermanence, accepting that things come and go, the death of the cosmos is perfectly acceptable, just as is our own death. This does not mean that we should not take action when confronted by a dangerous situation;

it means that we are at peace while undertaking the effort.[1] As we gain through shamanic and psycho-spiritual practices an awareness of impermanence, we learn how to live a full, vibrant life as authentic being.

A number of shamanic practices can help us more fully understand, integrate, prepare for, and live our death. These practices relate to the cycle of birth, life, death, and rebirth; the need to kill in order to feed our lives; preparing for and experiencing death; resolving unfinished business; dying to "who we are not"; the role of the shaman as psychopomp; and helping people who are dying.

THE CYCLE OF BIRTH, LIFE, DEATH, AND REBIRTH

The natural world around us can be characterized by a cycle of birth, life, death, and rebirth. This cycle plays out in the so-called living species on this planet, in our planet's geologic forms, and in the multitude of stars in the cosmos.

A simple shamanic journey can help us deepen our understanding of death and experience the organic, natural cycle of death and birth.

A Journey to Understand Death

With the intention of merging with a plant and experiencing its life cycle, walk outside in nature and let your senses become receptive to a plant calling you. Briefly journey to the plant's spirit and ask for its support and for permission to do the work. Then, standing, sitting, or lying beside the plant and led by its spirit, journey to merge with it. In merging you unite, become one, with the plant and its spirit. Start as a seed in the ground, and experience the entire life cycle of the plant. Take your time to fully experience each stage, from seed to seedling, from fully grown plant to withered husk spreading new seeds. When you are finished, thank the plant's spirit. If you like, you can leave an offering, such as a pinch of tobacco, sage, or cornmeal, next to the plant.

An aspect of our own life cycle as an animal species is that we need to kill in order to live. Every day we cause the death of plants or animals, directly or, more often, through surrogates, in order to feed ourselves. This is the nature of things. Yet we are seldom aware that daily we cause the death of other living beings. We tend to ignore or forget this fact and instead consider the beings that have died for us as "food stuff," neatly and conveniently packaged on grocery-store shelves.

Indeed, we tend to find value only in our own human life cycle and not in that of fellow creatures. Robert Bringhurst succinctly describes the barriers we erect between ourselves and the rest of the world: "I mean the barriers of law and of social convention which assign to the lives of human beings a theoretically infinite value while they treat the lives of wild creatures as theoretically zilch. I mean our way of assigning value to pets and livestock based on nothing but market price and human sentiment."[2] He adds, "[A] society happy to kill a billion birds or a hundred thousand cattle in the vague hope of saving a single unspecified human life, or to mow down a whole forest to make one day's worth of newsprint, or to sterilize a river in exchange for some ounces of gold, is a society that, I suspect, has lost its sense of what life and death are for: a society that has lost its admiration and its gratitude for life and death alike."[3]

Shamanic practice, with its awareness of the sacred in all, of spirit in everything, can help us transform into a sacred act our need to kill other species. This transformation is much needed to help bring harmony to our living planet and to regain a healthy view of our own personal death. We need not feel guilty, and we need not try to avoid killing other species to feed ourselves. It is a matter of asking permission to take another life to feed our own. It is a matter of appropriateness. It is a matter of impeccably crossing the boundary between ourselves and the species that feed us. It is a matter of gratitude. Through the shamanic awareness of the spiritual dimension in everything, eating and feeding ourselves can become a conscious manifestation of the interconnectedness of everything. On the physical level, the atoms and molecules from the bodies of the plants and animals we kill become part of our own bodies. On the spiritual level, this union manifests in the recognition that, indeed, we are all the One.

You may have your own ritual that you do or prayer that you say before you eat. Here is a simple ritual that recognizes the sacred and interconnectedness in the act of eating.

> ## A Brief Ritual of Gratitude before Eating
>
> As you prepare to eat, with your intention, briefly connect with the spirits of the plants and animals that are about to feed you. Express your gratitude for the fact that they gave up their lives to nourish you. Express your gratitude for the fact that they have offered you the atoms and molecules of their bodies to replenish your own body. Express your gratitude for the fact that they are raising your awareness of the interconnectedness of everything. You can add that when you die, you want to offer the atoms and molecules of your body to nourish plants and animals.

PREPARING FOR OUR OWN DEATH THROUGH SHAMANIC PRACTICES

Death can come to us unexpectedly at any moment. Therefore, preparing for our own death needs to be a daily, integral part of our shamanic practice. Preparing for death is also preparing for life, as it allows us to live more fully as authentic being. And when death comes, if we have prepared, we will be ready to open fully to the transition to the spiritual dimension that it brings.

Various shamanic journeys, rituals, and exercises, as well as the psycho-spiritual tools I described in the previous chapter, can help us in this important work. The purpose of reflecting on death and preparing for it is to bring about transformations in the way we live. These kinds of transformations often take place following near-death experiences. The aftereffects are usually a reduced fear and greater acceptance of death; an increased concern for helping others; an enhanced feeling of the importance of love; less interest in materialistic pursuits; a growing belief in the spiritual dimension and the spiritual meaning of life; a focus on living in the moment, in one's true power, as authentic being; and a greater openness to the afterlife. By reflecting on and preparing for death, we too can experience the same transformations and avoid old patterns and beliefs. We experience and learn what it is to disengage from the body, the temporal, and the impermanent, and to identify with pure consciousness, which is what happens at death. Preparing for death is part of the art of living.

All shamanic traditions emphasize death and rebirth initiations.[4] These are powerful ways of preparing for death, and I would like to share an initiation I experienced. It happened during a journey to the spirit of a Siberian shaman I have visited often; I use a recording of his power song to lead me to his spirit.

> I am wearing a sheepskin that the shaman gave me in an earlier journey. As I enter the shaman's hut, he greets me with a smile, calmly. I greet him, and he says it is time for me to undergo a death and rebirth initiation. He asks me to go outside, shapeshift into my ally elk, and run through the vast plains, hills, and woods surrounding the village. He says a group of hunters from the village will go after me in a hunt and I will experience my death. He tells me to remember to offer myself when it is time.

> Before I leave his hut, he asks me for my sheepskin, which he puts unceremoniously on the ground next to the central fire. I go outside and shapeshift into elk. I start running in the neighboring woods, feeling big, strong, and agile. Soon I see hunters on foot ahead of me, with guns. I change course, run in another direction, but again run into the hunters' path. I am experiencing the hunt vividly and bodily. At one point I feel surrounded. I wonder what to do, and I feel it is the end, but the hunters do not shoot at me; they just look at me. I run straight toward a group of them, where they are most dense, jump over some who are carrying a canvas as they squat on the ground, and run as fast as I can. This surprises the hunters, and I hear their exclamations.

> I come to a lake and run alongside it. But hunters show up in front and to the left, and I feel cornered again. Once more I run, turning back and moving to the right, through a group of hunters, who do not shoot but move aside as I run straight through them. Then I come to an opening in the wood, with smaller trees that are far apart. I see hunters again in various directions. I am starting to feel exhausted; saliva is running off the side of my mouth.

At one point I collapse, kneeling on all fours, but the hunters approach only slowly, without shooting. I get up and run again a little. I want to live.

I stop, exhausted, feeling the hunters very close. I decide to offer myself up, to let go. At that point, I feel a human hand touch my rump. I tremble—I experience the touch as both a signal of my death and a communication between "relatives." It has love in it. I also understand that that person is representing the community of humans who need my flesh. I give myself up to the hunters, and through them, to this community. I lower my head and wait.

A hunter raises his gun, fairly close to me, and shoots. I am hit in the breast; I collapse and feel my head turn to the side (in ordinary and nonordinary reality). I am still alive, in my body, without pain. Another hunter comes and plunges his knife into my side. My head falls, my body stretches, and I find myself look-ing down on my elk body. The head is still moving, raising itself a little. Another hunter takes his knife and cuts my throat. My head falls to the ground, and I am dead. I have a clear realization that the body below is not me, just matter I have inhabited. The realization is very clear and present.

The hunters put my body on the canvas and carry it to the village. They lay it on a large, flat stone, and several men and women start cutting it up. The skin is removed little by little, the insides removed and put in a big crock, and incisions are made in the flesh to cut the body into pieces. At one point the body is turned around, the skin fully removed. This is taking a long time; I am keenly interested in what they are doing, want them to do it cor-rectly, appropriately.

An old man cuts up the right rear leg and thigh, with the hoof still on, and puts it in a large bag. Then he takes the heart from the crock, puts it in the bag, and gives the bag to a small boy who brings it to the shaman's hut. I see the shaman put the leg in front of the fire, and the heart, and then place a decorated blanket on them. Then he respectfully puts the sheepskin on top. He starts singing, making gestures. At one point he reaches under the blanket with a small knife, cuts off a little piece of raw meat and eats it. I know it is not me.

Then he sings, and later pokes himself on the left hand with the tip of his knife, gets a few droplets of blood, lifts the blanket, and puts the blood on the leg. He then calls upon various spirits, and I see the hut fill with them. The shaman blows on the leg, makes a large gesture, and sings; all the spirits gather around, and I find myself rising in human form in front of him. The blanket is flat—there is nothing under it. I have the sheepskin around my shoulders. I feel good. I thank the shaman. He tells me the hunters pursued and killed me in the appropriate, sacred way, waiting for me to give myself up. As I offered myself, he says, this was not an individual act, but an act of cooperation. I come back to ordinary reality.

RESOLVING UNFINISHED BUSINESS

In the process of dying, an important task is to resolve unfinished business—unresolved issues—with other people, whether living or dead. I was first introduced to the concept of unfinished business with deceased individuals many years ago by shamanic teacher Sandra Ingerman. Indeed, resolving unfinished business is something best done throughout our life, as an important step in acknowledging our inevitable death and preparing for it and manifesting authentic being. People we have unfinished business with could be people we know—relatives, friends, colleagues, acquaintances—or people we do not know personally, such as political or societal leaders. It is also possible to have unfinished business, such as shame or regret, with other species or with parts of our natural environment.

When working with unfinished business with a person, it is good to use Byron Katie's projections practice, which I mentioned in the previous chapter; directions for this practice can be found in her book *Loving What Is.* We use this practice to focus on negative projections we have of that person. This often requires much self-forgiveness. This work can be followed by a shamanic exercise that further manifests our intention to resolve and let go of the unfinished business. In the case of a living person with whom we have unfinished business, I have found that a ritual in nature can be a powerful way to fully manifest our intention.

A Ritual to Resolve Unfinished Business with a Person Who Is Alive

First, do Byron Katie's projections work. Then find a place in nature that is sufficiently private to allow you to perform your ritual and speak aloud without being disturbed. Set up a sacred space by contacting the spirits of place and nature and asking their permission to work there. Also ask for their support as they witness your work.

Then speak aloud your unfinished business with the person, where it stands now, and how you feel about it now, as if you were talking directly to that person. When you have finished speaking, do a brief Middle World journey to connect with the authentic being of the person. Acknowledge and honor it, and offer love and positive energy; that is all.

Do a brief ending ritual, thanking the spirits of place and nature, and perhaps leave an offering.

If you can communicate directly with the living person in ordinary reality after you have done the projections work to clear your part in the unresolved issue, do so. Performing this ritual can prepare us to communicate with the person in a harmonious way.

A Ritual for Unresolved Business with a Person Who Is Deceased

Here is a ritual for resolving unresolved business that you were unable to finish before another person died. Here, too, start the work with a projections practice and do the speaking-aloud ritual in nature. Then do a brief journey, using your intention and asking your allies or teachers to lead you to the deceased person. You can usually meet them somewhere in the Upper World.

When you meet the person, greet and honor him or her and say you are done with your unfinished business. The authentic being in us is talking with the authentic being in the other person, and such a meeting is usually very peaceful and heartwarming.

In some cases, a dead person may not be available for contact or want to communicate with humans at this time. In this case, respect that and just send greetings with your intention.

Sometimes the spirit of an individual we want to connect with has not fully crossed out of ordinary reality. In this case, what is required is psychopomp work, which I will explain later in this chapter.

Resolving unfinished business with nonhuman entities can be done using the same approach as for humans. Normally this requires much self-forgiveness as well as acknowledging and honoring the sacredness of the entity.

DYING TO "WHO WE ARE NOT"

There is one more shamanic practice that can help us live authentically and prepare for our own death, a death ritual that we can practice throughout our life. In this ritual we die to "who we are not"—that is, release our attachment to our identity, our personal ego, and the mental pictures we create of ourselves, both for ourselves and others. Such pictures can be the position we hold at work, being the wife or the husband of someone, being the owner of this or that, or being a father, a mother, or a shamanic practitioner. These pictures are not who we truly are, our true nature. They are roles, functions, parts, or aspects of ourselves. As we die to "who we are not," those parts or aspects do not die, nor should they. What needs to die is our identification with them, our attachment to them as defining who we are. For example, our identity as a father or mother should not define us. These roles exist, but we need to let die our definition of ourselves *as these roles*. When we do, we see the truth: that we are authentic being having the experience of being a father or a mother.

A Dying to "Who We Are Not" Ritual

First journey to one of your teachers or allies to determine a single aspect of yourself that you tend to identify with—one that is not who you truly are and that is important for you to let go at this time. After you return to ordinary reality, go into nature and, using biodegradable materials, create with your intention a physical object, called a shamanic talisman, that is that aspect of yourself. You can use dead leaves, wood sticks, twigs, dried grass, and the like. Let your intention guide you. This shamanic talisman does not represent the part; it *is* the part.

Bring it to a place in nature that feels right for you. Set up a sacred space, and invoke the local spirits of nature. Then, holding your talisman, say out loud, "As authentic being, I am not [the aspect or part represented by the talisman]." Then leave your sacred space and take the talisman apart, returning the pieces to nature as the body returns to nature at death.

It is possible to do this work indoors and create a talisman by drawing the aspect of ourselves on a piece of paper. We can then cut up or tear the paper and recycle it.

It is good if you can perform this simple ritual with one or more friends or shamanic colleagues present to serve as witness. When you speak out loud, you speak to them as well as to the local spirits, and they can take the talisman apart.

PSYCHOPOMP

Another aspect of death that is an important part of shamanic practice is helping the souls of people who have died to cross fully out of ordinary reality; this is the classic role of the shaman as psychopomp.[5] In shamanic understanding, souls of people who have died usually move on harmoniously into the spirit world. This moving on is sometimes called "crossing to the other side" or "moving to the light." Some people who have left their bodies after death can get stuck in the Middle World, the nonordinary aspect of our physical world. They are in some ways still connected to this physical world. This is not the appropriate place for them, and they need to fully move to the light. They are perceived as ghosts or uncanny presences by the living, and at times they can try to reincarnate in a living body and possess that person.

There are diverse reasons for dead people to be stuck in the Middle World. This can happen when death is sudden or violent, in cases of suicide, and when people have resisted and denied death until the very last breath or have not felt ready to die. At times people may not know they are dead and may move about in a confused state. Some people who are aware they are dead may be lost, not knowing what to do. Others may feel a strong need to stick around in order to help loved ones, finish unfinished business, or for other reasons. The dead person in the Middle World is outside of time and not aware of its passage. Therefore, it is possible to do psychopomp work for people who, according to our ordinary-world time, died a long time ago.

The practice of psychopomp goes back millennia and is found in other spiritual traditions. One important question I have asked myself concerning souls stuck in the Middle World is this: if a soul, or authentic being, leaves a body that has died, and if the soul or authentic being is pure and divine, how can a soul be stuck, confused, lost, or guilty? These feelings or states are all characteristics of ordinary, dualistic reality, so how can authentic being, which sees itself only as the One, still be affected by them? What happens after death will always contain mystery for us living beings, but I feel it is important to try to make some sense of it, to more fully understand the art of dying and the practice of psychopomp. A useful concept to consider is that for some people after death, there remain constellations of emotions or traumas, psychic energies that stick to the soul. It is as if the soul is still partly incarnated, not in the body, but *in these constellations*. It is these constellations, coming from the ordinary-reality world, that keep the soul stuck in the Middle World, and that must be cleared away in order for the soul or authentic being to fully cross out of ordinary reality.

The purpose of the psychopomp is to convince the dead person to let go of the constellations and to offer to help him or her leave and go to the light. It is essential to work closely with one's allies and spirit teachers in doing psychopomp work, and to do the work with a clear and pure intention, working from the heart and leaving judgments behind. The Foundation for Shamanic Studies has for many years offered an excellent workshop that includes training in psychopomp work, and I highly recommend it if you are interested in psychopomp work.

Because of the level of violence in our world, the high rate of suicides, materialistic lifestyles, the frequency of wars and terrorist acts, and the increasing occurrences of natural catastrophes, the number of deceased persons' souls who are stuck in the Middle World is, unfortunately, quite large. Thus, while the work of psychopomp is not everyone's calling, it is shamanic work that is most important at this time. This is not only because it helps these souls move fully to the other side and to the light, which is their natural destiny, but also because the presence of souls stuck in the Middle World affects the wellbeing of the living and our planet Earth.

HELPING PEOPLE WHO ARE DYING AND THEIR SURVIVORS

Helping the dying and their survivors is a subject that our modern Western culture tends to ignore or delegate to specialists or trained professionals. Yet it is highly likely that most of us will, more than once in our lives, find ourselves in a situation where our presence and assistance are desirable as someone in our family or a close friend is dying. We could even find ourselves in this situation with a complete stranger.

Helping people who face death to die a good, natural, peaceful death and move easily to the light can be challenging. Many of us feel inadequate or fearful in undertaking this task, not knowing what to do. Yet helping someone face death is a privilege, a sacred task, and a wonderful and priceless gift from the heart, a way to express love. And accompanying the survivors—through their experience of their loved one's death, through their grief—is also a loving task.

Shamanic practitioners, because of their awareness and knowledge of nonordinary reality and death, have a good foundation from which to acquire capabilities for this work. There are many excellent books on the subject; I particularly like Kathleen Dowling Singh's book *The Grace in Dying: How We Are Transformed Spiritually as We Die.* And being present with someone in the process of their dying is the best way to learn.

LOSS AND GRIEF

Loss and grief is the lot of the survivors after the death of a loved one. Those who have died, if they have made a good transition, are pure essence, having returned to the One; there is no loss or grief for them. But for survivors, grieving is an important part of the life-and-death cycle, allowing those left behind to express their feelings when a person, several or many people, or a member of another species has or have left the physical world and the community of the living. There can be deep sorrow and pain at the loss of the departed. Yet for those who understand the certainty of death and know that it is a natural transition—one in which the soul or authentic being persists and leaves its material form to move to its destiny with the One—grieving for the departed can contain joy as well as the sorrow and pain of loss.

There are two ways to be with loss and grief: at the level of our identification with ego and at the level of authentic being. Apprehending loss with fear only feeds our ego, which thrives on reminiscing about the pain-filled past and fearing the future. Apprehending loss as authentic being allows grief to be expressed naturally and authentically, with the knowledge that death is but a transition, part of the impermanence of life, and that the permanent One is all there really is. Shamanic rituals, especially those given to you by your own spirit helpers, can be beautiful and powerful avenues for expressing grief. There is no rehearsing of loss and grief because we do not know where we will be when they occur or what resources will be present. What is asked from us, then, is to be in the moment.

5

The Art of Healing

o ❍ o

For the shamanic practitioner, self-healing is often part of a personal spiritual path. But as I mentioned in chapter 2, a shamanic practice also includes a service path, and helping others in their self-healing is a central part of that shamanic service path.

Over the many years I have practiced shamanism, I have had the privilege of performing hundreds of shamanic healings. I have never advertised myself as a shamanic healer, however, and the people I work with come primarily from three sources: friends and relatives, referrals from people I know, and psychotherapist referrals. Most of these healings—and here I can take no credit, as all the credit goes to the spirits and the patients—have had powerful beneficial effects on the patients' health and wellbeing and the way they approach life. For me, these effects have demonstrated powerfully how traditional shamanic healing methods, adapted to modern culture, can complement Western medicine and psychotherapy and help people face life's many challenges.

This has been particularly evident with the psychotherapy patients I see. I am not privy to any information related to the psychotherapy work itself, but at the patient's request, the therapist often participates in our healing sessions, as a witness and sometimes as a drummer, and is then able to integrate shamanic healing and psychotherapeutic healing along with the patient.

This chapter explores shamanic healing work with individuals, specifically those aspects of shamanic healing that I have come to appreciate in my own practice and that I believe are important considerations for work-ing with others: the nature of shamanic healing, the roles of the healer and patient and the relationship between them, the importance of audience participation, and the dangers inherent in the healing practice.

TRADITIONAL SHAMANIC HEALING METHODS

Healing is inherent to the shamanic tradition and has always been a fore-most aspect of all shamanic cultures. Mircea Eliade, in his classic book reviewing the anthropological literature on shamanism, documents the central role of healing: "[A]ll through Asia and North America, and else-where as well (e.g., Indonesia), the shaman performs the function of doctor and healer." He adds, "As everywhere else, the essential and strictly per-sonal function of the South American shaman remains healing."[1] Michael Harner says, in his classic book on shamanism, "Shamans . . . are the keep-ers of a remarkable body of ancient techniques that they use to achieve and maintain well-being and healing for themselves and their communities."[2]

In one sense, there are as many shamanic healing methods as there are practitioners; the shaman often seeks guidance and instruction from his or her spirit helpers about how to perform healing for a patient, and such advice can differ. There are, however, a number of traditional, even universal, shamanic healing methods that have probably been practiced for thousands of years. I have briefly mentioned some of these in chapter 1. There are excellent books that discuss at length these methods as they can be practiced in the modern world. Workshops are offered in many countries for those interested in training in these methods.

Among traditional shamanic healing methods is *ally retrieval.* Here the shamanic practitioner journeys in nonordinary reality to recover or retrieve an ally for the patient. This helps restore the patient's power and vitality, helping him or her to self-heal, fend off future illnesses and mal-aises, avoid chronic problems, and in general acquire more confidence and energy in everyday life.

Another method is *shamanic extraction,* in which the shamanic practi-tioner extracts a spirit intrusion from the patient. The intrusion is a spirit entity or foreign energy that does not belong there and can contribute to localized pain or illness, such as infection, cancer, and injury.

In *soul retrieval,* another major method, the practitioner journeys to recover a part of the patient's soul that is somehow no longer available or accessible to him or her. This is usually the result of a trauma or a difficult or disharmonious interaction with another person; in shamanic parlance it is designated "soul loss" or "soul theft." Such lack of accessibility to parts of one's soul or authentic being can make one feel fragmented, disassociated, ill at ease, and vulnerable to various psychological or physical diseases. The reintroduction of soul-retrieval healing in the modern world can be largely attributed to the work of Sandra Ingerman.

The method known as *depossession,* which is also practiced in other spiritual traditions, is necessary when an individual becomes possessed by the presence of the soul of a deceased person that has not crossed over to the light. This method requires psychopomp work, discussed in chapter 4.

THE NATURE OF SHAMANIC HEALING

Shamanic healing probably has roots going back tens of thousands of years. Much information on the topic has been passed down orally and in written form. What I share here, to add to our collective knowledge, is what I have personally learned about healing through my own experiences with illnesses and injuries, through my work performing shamanic healings, and as a shamanic teacher and mentor.

Each of us is one being comprising body, mind, ego, and authentic being. We are not independent, separate parts. For me, then, healing means bringing forth harmony between the biological, the psychological, and the spiritual. It includes integrating polarities, light and shadow. It is a transformation, which is always a return to living in the moment. And while healing can at times include the restoration of physical health or a physical cure, this transformation is what counts.

Much academic shamanic literature describes illness as the result of malevolent spirits. As I noted in chapter 1, for me there are no beneficial or malevolent spirits. Spirits and spiritual forces exist in the nondual dimension, outside the physical world of ordinary reality. It is tempting to project onto the spirit world the dualistic, and often anthropomorphic, characteristics of our ordinary physical world—good and bad, happy and unhappy, kind and angry, and the like. However, *intention* on the part of the shamanic practitioner can be good or bad, and spiritual forces can be misused to cause harm to others. The reference to evil spirits as the cause of illness in the shamanic literature is likely a cultural projection on the part of the anthropologist/observer, the shaman's way of speaking of healing, or perhaps a belief system found in some shamanic cultures as well as other spiritual traditions and established religions. For me, a spiritual force that is out of balance with our body/mind/ego can lead to sickness, as is the case for intrusions. But this imbalance does not mean the spiritual force or intrusion is malevolent or evil.

A most important aspect of healing that Western culture often misunderstands or ignores is that the only kind of healing that exists, whether shamanic or of any other kind, is self-healing. The word *healer* is, in a sense, a misnomer. When we are sick or injured and seek any mode of help from modern medicine—whether surgery, medication, or dietary advice—we tend to say, "Doctor, heal me. Doctor, fix me." Yet the physician, like any healer, is there merely to facilitate the patient's self-healing. The body heals itself.

The shamanic tradition has always understood that healing needs to occur at all levels of our being: spiritual, psychological, and physical. Shamanic healing works at the spiritual level; it does not replace traditional medical or psychological healing, but instead complements and empowers both.

According to Eliade, for the traditional shaman "[T]he recovery of physical health is closely dependent on restoring the balance of spiritual forces."[3] Too often, Western medical and mental-health practices ignore this spiritual component. This is why shamanic practice offers such a significant contribution to healing: it reestablishes the essential link between spiritual, physical, and psychological healing. It is encouraging to see that in the United States, collaboration between Native American shamans and healers and Western physicians is taking place in some major hospitals, a trend that one can only hope will spread.

AN EXPERIENCE AS PATIENT

I had a strange medical experience more than twenty years ago that taught me much about healing. At that time, I named it my "birth and redeath experience."

Noëlle and I were participating in a weekend workshop on ancient pre-dynastic Egyptian Huna spiritual traditions, which are strongly rooted in shamanic tradition. I had been under stress and was very anxious because doctors had recently discovered that Noëlle had a small melanoma (skin cancer).

At one point on the first day of the workshop, I felt intense sensations in my stomach, as if my insides were exploding into a thousand pieces. I was nauseous and simultaneously needed to vomit and excrete. I did not throw up, but I had a large bowel movement and noticed that my stools were black and sticky, like tar. I stayed through the rest of the weekend session, feeling fatigued and dizzy at times but otherwise okay. I had no pain. I attributed my sudden illness to a possible food poisoning.

That night Noëlle and I and some friends each pulled a card from the Medicine Wheel Tarot deck, which is based on the animal world. I pulled the elk, a card that represents masculine qualities and the wisdom of the elders who teach from their own life experiences. It was only later that I understood the card's message.

Back home on the following Monday, I decided to see my doctor. After he examined me, his expression was grave. He told me I had a bleeding ulcer, had lost about half of my blood, and that I should not even be able to stand up in such a state. He admitted me to the hospital, where I stayed a few days. While there, I opted not to have a blood transfusion, preferring to restore my blood levels to normal on my own. I had a whole series of tests, including chest X-rays.

On the second day, my physician, appearing concerned, asked me if I smoked. I told him I had occasionally smoked a pipe when I was younger, as well as occasional small cigarillos, but had never smoked cigarettes. But I understood immediately what his question meant and felt a tremor vibrate through my entire body. The X-rays had shown a spot on my lung that very much looked like lung cancer. My doctor recommended immediate surgery to find out whether the cancer had spread into the lymph nodes or elsewhere. But I would not be able to undergo surgery for about a month since I needed to regain my strength first.

After I left the hospital, I sought a second opinion. According to this second doctor, it seemed I had three choices. The first was to do nothing and hope the spot on my lung was not cancer. The second was to have a long needle inserted in my lung to remove tissue for testing. If the tests were positive, it would be clear that the spot was cancerous. However, if they turned out negative, there would still be uncertainty, because the needle might have missed any tumorous tissue. The third option was to have surgery. Only this would give me a definite answer.

There was a 1 percent chance of dying from this operation and the general anesthesia it required. I spent considerable time contacting my allies and spirit teachers, asking for support and counsel. I also sought counsel from Noëlle and close friends. I had a strong sense that these choices were truly my own, that healing was my responsibility, and that there were no clear answers.

I was in my early fifties then and was fortunate never to have suffered a major illness or injury in my life. I had not spent a night in a hospital until this bleeding-ulcer event, which by now I attributed to the stress I was under. While I had dealt with death and dying in my shamanic work and had faced death as a child during the Second World War in Belgium, I had never as an adult faced the real possibility of my impending death. This was a profound and emotional experience that for the first time in my life placed me squarely before my own vulnerability, deepened my understanding of life and death, opened me further to the notion of impeccability, and ushered me into a deep inquiry into the meaning of healing.

I decided that I wanted to know for sure what was going on, opted for the surgery, and went to see the surgeon my personal physician recommended. Because I still needed to regain my strength, he scheduled the surgery four weeks after my appointment with him. I told him that I planned to do healing work in the meantime. I used the words *shamanic healing, energy,* and *spiritual healing.* To my surprise, he said that although he was not familiar with these forms of healing, he could order X-rays in two weeks to see if any change might be occurring.

In the following weeks, I worked intensely with my spirit helpers and sought healings from others. Michael Harner did a shamanic extraction for me and gave me very wise advice. He told me to put the various healings I was doing, along with the Western medicine procedures and pending operation, in my personal medicine bag. Combined there, they would complement one another. This confirmed my sense that my healing was my responsibility and nobody else's, and that the shamanic healing would complement, not replace, medical treatment.

During this time I also learned to say no to some offers of nontraditional healing. I understood that it was important for patients to choose healers they feel comfortable with. Many friends and shamanic colleagues offered to do healings, and some recommended healers they knew and highly valued. While I knew that these offers came from the heart, and I much appreciated that, I turned down several of them because they did not feel right for what I needed. Saying no to my friends and colleagues was not easy.

I was also starting to learn of the wisdom and intuition of the body; in many cases, my body immediately told me, somehow, whether an offer of healing was appropriate for me. All the while, Noëlle and my four children, all in their twenties, were immensely supportive. While I knew they fully realized there was a distinct possibility that I may not be alive for much longer, they were centered, and I felt their strong love.

After two weeks, I went for my scheduled X-rays. There was no change. The spot was still there. I continued with my healing and prepared myself for the operation, working with my spirit helpers. My mother, who lived in Belgium, decided to come to California to be there for the operation and the postoperative recovery.

On the day of the operation, we drove to the hospital. All my children were there. The medical staff took another set of chest X-rays and prepared me for surgery. I was lying on a stretcher next to the operating room, waiting to be rolled in and receive anesthesia, when my surgeon came running down the hall, calling for the nurses to stop. He walked up to me and said, "The X-rays no longer show a spot. You are clean. I've cancelled the operation." I sat up, shaken, elated, and in some disbelief. As the surgeon was walking away, he turned around with a smile and said, "Don't tell me your Indian friends [his notion of shamanic practitioners] did this!" He suggested we take another set of X-rays in two weeks, just to make sure everything was still clear.

The next two weeks were filled with joy, grace, and gratitude. I journeyed many times to thank spirits and express my gratitude. Then, dutifully, I went in for the X-rays and waited for the results in the surgeon's office. When he walked in, I could see in his sad face that the news was not good. "The spot is back," he told me. "I think we need to operate after all." I was startled and confused—I didn't know what to think. The surgeon couldn't schedule me in for another three and a half weeks, but because I wanted to continue to work with him, we set a date.

I entered the hardest period of my life. The abrupt shift from elation to the stark reality of facing a major illness—again—was shocking.

The possibility of death seemed more real than ever. And my belief systems were challenged as never before. What was the meaning of all the healing work I had done, for myself and others? Did it mean anything? Were the spirits really helping? Did spirits really exist? If I really had lung cancer and might die soon, was it worth living through this desolate experience?

A walk in the surrounding hills with my oldest son, Eric, began to bring me out of this darkness when he said, "Well, Dad, it looks like spirits have hit you with a double whammy!" The humor in the statement shook me loose from my despair. Perhaps the spirits were testing me? Was this some kind of initiation? What were the spirits trying to teach me?

I had regained my full strength since the bleeding-ulcer episode, and I spent a lot of time hiking in nature. The spirits of nature helped me accept the reality of my situation, center myself again, and deepen my understanding of the nature of healing and its differentiation from a simple cure of the body. I performed and received further healings, being very selective in what I did and whom I worked with, and spent much time with family. I learned more about the wisdom of the body: how learning often first comes through the body before the mind can make sense of it, and how my body was cooperating, almost organically, with spirits.

I also learned, through direct experience, and perhaps for the first time in such a deep way, that it was possible to experience polarities, which I tended to consider mutually exclusive, at the same time. I simultaneously experienced deep sadness and deep joy. I felt fear and confidence, doubt and certainty, anxiety and joyful anticipation. The polarities did not disappear or blend into one another; they were both present. But the resulting sensation was one of truth, clarity, and authenticity. They were moments of pure grace, and my body always reacted, wanting to express the experience through dance, movement, or song. At such moments, I felt healed.

When the day of the operation came, I felt ready, at peace. My family came with me to the hospital again. As I lay on a stretcher, waiting to be rolled into the operating room, I called upon all my allies to be with me. I could almost see them, hear them, and feel them as they lay on the table with me, with one literally lying on top of me. I asked that they protect my body during the operation and that, wherever my own spirit might go, they teach me more about healing.

Following the operation, Noëlle sat with me as I slowly returned to full consciousness. She later told me that as I was awaking, I repeated several times, "This is wonderful. This is amazing!" I do not recall saying this. But whatever I learned during that operation is in me today, I know.

When I was fully awake, I learned from Noëlle, with great relief and gratitude, that I did not have lung cancer after all. The spot was a scar, probably the remains of a past infection. The surgeon, who had cut off and removed the scarred tissue, later confirmed this, but did not know what had produced the infection. My daughter Ann, who was a resident physician, did some research and concluded that the most likely cause was a past incident of desert fever, which is caused by a fungus that infects the lungs and is prevalent in the southwestern deserts of the United States where I had spent some time.

I learned more about the nature of healing, self-healing, and the difference between healing and curing through this experience than I ever did from books, lectures, or workshops. It confirmed for me the importance of opening up to the shaman within. As is the case for shamanism in general, direct personal experience is the greatest teacher. I learned that I was in charge of my own healing and of combining shamanic healing, other forms of nontraditional healing, and Western medicine: one form does not replace the other; they complement one another. My experience confirmed the importance of continually seeking counsel and support from my spirit helpers, and I also found spirits of nature to be of great help in my self-healing. I learned that spirits sometimes teach us through initiations that are grueling; perhaps this is necessary to break our resistance and denial. And my experience also shows that even long-time shamanic practitioners can have doubts about spirits and spirit work.

I learned that healing is all about transformation; it is a return to authenticity. I also learned the importance of choosing healers, including shamanic healers, with whom you feel comfortable; reputation and recommendations from others are not sufficient. And it is important to say no to offers of nontraditional healing when those do not seem right to you. In all these cases, it is important to seek advice from your spirit helpers. Finally, I learned about the body's wisdom, its power to heal itself, and its organic cooperation with spirits.

THE ROLES OF, AND RELATIONSHIP BETWEEN, HEALER AND PATIENT

If there is only self-healing, what, then, are the role and function of the shamanic healer when helping others? Shamanic healers are facilitators, guides, and helpers who help patients self-heal. They do this by crossing the boundary between ordinary and nonordinary reality and interceding with spirits, so their patients can access and utilize spiritual forces in their self-healing. To perform this function impeccably, shamanic healers need to be authentic being and let the ego recede. Authentic being is contagious; to the extent that healers manifest authentic being, patients can manifest it too, thereby enhancing self-healing.

Shamanic healers need to embody honesty and humility, putting aside agendas and expectations and knowing that healing will occur through the work of spirits. Before a healing session, shamanic healers must verify with spirits that it is appropriate to do the healing and what kind of healing is appropriate. Sometimes the kind of healing the spirits suggest differs from what patients request. While it is up to patients to describe what they want, it is essential that both healer and patient are true to their inner guidance. During a healing session, shamanic healers collaborate closely with spirits, continuously seeking guidance and support from them. And it is important that as the shamanic practitioners do their healing work, they take care of themselves and utilize some sort of spiritual or psychic protection in order to not take on anything that does not belong to them.

The role of the patient is no less important than that of the healer. Patients must impeccably assume responsibility for their own self-healing and be clear that they want to heal and accept the consequences. They need to be open and receptive to the spiritual energies that become accessible through the intercession of the shamanic healer, and they must make use of these energies. When I do a shamanic healing, I ask patients to be in their bodies, in the here and now, and I remind them that the healing will take place primarily after the shamanic healing ceremony, through their own work of self-healing.

Because there is a "healer" and a "patient," shamanic healing contains the essential elements of a relationship, which implies the presence of boundaries and, thus, the elements of boundary crossing discussed in chapter 3. Not only do shamanic healers cross the boundary between ordinary and nonordinary reality, but they must also cross, with impeccability, the boundary between themselves and their patients. And patients need to reciprocate. Both this crossing of boundaries and the relationship it establishes between healer and patient needs to be I-Thou (also discussed in chapter 3). The healing then becomes a direct relationship between authentic beings, and this is how spiritual energy can be transferred, accessed, and lead to healing. A healer and patient in an I-Thou relationship manifest the interconnectedness of all and empower healing. There is complete equality between the shamanic healer and the patient. There is mutuality in giving, receiving, appreciation, and healing.

Healing practices are inherently paradoxical since healing requires both unity and individual responsibility from both parties. The patient self-heals, and the self-healing is made possible and empowered by the work of the healer.

AN ESSENTIAL INGREDIENT: AUDIENCE PARTICIPATION

The importance of audience participation and community in a shamanic-healing ceremony cannot be overstated. It was Sandra Ingerman who showed me just how valuable others are to the shamanic-healing process. Today when I perform a healing, I always ask the individual to bring along relatives or friends, and it does not matter whether the invited participants practice shamanism or not. The presence and participation of an audience in a healing ceremony manifest the interconnectedness of all more fully than the healer and patient alone and thus further empower self-healing. Audience participation also adds the social component of community to healing.

Besides being physically present to support a loved one, participants in a healing ceremony have specific roles that I always describe to them. They can hold the energy, each in their own way, and through such inner participation greatly contribute to the healing process. Very importantly, they serve as witnesses and help "anchor" the healing. Having witnessed what can be a very intimate moment for the patient, friends and family can build on this shared experience and continue to support the patient's self-healing after the ceremony. Participants also represent the larger community, the human species, other species, and the planet. Healing is not an individual event; it is a collective one. As each one of us heals, so do the rest of humanity and the planet. At their choice, I offer friends and family the option to drum or sing as appropriate. Then, immediately following the ceremony, after I have described to the patient my own journey and my intercession with spirits, I invite the friends and family in attendance to describe, if they wish, their inner experience as well—their own inner journey. This information is almost always important for the patient and contributes to the self-healing.

ETHICS AND POTENTIAL DANGERS IN SHAMANIC HEALING

Ethics are of primary importance in shamanic healing, as they are with all shamanic work. It is essential to always obtain permission from the person and from spirit to do a healing. There can be no psychic intrusion; instead, we must approach and move across the boundary between healer and patient with courtesy and authenticity. It is essential to strive for impeccability, to collaborate with spirits, and to adequately protect and take care of yourself. This includes being conscious of and inquiring into the potential dangers and obstacles.

Several dangers are inherent in the shamanic healing practice. Noëlle stresses that there is a negative and often unconscious shadow side to shamanic service—codependency—that coexists in all of us along with altruism. This is true of both individual shamanic healing and world work. Codependency in service can manifest itself in many ways: a need to fix others or the world; a need to correct a situation in order to alleviate our own discomfort or anxiety as a witness to it or to feel self-important or useful; the need to take care of others to make up for not receiving sufficient attention ourselves earlier in life; an attempt to avoid the responsibility of taking care of ourselves by focusing on others instead; a feeling of responsibility for the success or failure of the service we provide; and the fear that others are doing a better job of serving others than we are.

Healers may see themselves as the ones who do or cause healing. They may let various aspects of the ego take over and fail to cooperate with spirits, thereby preventing the spirits from doing the work. They may work from a place that is not authentic being, inappropriately cross the boundary between themselves and their patients, and forgo an I-Thou attitude for an I-It attitude toward patients. Recalling our discussion of the inner family of self and the role of the mind in chapter 3, there is the danger of the mind teaming up with "the one who wants to heal" or with "the narcissist" or with "the one who wants to do good," and wresting control from spirits and authentic being. There is also the subtle danger of the shamanic ego taking over and masquerading as authentic being in the process of healing.

An additional danger is that the patient may want or expect the healing to come from the healer, thus renouncing self-healing. Healer and patient can thus mutually reinforce each other in abandoning their true roles and responsibilities. The patient can also put up obstacles to self-healing, such as identifying him- or herself as "the victim" or "the oppressor." As Noëlle says, the patient can remain in the mind and its stories; avoid the here and now, looking to the past and fearing the future; or wallow in pain, thus reinforcing suffering.

It is the subtle, sometime unconscious manifestation of these dangers that we need to be conscious of and watch for. It is important for shamanic healers to honestly inquire into these potential dangers, working with their spirit guides and using the psycho-spiritual tools I mentioned in chapter 3. It is also important for them to help their patients confront and deal with potential obstacles they may construct to their own self-healing.

6

The Art of Shapeshifting

◦ ◗ ◦

Many years ago I was exploring advanced shamanic practices with a group of shamanic practitioners in Northern California. Sandra Ingerman, an ordinary-reality teacher I have mentioned before, led us in a journey in which we were to ask one of our spirit teachers what we saw as impossible in our shamanic practice. I was intrigued by the question, and when I asked it of my spirit teacher, the response came back immediately: shapeshifting.

That answer was like a blow that deeply shook my entire being. Until then I had given little thought to the subject of shapeshifting, except for coming across brief references to it in books or in myths and legends. And my spirit teacher was right: it indeed seemed impossible for me. I feared losing myself if I shapeshifted; what would become of *me*? My teacher said that my fear was part of my sense of impossibility and that by shapeshifting I would connect with the greater whole and actually become more myself.

While it took many years of practice before I fully and deeply understood my teacher's words, they encapsulate the meaning of shapeshifting as a spiritual practice. Shapeshifting allows us to directly experience the illusory nature of separation and duality and the interconnectedness and unity of all that is. It awakens us to our true nature and helps us fully incarnate authentic being.

Shapeshifting requires a high level of impeccability, and practicing on a regular basis is an effective way to learn and manifest impeccability in both nonordinary and ordinary reality. It is a wonderful way to live our deep and essential connection with nature, and for me it has enriched and enhanced my relationship with all of nature. Not only that, but a regular shapeshifting practice greatly facilitates the remembrance and awareness of the continuous presence of spirits.

Shapeshifting is not a beginning practice; it is very advanced and not for everyone. However, because it can powerfully awaken us to the sacred and the connectedness of everything in a way that is at once mystical, fully embodied, and oriented toward service to the world, it is a wonderful way to evoke the shaman within. It is a practice that happens in both nonordinary and ordinary reality simultaneously.

Following my memorable journey proposed by Sandra Ingerman, I was quickly led to a shapeshifting teacher in nonordinary reality: an ancient shaman who once lived in the southern part of Central Asia. I have visited him every single day since then. When I first began to do so during my daily morning ritual, he taught me the many intricacies of shapeshifting practice, along with innumerable exercises. I spent much of the day practicing. At first we worked on shapeshifting into one of my allies that my teacher selected, and this practice lasted for almost two years. There were times when, for several weeks or months in a row, he would ask me to repeat the same exercise as the day before. I was impatient to receive the next practice, so this repetition took much discipline on my part. But now I know that it served me well, for there is no other way to master this profound and powerful practice.

At length my teacher suggested I start working with another ally and, over time, all my other allies. Later he led me into shapeshifting into other animals, multiple shapeshifting, and finally shapeshifting into beings other than animals, such as plants, trees, rocks, rivers, mountains, or the ocean. Shapeshifting became not only my principal daily spiritual path, but also an integral part of all my shamanic work, greatly enhancing its power and integrity.

Because I know from firsthand experience that shapeshifting can have a major impact on all aspects of spiritual and ordinary life, I want to explain fully what it is and why you may want to practice it, introduce the techniques I was taught by my spirit guides, and share my personal experiences of shapeshifting into allies and a number of different nature beings.

WHAT IS SHAPESHIFTING?

Shapeshifting is an ancient practice found in almost all shamanic cultures and traditions worldwide. Still, scant information has been shared about it except through stories, myths, and legends. It has always been one of the most secretive of shamanic practices, and for very good reasons: to successfully practice shapeshifting requires great inner containment, humility, and impeccability in intention, thought process, and action. Boasting about or misusing one's shapeshifting practice will render one incapable of shapeshifting again. This need for impeccability in both ordinary and nonordinary realities is an important—if not the main—reason to embrace the shapeshifting path.

What shamanic practitioners usually call *merging* is also a fairly universal practice. But while there are similarities between the two, it is important to understand that they are not the same. Merging—be it with one's spirit teacher or ally, a tree, or the element of water—has its roots in the wonder of connecting with spirit and in the love and quest for the union that emanates from that connection. It is the uniting or combining of our identity with that of another being. It allows us to manifest and experience the essence of the other and is a powerful practice in healing, divination, and rituals. I have done much merging in my shamanic practice, and for me, shapeshifting has allowed me to go further than merging in my awareness of authentic being, interconnectedness, and impeccability. By its very nature, it opens up and heightens our experience of being part of the One, of being One. Indeed, if we were separate, shapeshifting would not be possible.

The only way to really understand the difference between merging and shapeshifting is to experience both, but one way I can express this difference is by saying that in merging with an ally, for example, both the ally's and your own essence are present in a new energy entity that is a complete union of the two. When you shapeshift into an ally, there is only one energy entity: that of the ally. It is a metamorphosis. You are your ally, yet you are also still you. This is a great mystery that can only be experienced.

I have found no teachings about shapeshifting practice in books on shamanism. The word is used in many different contexts and takes on a wide spectrum of meanings. It is often used to denote any kind of transformation at all. But here I use the term in the classic, traditional shamanic context to denote a complete metamorphosis into another being.

Among the shamans I have met around the world, I am fairly sure that some, like the Q'ero in the Peruvian Andes, engage in the practice, yet none have taught me anything about it or even mentioned it. Here I am sharing what I have learned through personal experience, principally through the guidance of my primary shapeshifting teacher and my allies and other spirits. My teacher has given me permission to share some of this knowledge here.

In chapter 1, I mentioned the importance of intention, attention, and trust in achieving the nonordinary state of consciousness that is central to shamanic practice. Shapeshifting requires an ultimate level of impeccability in intention, attention, and trust; thus, it provides a demanding but effective way to reach that level of impeccability. To shapeshift fully, you must have an absolutely clear intention to shapeshift, including clarity about why you want to do so. You must devote complete attention, with every part of yourself fully present, in the here and now. And you must fully trust the spirits, for shapeshifting can be scary at times. In shapeshifting, attention is energy, intention is transformation, and trust is the heart.

This experience is fully beyond the ego mind. The great spiritual teacher Jiddu Krishnamurti spoke about attention in a small book on meditation in ways I thought were very applicable to shapeshifting: "If you give complete attention (to something), with your body, with your nerves, with your eyes, with your ears, with your mind, with your whole being, there is no center from which you are attending, there is only attention. That attention is complete silence."[1]

Shapeshifting work requires daily attention and practice. You must almost continually be in and out of the spirit world. This is very difficult for most of us humans; it is not easy to remember to work shamanically, to do the practice. And this is part of the learning, part of the path. What has worked for me is this practice: I do a small morning ritual each day when I awake. I create protection for myself for the rest of the day, contact spirits that I will be working with during the day, and do shapeshifting work with one of my allies. I have learned not to miss a single day, just as I do not miss brushing my teeth daily.

A possible obstacle to shapeshifting is the sense that we possess our bodies. We tend to feel deeply that "This body is mine. I am my body. This is me." It is important that we become consciously aware that this is not so; the body is part of the earth, part of the interconnecting web that is the One. In chapter 10 I will explain how, in the science of cosmology, our bodies are just aggregates, albeit extraordinary ones, of particles created in the big bang, in stars, and in supernova explosions. This awareness that we are not our bodies, that our bodies do not belong to us, can intensify our shapeshifting practice.

THE PURPOSES OF SHAPESHIFTING

Ancient myths and stories from around the world speak to the purposes of shapeshifting. In a Northwest American Indian story, related in a poem called "Salmon Boy" by American poet David Wagoner, a young boy, hungry and desiring to explore, shapeshifts into a salmon in the river. He swims downriver with the other salmon toward the ocean, discovers a marvelous world as he travels, and at last reaches the ocean, where he feasts on herring eggs. When it is time to swim back upriver, the salmon boy is exhilarated, full of energy and feeling he is capable of anything—until his human father spears him during the annual salmon catch. His parents dry him, and he becomes food. In this culture, dried salmon represents not only material food but also spiritual food that nourishes and sustains the people.[2]

In an ancient Celtic story from Wales, the goddess of wisdom, Ceridwen, asks the young child Gwion Bach to watch over a cauldron in which she is preparing a special brew for her son. Whoever drinks first of the brew will acquire all knowledge and wisdom. She admonishes the boy not to touch the hot liquid, but when the goddess is away, three drops fall accidentally on the boy's thumb. The boy sucks his thumb and thus acquires the knowledge and wisdom the goddess had meant for her son. She is furious! To escape her, the boy shapeshifts into various animals, but she also shapeshifts and closes in on him. Finally he shapeshifts into a grain of wheat, and the goddess swallows him while she is in the form of a hen. She becomes pregnant and gives birth to a beautiful, radiant boy, whom she casts into the ocean in a leather bag. The boy is rescued by a fisherman, who names him Taliesin ("Radiant Brow" in Gaelic), and he goes on to serve the people of his land as a great bard, poet, and shaman.[3]

In both stories, the ultimate purpose of the transformation is for the individual to be of service to his or her community, humankind, and the universe. Both stories involve an initiation process and the work or intervention of spirit. In "Salmon Boy," the final transformation is achieved through the administration of a wound—in the wounded-healer tradition—administered intimately by the father, who represents the people. In the Taliesin story, the final transformation is achieved through a death-and-rebirth initiation.

It is important to understand that shapeshifting is not an end in itself; turning into an animal is not the point. Nor should it be done to prove to ourselves or others that it is real. It certainly should not be done to impress others or for personal purposes, such as Gwion's desire to escape or the salmon boy's hunger and desire for adventure. Shapeshifting is a spiritual path, a tool used to grow spiritually, to become a more complete human being, fully manifest authentic being, and serve. In shapeshifting, the personal ego recedes, and the divine presence is manifested. Becoming one's ally is experiencing the One.

In a journey I did on the Scottish isle of Iona, one of my Celtic ancestors told me that a purpose of shapeshifting is to help maintain the unity, interconnectedness, and harmony of our ordinary-reality world by manifesting and experiencing those qualities fully.

Recall that the shaman or shamanic practitioner follows both an inner spiritual path and a public-service path. On this planet Earth where we are incarnated entities, manifesting authentic being is not an isolated purpose or endeavor; we do it so we can be of service to the Whole and to all other incarnated beings. It is as simple and beautiful as that.

Finally, there are other aspects of shapeshifting that I have found very beneficial: it teaches us how to work continuously with spirits, deepen our work with them, quickly shift between ordinary reality and nonordinary reality, and integrate shamanism into daily life. In all these ways shapeshifting has profoundly impacted and benefited my overall shamanic practice. I use shapeshifting in every shamanic journey and in all my divination, healing, and world work. It has greatly enhanced the overall quality of my shamanic work, and I have heard similar comments from many shamanic practitioners who have attended my workshops on shapeshifting.

SHAPESHIFTING INTO AN ALLY THROUGH SUBTLE ENERGY WORK

My shapeshifting teacher taught me a method that is based on working with the *energy body*, the energy field that is unique to each of us; it is sometimes referred to as *subtle energies*. Shapeshifting is the transformation of our entire being, and the initial manifestation is the transformation of the energy body. You could call this partial shapeshifting. Energy-body transformation, like physical-body transformation, can also be partial itself.

Different spiritual and healing traditions offer various models that describe the energy field or energy body. I call them "models" because they are symbols, using physical-world concepts, of what is, in reality, outside the physical world and hence not fully describable with ordinary language and concepts. These models are very useful, however, because they can help us work with our energy bodies.

The energy-body model I use is that of the *chakras,* or *energy centers.* They are identified and activated at different locations in the physical body, and each chakra has a specific meaning or purpose in relation to the energy body as a whole. A popular model identifies seven major chakras, ranging from the base of the spine to the top of the head: (1) the root chakra; (2) the womb or sexual chakra; (3) the solar plexus, power, or will chakra; (4) the heart chakra; (5) the throat chakra; (6) the third eye chakra; and (7) the crown chakra. It is useful to think of them as constituting a musical energy instrument, like a flute. Through intention and attention, we awaken or activate these chakras, by themselves or in combination, as if playing a musical instrument.[4]

Intention is particularly linked with the third, or will, chakra, and this energy center is used extensively in shapeshifting work. It is also connected to power and personal identity. The will chakra can be problematic for Westerners, because in the Western world, generations have misused this energy: there has been rampant abuse of power, the view of power as power over others and over our natural environment, the emphasis on individuality, and fear of assuming one's own inner power. It is not surprising that many in today's world either overemphasize and misuse the energy of the third chakra or fear and shy away from it. Yet shapeshifting requires the appropriate and sacred use of the third chakra.

The power of the intention to shapeshift comes from the interconnection between ourselves and the ally we are shapeshifting into. Attention and trust give us the awareness of and an opening to this connection. In all shamanic practices, the intention that we formulate and put forward is what allows us to cross the boundary between ordinary and nonordinary reality and work collaboratively with spirits. In shapeshifting, intention allows transformation to proceed.

Shapeshifting into an Ally

The first shapeshifting practice I learned was shapeshifting into an ally. Here is the method my shapeshifting teacher taught me:

- Be in as complete a state of attention and trust as you can.
- Clearly declare your intention to shapeshift.
- Focus your attention on your will chakra and activate it.
- Shift into nonordinary reality, in the Middle World, right where you are.
- Call the ally you are working with; it is good to see, hear, sense, or feel the ally clearly in front you.
- With your intention, and with full attention and trust, align your will chakra with that of the ally.
- Align your will, or third chakra, with the will of the Universe, of the One, through the ally.
- Seeing or sensing the ally in front of you, activate and align each of your other chakras with those of the ally, in whatever order seems most appropriate, taking time to focus on each chakra with intention and full attention.

Ethics play an essential role in shapeshifting; always ask the permission of the ally before shapeshifting into it. (This is also necessary when shapeshifting into any other animal or entity.) Ethics require that shapeshifting be practiced in harmony with the Universe. It should be practiced for spiritual growth and to be of service to others and to the world, not to satisfy personal, selfish needs, seek power that leads to abuse of power, or meet self-aggrandizing, narcissistic needs.

Once I had learned the method I have just described, my teacher, as I mentioned earlier, had me spend considerable time—weeks or months—on each step. Over time, the steps became naturally integrated and flowed easily as one practice, and yet the essence of each step fully remained. My teacher also explained to me the importance of aligning with the will of the Universe, the Whole, the One. I know I am aligned when I feel a strong sense of grace, peace, harmony, and centeredness.

Experiencing the Transformation

As I practiced shapeshifting into my ally each day, I could feel transformations occurring in me, without any effort on my part. This occurred at many different levels—my energy field, my emotions and feelings, my mind, my thoughts, and my bodily feelings. While these changes varied in kind and intensity depending on the day and on my intentions for shapeshifting, many sensations recurred. I felt a difference in my relationship to the outside world, my place in it, and my feelings toward it. My mind quieted down; my thoughts were spontaneous, in the now, and usually related to observations of what was. All of my senses were strongly impacted, as I perceived the external world quite differently from my usual human sensory perception. And as I expanded from one ally into shapeshifting with others, I noticed that my sensory experience differed with each.

I also felt strong physical sensations and physiological changes in my head, feet, legs, skin, and arms, associated with transformations into the ally's features. I moved differently; the sound of my voice changed. I learned to let my body express what it was experiencing. While I had learned that the initial transformations in the shapeshifting practice occur at the energy-body level, I soon saw that changes in the energy body are immediately felt or reflected in the physical body as well.

During my training, I found it particularly helpful to shapeshift while walking outside in nature. In this way, I could observe how my experience of the world around me was different, how my sensitivity to the world had changed. I noticed omens or signs from nature in an almost organic, effortless way. I was much more aware than usual of the presence of spirits in everything around me, and I connected with them, feeling deeply my intertwining with all else.

I have been particularly struck by how animals react to my presence while I am shapeshifted, even when only my energy body is involved. Wild animals come incredibly close to me, look at me, and behave in ways that I have never experienced as a normal human. It appears that animals are very sensitive to and perceptive of changes in our energy bodies, and I have used animal reactions as a gauge of sorts in practicing shapeshifting.

My first encounter with an animal while I was shapeshifted, early in my shapeshifting apprenticeship, was quite striking. I had been backpacking with Noëlle in the high Sierras of California for about twelve days, and we were coming down from the mountains into a long, wide, gently sloping valley. I had been shapeshifted into my ally tiger for about two hours, experiencing what it was like to walk in the wilderness as a tiger.

Noëlle was about two hundred feet ahead of me on the trail when I noticed a group of people on horseback coming up the valley, a cowboy guide riding in front. I watched them pass Noëlle, people tipping their hats or waving to say hello. As the group approached me and the guide was about thirty feet away, his horse suddenly let loose a loud whinny, reared, and nearly threw the poor cowboy to the ground. The other horses either stopped or moved backward.

The cowboy, clearly somewhat embarrassed, got control of his horse; looking at me with a strange stare, a mix of anger and confusion, he led the group in a wide arc around me. As they got back on the trail, several people turned and looked back at me with puzzled expressions. I was puzzled myself until I realized that the horses must have somehow perceived my shapeshifted form and had reacted as any horses would when sensing a tiger. This incident not only taught me about animal sensitivity to energy-body transformations, but also about the importance of varying, through intention, the level of shapeshifting so as to be appropriate to the situation at hand. I will say more about this later.

The metamorphosis into an ally is a very intimate, direct-knowledge experience. In becoming an ally, one learns about the animal in a way that is completely different from reading about or observing the animal in ordinary reality. I have gained a profound appreciation for the wonderful and awe-inspiring qualities of the many animals I have been honored to shapeshift into.

My shapeshifting teacher also instructed me to seek from each of my allies the quality or qualities that ally could bring to me to help me grow and become a fuller human being. I can sense those qualities as I shapeshift, and I continue to sense and embody them as I return to my human form.

Shapeshifting also offers a very different way of communicating with our allies. Because I have learned over time to use my visual, auditory, and kinesthetic senses in nonordinary reality, during a regular journey with an ally I usually see and sense my ally, and when I ask a question, the answer comes back through words or images. When I shapeshift into an ally and I have a question, either one I have formulated in advance or one that arises from the experience, I simply know the answer, naturally and immediately. I suspect that shapeshifting, as it was practiced by my ancient European Celtic ancestors and is still practiced by other indigenous cultures, serves as a powerful shamanic divination technique.

I would like to stress the importance of retransformation, or shapeshifting back into yourself after you have shapeshifted into an ally. As with transformation, it is important to do this consciously, with clarity of attention, intention, and trust. Over the years it has become more and more obvious to me that the whole point of shapeshifting into an ally or any other being is to be able to shapeshift back into our beautiful human form, manifesting through this form authentic being.

It is also possible to shapeshift into an ally while in a shamanic journey in the Upper, Middle, or Lower worlds, by using the chakra-alignment method described earlier, and to journey in the shapeshifted form. Shapeshifting back and forth during a journey is an excellent skill-building exercise. For example, you could do a regular journey to meet a spirit teacher, say in the Upper World, then shapeshift into an ally at the teacher's place and journey back as the ally to the Middle World, where your body is. Then you could shift to ordinary reality as the ally and shapeshift back into your human form. Alternatively, you could shapeshift into an ally before the journey, then journey as the ally to the Upper World to meet a spirit teacher, then shapeshift back into human form at the teacher's place and journey back to ordinary reality in human form. There are many possible variations.

Let me return to the point I made in the tiger story: we need to acquire the ability to vary, through intention, the level of our shapeshifting according to what is appropriate in the situation at hand. This is important when you do shamanic work for another person who is present or when you work with a group such as a drumming circle. It is particularly important when you do shamanic healing—retrieving an ally, a shamanic extraction, a soul retrieval, or some other form of healing—for another person. Being able to adjust our level of shapeshifting is an aspect of impeccability in doing shamanic and shapeshifting work.

For example, I have found that in searching for and recovering a lost ally or a lost soul part, or in extracting a spirit intrusion, the quality of my work is greatly enhanced if I carry out the healing in a shapeshifted form. However, it serves no good purpose and is inappropriate if the person for whom the healing is being performed somehow perceives the shapeshifting and becomes alarmed or confused.

A remarkable film called *Palos Brudefoerd* (or *Palo's Wedding*), made by Knud Rasmussen in 1933 in the Ammassalik district of East Greenland, depicts the life of the local Inuit. There is a scene in which a shaman performs an extraction healing for a young man who has been severely wounded. The shaman shapeshifts into a bear to do the healing, and as you watch the film, it is difficult to say whether the shaman is a man or a bear. This deep level of shapeshifting is appropriate for the Inuit culture, where shamanism and spirits are an integral part of daily life. For most of the people I do shamanic healing with, often in my living room, this level of shapeshifting is not appropriate. So I have learned to adjust the level as appropriate for the person I am working with and any other people present.

As I noted in chapter 1, an ally is not a specific, individual animal, but the spirit or essence of the species. When we shapeshift into an ally, we start with the spirit or essence and, in the practice, transform into a specific animal, for example male or female, young or old, of a specific color. I shapeshifted into my ally, tiger, in order to experience being a tiger. This is the power and mystery of the shapeshifting practice. As we shapeshift, we are the One, and we are an individual, although from another species. We experience both unity and individuality at the same time. The same applies when we shapeshift into entities other than animals. This is why shapeshifting is a profound spiritual practice.

Learning the shapeshifting practice by starting with an ally is important, because we already have an intimate relationship with the ally. As I noted earlier, over time my shapeshifting teacher led me to shapeshift into other allies of mine and later into animals that are not my allies.

SHAPESHIFTING INTO OTHER ENTITIES

After I had practiced shapeshifting into allies and other animals for many years, my shapeshifting teacher began teaching me how to shapeshift into other entities, such as rocks, trees, mountains, rivers, and oceans. Because the human species is part of the animal kingdom, there is a genetic affinity with other animal species. The experience of shapeshifting into a rock, a tree, or a body of water is profoundly different because we are dealing with fundamentally different forms of being. It is an experience of delving into the unknown, the unfamiliar. But interconnectedness is not limited to our connection to other animal species; we are connected to all that is. Because these other entities are so different from us, shapeshifting into them is a powerful and distinct way to put aside our ego mind and awaken to pure consciousness, authentic being, or being One. I will share some of my experiences of shapeshifting into such nonanimal entities and, with my teacher's permission, describe the techniques I was taught for doing so.

These methods all involve and start with energy work and use the energy-center or chakra model of the energy body. Like the method for shapeshifting into an animal, they involve transforming our energy bodies and experiencing the related transformations of our physical body and our consciousness. The energy work I have been taught to initiate shapeshifting differs for shapeshifting into animals, trees, rocks, mountains, or other beings or entities. My teacher repeatedly urged me to be open, to experience, to observe, and to put aside rational questions or explanations as I explored this unknown terrain.

Shapeshifting into a Rock

I always have had a special relationship with rocks, and one of the first techniques I learned in this phase of my exploration was shapeshifting into a rock or a rock formation. This can be done near a particular physical rock, on that rock, or from a distance. If you're doing the shapeshifting from a distance, it is important to have a relationship with the rock or rock formation—that is, to have been close to it and communicated with it. Here again it is the intention to shapeshift that allows the metamorphosis to proceed, and you need to be in as complete a state of attention and trust as possible.

Shapeshifting into a Rock

First, journey in the Middle World to the spirit of the rock or rock formation you have chosen and ask for its sacred name. You need to know this name to shapeshift into it; if the rock tells you its sacred name, you have permission to shapeshift. And it is important to remember the name of each rock you will shapeshift into, as a way of honoring the rock.

After you return from the journey to the rock spirit, with full attention and trust in the rock spirit and your own spirits, declare your intention to shapeshift. Focus on the third chakra and, with intention, bring its frequency of vibration to the rock's level of vibration. As that happens, bring the frequency of vibration of all the other chakras to the frequency of the rock's vibration, so all chakras vibrate at the rock's frequency. You may say the rock's sacred name as you work with the chakras, but it is not necessary. When it is time, slowly shift back to yourself and thank the rock spirit.

The first time I shapeshifted into a rock, I was hiking in the hills not far from my home. I had received a message from spirit a few days earlier, saying that it was time for me to shapeshift into a rock. I was apprehensive, not knowing what would happen and fearing that I might lose my identity. I was hiking shapeshifted into my ally hawk, and I watched as a hawk flew overhead and landed nearby. Then it arose again and flew in front of me, as if leading me. I followed it down a side trail, and when I arrived at a small rock formation, I knew this was where I needed to do the work. Just then a turkey vulture flew close by, and I felt supported.

I sat on top of the rock and journeyed to its spirit in the Middle World. As soon as the spirit showed itself, it told me its sacred name and said it was happy I was going to shapeshift into it. I thanked the spirit and came back to ordinary reality from my hawk form, returning fully to my human form with full attention in the here and now. I felt trust in the rock spirit, my spirits, the surrounding nature spirits, and my shapeshifting teacher.

With the intention to shapeshift into the rock, and repeating the rock's sacred name aloud, I started to bring my third chakra's energetic vibration to the level of that of the rock. Then I brought the frequency of my other chakras' vibration to that of the rock. Fairly quickly I felt I had become massive—and paralyzed. My face felt dense and my mouth shut, lips and jaw compressed. I could no longer utter the rock's sacred name as I experienced the unfamiliar sensation of becoming rock. I had no thoughts; I simply was. I lost all sense of time, as if I were dwelling in an eternal present moment. I sensed the wind on my rock faces, the change of day to night, the presence and growth of moss, the presence of animals, and these changes did not disturb my sense of being fully in the present. These changes were happening, but not in time. I felt solid, heavy, compacted, yet in a powerful and intensely peaceful state.

After a while, I used my intention to slowly come back to myself. I opened my eyes and felt a great calm. All was peace and quiet. I felt connected to everything around me; there was no separation. My human ego and all its attendant issues felt of little importance to me. I thanked the spirit of the rock, got up, and left, feeling changed in a strange yet wonderful way.

Shapeshifting into a Tree

My profound affinity for trees dates back to when I was a small child, and anyone who knows me well is aware of this. Years before I learned about shapeshifting, my children joked that when I retired I would turn into a tree. Hence, I was excited as well as apprehensive when my shapeshifting teacher gave me the instructions for shapeshifting into a tree. As with shapeshifting into a rock, you can do this while next to a tree or at a distance from a tree you know.

Shapeshifting into a Tree

Shapeshifting into a tree, as I learned to do it, involves two other chakras in addition to the seven chakras described earlier. I call these the transpersonal and transterrenial chakras. They are located, respectively, a few inches above the head and a few inches below the feet.

When shapeshifting outdoors into a tree, it is always good to stand next to the tree, look at it, observe it, make contact with it, get to know it in ordinary reality first. Next, greet and honor the tree spirit in the Middle World and ask it for permission to do the work; if you are working from a distance, do a Middle World journey to the tree to ask permission. It is good to start this work as yourself as opposed to being shapeshifted into an ally.

Place your attention on all of your chakras—nine in all—and become aware of each of them breathing. You may do this one chakra at a time (the order does not matter) or by focusing on all of them at once. Then, using the third chakra, put the intention forward to shapeshift and call the spirit of the tree, asking that it make the breathing of your chakras its own breathing.

When it is time to return, slowly shapeshift back into yourself and thank the tree.

The first time I shapeshifted into a tree, I was in Europe teaching, and the experience was both unexpected and deeply moving. I was spending a few days between workshops in the Condroz of Belgium, in the village and countryside where I spent many of my happier childhood days. I was taking a walk though some woods nearby where I had gone as a child. It was March, and the trees were bare. I walked toward a spot where a beautiful great elm had lived, an elm that had become an important friend when I was little, and which I had called the Twins because of its huge double trunk. The tree, unfortunately, had been cut down several years earlier.

I passed by several large, single-trunk elms and thought they might be relatives or descendants of the Twins. I had been thinking about doing my first shapeshifting into a tree since entering the woods, and I decided to do the work with one of these big elms. I was attracted by a large tree, approached it, and spent some time getting to know it. I put my forehead on it and asked the tree spirit's permission to shapeshift. The spirit showed itself as an old man and said I could. I leaned my back against the tree trunk, placed my attention on my chakras' breathing, put forth with my third chakra my intention to shapeshift, and called the spirit of the tree to make my chakras' breathing its own.

I entered into an utterly unfamiliar state, different from experiences of shapeshifting into a rock or an ally. I did not, as I had perhaps expected, strongly feel roots or branches. My experience was primarily auditory; immediately I heard other trees talking, and one in particular, in front of me and to the right. Its voice was a very loud sound, remarkable, like sharp groans, like hardwood rubbing against itself deep inside the tree. I began "speaking" too, communicating with the tree and the others around me, who also seemed to speak. I spoke from inside my trunk, where the sap was rising and the cells that channeled the sap were vibrating, making a sound. I had absolutely no thoughts, no mind or sense of sight, just a sense of hearing. I was strongly linked to the trees around me. I leaned away from the tree and continued shapeshifting. I was incredibly awake and linked to the other trees in community, but without dependence. It was a raw, pure state of love.

I shapeshifted back into myself, quickly and easily. I felt more whole, and I had a need to walk deeply into the forest. It started raining, and I did not care. I wanted to be in that forest, to live there.

Shapeshifting into a Mountain

Some years ago, Noëlle and I were hiking up Mount Ausangate in Peru with a group of Q'ero shamans from the Peruvian Andes. Following a sacred ceremony at more than sixteen thousand feet on the flanks of the mountain, we saw one of the older shamans shapeshift into the mountain. He was some distance away, and we watched as he took the shape of the mountain, became the mountain. This shaman later became a teacher for me in nonordinary reality and taught me how to shapeshift into a mountain or a hill. He told me that shapeshifting into a mountain was not an obvious thing; he urged me to be open and trusting and to know that in this kind of work, rational questions have no answer. He instructed me to leave my rational mind aside and delve into the mystery.

Shapeshifting into a Mountain

You can do this work close to a mountain you can see or at a distance from a mountain you know. It is nice to do it outdoors with the mountain in view. What is important is to feel the energy and presence of the mountain, and this is easier to do when you are in direct contact with the mountain and can see it. However, as with a rock or tree, you can also do it by visualizing the mountain and journeying to it in the Middle World.

The first thing to do is to empty yourself of all heavy energy in your energy field; it is important that your energy be very light. According to the Q'ero tradition, heavy energy, which they call Utcha, is not bad energy; it is simply energy that causes disharmony, disturbances, or a feeling of toxicity in your energy field and, therefore, in your being. A Q'ero method to cleanse heavy energy involves breathing the heavy energy into your spiritual stomach, which the Q'ero call Cusco, where it is digested. You then offer the digested heavy energy to the Mother Earth, the Pachamama, through your feet with your out-breath. The Q'ero say the Pachamama relishes that digested energy.

Next, do a Middle World journey to the spirit of the mountain to ask the spirit permission to do the shapeshifting work. If the mountain spirit agrees, ask the spirit for one or more words to use in shapeshifting. This is important and a key to this work. The words you receive are power words—sacred words that enable the shapeshifting to take place.

When you are ready to shapeshift and are in a state of full attention and trust, begin repeating the sacred words aloud, focusing your intention on shapeshifting into the mountain, and aligning the will, heart, and root chakras with those of the mountain. As my Q'ero teacher told me, the heart chakra is especially important in this work; mountains have big heart energy. Continue repeating the words aloud as you use intention to align these three chakras.

When it is time to return, it is important to retransform slowly, without rushing, until you feel fully human again. Thank the mountain.

The first time I shapeshifted into a mountain, I was not far from my home in the Marin Hills, sitting on a rock and looking at Mount Tamalpais. I had worked with the spirit of Mount Tam, as we call her, for some time, and she had indicated it would be good to start my shapeshifting-into-a-mountain practice with her. I cleansed my heavy energy and did a Middle World journey to a power spot on a trail up the mountain. I called the spirit of Mount Tam, and the spirit said it was good for me to shapeshift at this time.

Immediately, and before I asked for them, the spirit gave me three sacred words. I came back to my place on the rock, aligned my three chakras, and repeated the three words aloud, slowly. Very quickly I felt my entire body become stiff, as if frozen in time. I could hardly move my jaw, and my words came out slower and slower until I could no longer speak. I continued to say the words silently until that, too, became impossible. I felt heavy, dense, and immense. My hands, hanging over my knees, felt extremely heavy and seemed to get longer at the fingertips, as if they were stalactites, until they connected with the ground. I felt the wind upon my sides. I felt deep compassion for all creatures and beings living upon me—trees, bushes, mammals, birds, snakes, insects, humans. I felt love, and I cared for all. I knew I was being taught being, becoming, and compassion and that these qualities were somehow being imprinted in me. I retransformed very slowly and thanked the mountain. I felt peaceful and connected, part of the One.

Shapeshifting into the Ocean

The first time I was led by my spirits to experience shapeshifting into the ocean, it was a major initiation for me. I found it beautiful, meaningful, and profound.

Noëlle and I were spending a few weeks at a friend's house near the ocean north of San Francisco. For a couple of days I had been getting messages from my shapeshifting teacher, my allies, nature spirits, and the spirit of the ocean—whom I call Yamaha and with whom I had worked for many years—saying that I was ready to learn and experience shapeshifting into the ocean. My teacher had told me that Yamaha would teach me. He also had said that the spirit of Greenland, whom I call Mother and with whom I had worked when we kayaked in the Ammassalik region of East Greenland the year before, would also help.

I started walking on the beach at low tide, thinking I would go to an isolated stretch about a mile away. I had trepidation about entering into the unknown, and I felt vulnerable. Along the way, various animals—a seal, two blue herons, turkey vultures, crows—were behaving in unusual ways, approaching me, looking at me, flying or swimming ahead of me, as if leading me on. I felt the animals supporting me, guiding me, taking me through portals. I understood it was important to let go of my ego, my beliefs, my expectations; to be clean, open, empty, authentic being; and to trust spirit. My allies asked if I was ready to let go of the old, to literally die. It was terrifying to realize I could vanish, cease to be. I took a deep breath and told the universe I was ready to let go, and I put my trust in my own spirits and the spirit of the ocean.

As I came around a bend of the beach, I had in mind a spot where I would do the shapeshifting. Then a turkey vulture came flying toward me at low altitude, and as he reached me, he turned around and flew low over the beach ahead. He went past the spot I had picked, slowly flew over a rock wall straddling the beach, and disappeared. I climbed the wall and saw the turkey vulture land at a spot a little farther off, beside a rock alongside a cliff. As I looked at him, the bird lifted off again and joined a number of other turkey vultures and crows far off down the beach.

I knew that the place the vulture had just left was where I was to shapeshift into the ocean. I spotted a plank against the cliff, about a yard and a half long, retrieved it, and carried it to the spot, laying it on two small rocks for stability. I sat, feeling both open and vulnerable. I put my trust in Yamaha and the spirits.

I journeyed to my shapeshifting teacher, who told me again that Yamaha would teach me this lesson. I took a deep breath, shapeshifted into my ally seal, and went to Yamaha, swimming out into the ocean in the Middle World. I felt her presence strongly. I honored her and asked permission to shapeshift into the ocean, and she said I could. I asked if she could teach me now. Immediately, it was serious business.

She told me to lie down, enter a state of full attention and trust, and put my intention into shapeshifting into the ocean. Then I was to awaken all my chakras so my energy field would be fully alert. Next, I was to call her, the spirit of the ocean. She would come and "cover" me, as water surrounds a body, and the spirit would "extinguish" all my chakras. When my energy field completely disappeared, I would become the ocean. My energy field would not align with the ocean as it did with other entities; it would be abolished, extinguished. The complete disappearance of my energy field would indeed be death. Nothing would be left of me; I would be the ocean.

I asked Yamaha when and how I would be able to shapeshift back into myself. She replied that I needed to call Mother, the spirit of Greenland, with my intention, and Mother would come and recreate me, rebirthing my energy field. She also told me I did not need to contact Mother before shapeshifting; the spirit was aware of what was happening and would come to help me when called.

I returned from my journey to Yamaha, came back to ordinary reality, and fully shapeshifted back into myself. I lay down on the plank with my head facing east and my hands lightly touching the sand at my sides, and started the work. I activated all my chakras. I called Yamaha and immediately felt surrounded by a light fluid. I could feel my chakras being extinguished, my energy body disappearing. This is almost impossible to describe: it was a feeling of "not being," of death.

Every now and then my body shook, as if resisting my disappearance as I went deeper. Then it quieted, and the only sensation I felt was of my hands lightly touching the sand, small pebbles, and rocks. But it did not feel like human touch; it was an experience of water lapping over a sandy bottom. I knew that the ocean waves, the surf, the ocean color, the swirling water touching the bottom, the rocks—these were not the ocean. They were movement, the action of wind, heat, moon, earth rocks, and mantle on the ocean, not the ocean itself. The ocean was something else—a not-being. I felt a deep peace, yet that peace had a different quality from peace I had experienced before; this was a not-being peace. I felt joy, but without expressing it. I knew that all emotions, all expressions, my mind, everything was contained in me, Ocean, yet need not be expressed. I was pure consciousness; I was the One.

I called Mother and felt her come to me. She recreated my chakras, the me, and I slowly opened my eyes. I felt strangely numb, silent, calm, slow, and yet with a deep longing for where I had come from. I thanked Yamaha and Mother and slowly stood. As I walked back, observing without thought my surroundings, I still felt that strange sensation of the ocean. Two turkey vultures came and circled overhead. The two blue herons I had passed earlier watched me walk by.

Shapeshifting into the Ocean

You can do this work outdoors at the ocean, on a beach or a cliff, as long as you can be assured you will not be disturbed. Or you can do it from a distance, indoors or outdoors.

You first need to do some preparatory work. Contact the spirit of the ocean, honor the spirit, ask for permission to do the shapeshifting, and ask the spirit which other spirit you will need to invoke to bring you back to human form when it is time to retransform. This could be a spirit you already know, such as a guide, or it could be one you have not encountered before; the spirit of the ocean will tell you. You do not need to contact the spirit who will bring you back yet; it will come when you invoke it. When you are finished with the preparatory work, come back and prepare for shapeshifting.

If you work from a distance, do a Middle World journey to a spot by the ocean, contact the spirit of the ocean, do the preparatory work, and come back.

Now follow the instructions Yamaha gave to me. Lie down, and with full attention and trust, put your intention into shapeshifting into the ocean. Awaken all your chakras and when you feel they are fully engaged, call the spirit of the ocean. Gently surrender as the water inundates your energy field and you become the ocean.

When you are ready to shapeshift back, call the spirit that will regenerate your unique energy field and return to yourself.

While shapeshifting into allies can be a frequent practice, it is best not to overdo it with beings other than animals. This kind of work needs to be done only when appropriate and with spirits' guidance. Each shapeshifting experience can be very profound, and you will need time to integrate it. This integration occurs consciously and unconsciously in your body, your energy field, and your consciousness. I typically let several months elapse between sessions of shapeshifting into a rock or a tree, and longer— sometimes years—between sessions of shapeshifting into the ocean.

MULTIPLE SHAPESHIFTING

At one point my shapeshifting teacher introduced me to what he called multiple shapeshifting: shapeshifting into several allies consecutively until I was shapeshifted into all of them simultaneously. As with other shapeshifting experiences, my teacher advises that it is important not to try to think about or understand this practice rationally, but to live it.

In many ancient mythologies and varieties of art, there are mythic forms representing beings that are partly human and partly animal, with two or more animal forms present. We find this in ancient Egyptian art, and it is also strikingly evident in recent Inuit sculptures, often carved in serpentine, that represent a man or woman whose body is partly bear and partly bird, or partly seal and partly bear, or other combinations.[5] It is possible that these are artistic representations of multiple shapeshifting.

When I do multiple shapeshifting, it is usually with two or three allies. The experience is one of presence and strong connection with the world around me. It is a different feeling from shapeshifting with one ally, less marked by the characteristics of a single animal, more alive and in the moment. There is a feeling of lightness of being, a beingness that is pure, without judgment about anything that surrounds me or is going on in the mind. I feel joy and a sense of harmony with everything around me, which all seems very familiar and intimate.

You can do this exercise anywhere. I have enjoyed it while walking alone in nature. As I shapeshift into several allies, I feel unusually close to the natural world around me and very easily able to connect completely with it. As I practiced multiple shapeshifting, my shapeshifting teacher asked that I also shapeshift back into myself while staying shapeshifted into the allies; my human self thus became part of the multiple shapeshifting. This state of being is one of pure, light, and joyful awareness of myself and of the surrounding world.

SHAPESHIFTING AS A SPIRITUAL PATH

Shapeshifting can be a deep, profound spiritual practice. The fundamental purpose of the work, as I mentioned earlier, is to help us know and be interconnected with everything so we can be of service to the universe as authentic being. This is what we and our modern world so desperately need today. Shapeshifting reinforces our awareness of the Oneness of the universe and the sacredness and interconnectedness of everything through direct whole-body, whole-being experience. It helps us realize our true divine nature, as part of the One, as being the One. It can be used as a personal spiritual path or incorporated in other shamanic practices. Both uses ultimately relate to being of service to the world and our fellow human beings.

Joseph Campbell, in speaking about the sacred dance honoring the Hindu goddess Shiva, gives an eloquent description of shapeshifting, though he does not use the word.[6] In the sacred dance, he says, "the god is the dancer, and you have to become the god to worship the god, to find that god in yourself. . . . No matter what you call the god or think it is, the god you worship is the one you are capable of becoming. The power of a deity is that it personifies a power that is in Nature and in your nature."

The contemporary nondualism teacher Adyashanti says, "True relationship is not what happens between two or more entities. True relationship is the Oneness dancing with itself."[7] This for me is a wonderful way of describing shapeshifting. In many ways shapeshifting is a sacred dance.

It is important to remember that when we talk about shapeshifting, we are limited by language that was created to describe the ordinary physical world. Our words and concepts are often inadequate to fully express spiritual experiences, insights, or knowledge. This is why it is important not to become stuck in the rationality and logic, or the lack thereof, that we find in the words we read, hear, or use when discussing shapeshifting.

As we deepen our shapeshifting practice, we delve into the mystery of life. As all spiritual traditions tell us, the more we learn and know, the more we realize that we do not know. Spiritual traditions speak of the true nature that we are, the authentic being that we are, of being one with everything instead of being the ego or persona we think we are and identify with. In shapeshifting, we become the One, and therefore our true selves, by becoming another: *we awaken to the One we are.*

As Campbell said, "[Y]ou have to become the god to worship the god, to find that god in yourself." Shapeshifting can thus be looked upon as a form of worship. In shapeshifting we worship the transcendent, the divine as represented by what we shapeshift into. We cannot worship the transcendent of what we do not become, of what we are not already. Shapeshifting into animals, mountains, trees, oceans, connects us with the transcendent aspects of nature, with the powers of the universe. If we shapeshift into these powers, then we have them in us; we are them.

When we become aware of who we truly are, which shapeshifting practice can help us do, we learn how to be fully in the here and now and realize that every moment is a precious opportunity. In being who we truly are, we can freely choose how to be and act instead of being carried by the current of life flowing around us. We can learn to *be* the current of our life, and everything we do is transformed.

While shapeshifting is ultimately a personal, individual quest, as we awaken to our divinity and build or regain personal inner harmony, we help build world harmony, because everything in the world is interconnected. By manifesting this interconnectedness, we also serve the universe by awakening, or lighting up, the threads of the web of life, the web of being. Here I can use the quantum-physics analogy of the interpenetration of matter through the infinite probability wave functions. Just so is personal harmony transmitted throughout the world through the web of interconnections. Yet when we are awakened to authentic being, interconnectedness takes on an even deeper meaning. It is more than being linked; it is *being*, within ourselves, all that is.

PART II

Shamanism in the Twenty-First Century

7

Shamanism in Family and Daily Life

◦ ◖ ◦

THE CHALLENGES OF MODERN LIFE

We live in an increasingly materialistic culture in which we are increasingly isolated from nature and increasingly separated from one another. For many of us, the days look like recurring film clips of endless activities where the key word is *busy*. We are continuously preoccupied with making sure we can make ends meet or checking our long list of to-dos, which include working, making money, meeting family needs, maintaining a house and car, fulfilling legal obligations, answering emails—on and on it goes. We find ourselves multitasking, tossed between feeling satisfaction and pride at carrying out multiple activities at once, and feeling reduced to automatons. At the same time, many in our society experience a recurring sense of boredom, even if they are very busy. This boredom leads to feelings of isolation; a sense of meaninglessness in our lives, our world, and our place in it; and feelings of frustration.

Time, which for the largest part of human evolution and history aligned human cycles with the other cycles of nature, has in an abruptly short period become an abstract concept defined by the clock and the pages of the appointment calendar. We are in many ways enslaved to this abstract ticking time that runs our lives with inescapable authority. Advances in mass production and technological innovation are giving rise to the faster and faster creation and distribution of technologies and machines. These new gadgets and devices increasingly do just about anything and allow us to do things faster and faster. Everything is going faster and faster, to the point that time itself seems to be accelerating. And most of us feel the need to go faster still.[1]

Technology is a double-edged sword. Since its emergence millions of years ago, the human species has been characterized by our great capacities for toolmaking—and our increasingly complex technologies are just increasingly sophisticated tools. These technologies have brought us many benefits—such as survival, health, welfare, and cultural benefits—in addition to our understanding of the universe we live in. Recent inventions such as cell phones and the Internet have dramatically improved our capacities for communication across the entire planet and given us unprecedented access to information and knowledge. Global communications technologies available to nearly all have brought forth benefits such as greater attention to social justice issues, increased solidarity and mutual aid, and enhanced connections among dispersed families and communities.

Yet technology has also given us the means to cause massive havoc to the environment and to mercilessly destroy one another. It has also contributed to our alienation from the rest of nature and isolation from one another, leading to a pervasive sense of separateness. We have also become increasingly dependent on—and addicted to—technology. Thomas Berry, author of *The Dream of the Earth,* has called this "a technological entrancement, an altered state, a mental fixation."[2] The image of people chatting on their cell phones as they navigate a busy street or hike in a park is a symbol of how we have become cut off from our immediate environment and each other.

Technology itself is neither good nor bad. What matters is how we use these tools: Are we engaging with technology mindlessly, leading to destruction, isolation, and alienation? Or are we engaging with technology with awareness and intention, leading to enhancement and greater wellbeing of all that is—humans and the rest of nature?

Modern economic systems have also contributed to materialization and a sense of separateness. In the United States it is generally acknowledged that the strength of the economy depends on consumer spending. Our consumption economy has contributed to our alienation from nature despite the fact that all consumer products originate in the natural environment. It ceaselessly urges people to spend and consume, and it promotes products that quickly become obsolete, leading to a frenzy to buy more and make sure we have the newest gadget on the market.

We and our families dwell in this frenetic, alienated, consumptive environment. Family, and community, its natural extension, has been at the core of daily life for as far back as we can see. And while forms of family have evolved in the past few generations—to include traditional, single-parent, and same-sex-parent families—the most widespread form in most of the modern Western world is the nuclear family, with parents and children living apart from other close relatives. This kind of family has led to further isolation, which often spills over into the community; nuclear families in countless urban and suburban neighborhoods barely know or relate to their neighbors.

The characteristics of modern life I have just described also contribute to the dearth of a spiritual life in most families. Rituals in particular, which I believe are an essential element of a healthy and thriving family environment, have by and large disappeared from daily family living. Traditional religious rituals, once an accepted part of family and community life, have lost their appeal for many and have seldom if ever been replaced. Even the simple daily ritual of family meals, characterized by attentive and conscious participation, has largely disappeared. This is particularly true in the United States, where family members often eat separately, on the fly, or in front of the television.

Shamanism and a shamanic practice provide ways to address these imbalances and disharmonies in the way we live. Embracing a shamanic practice and worldview in modern life does not mean rejecting technology or somehow changing the world we live in; instead, it means *reconsecrating modern life*—changing the way we perceive and relate to the world. The basic principle of shamanism, that everything has a spiritual dimension, means that shamanism can help us see the sacred in everything. And just as the shamanic perspective has traditionally recognized the sacred in our natural environment—trees, rocks, animals, the wind, a mountain—it can help us recognize the spiritual dimension of the man-made environment in which we live.

Cities, buildings, cars, computers, and cell phones are all made of earth stuff. If we see the sacred in these things, our use of them and our lives with and among them take on a completely different character. We can approach our use of modern technology with awareness and the right intention, acknowledging the sacred in it, communicating with the spiritual dimension that is part of its broader reality. Perhaps a shamanic perspective is now more relevant than ever.

How would your life change if you decided to integrate shamanic practices into everyday modern living? To help you imagine the possibilities, allow me to share stories of how shamanism has been a part of my family life and other aspects of daily life.

SHAMANISM IN FAMILY LIFE

I have been blessed with eight beautiful grandchildren. They have been my students, my teachers, and most of all my tireless playmates. Before each of them was born, usually in the third trimester of pregnancy and with the permission of the parents, I undertook a shamanic journey to meet the spirit or soul of the being who was about to incarnate. I introduced myself to the spirit, said that I was its grandfather, told the spirit that I was happy it had chosen my family to join in this world, and welcomed it.

Spirits are formless, while physical form is a part of ordinary reality. In my experience and understanding, the way spirits show themselves to us in a shamanic journey or state of consciousness—the form spirits assume and that we perceive as we encounter them—is part of their communication with us. It is part of the message they convey. When I journeyed to meet my grandchildren's spirits before they were born, they showed themselves as young children, either boy or girl. Each time I felt a strong connection with their essence, and my perception of the sex of the child I met always turned out to be correct.

My children didn't always believe some of the details I offered when I shared my experiences. One of my grandchildren appeared to me as a small young boy with a thick tuft of blond hair. He already had an older brother with very dark hair, and his parents raised an eyebrow when I mentioned the blond hair. But when he emerged from the womb, sure enough, he had a beautiful crown of blond hair.

The real test came with my last grandchild. The parents had decided not to find out ahead of time what sex the child was, and they were convinced they would have a girl; the baby moved in the womb the way their first daughter had. My other children were also certain it would be a girl, and they all challenged my account that the spirit had manifested itself to me as a boy. When my grandson was born and we met again, he almost seemed to wink.

Before they were born, the spirits of each of my grandchildren shared with me an essential aspect of their nature, of who they would become in this lifetime. This was usually conveyed in a symbolic or metaphorical way. One grandchild told me she would be an elf. Another said he would be a warrior dancer. Another said he would incarnate the essence of the Celtic god Pan. One grew a long nose, à la Pinocchio, and told me she would tell lies in this life but would then overcome this and acquire the power to turn matter into spirit. Another said that northwest would be an important direction for her, and moon energy and moonlight would be important for her as well. I shared this information with the parents, who, no matter how skeptically they may have viewed it, always wanted it. In every case, the characteristics the spirit showed me revealed themselves in the growing child.

All of these meetings were profound experiences for me, nurturing and deeply touching. Each time I felt privileged and blessed to have such intimate contact. I am convinced that these initial contacts have continued to permeate my relationships with my grandchildren as they have grown, in a subtle and indescribable way, grounding my role as grandfather. It is as if from the start we have mutually acknowledged one another.

Children and Shamanic Practice

Noëlle and I have hosted an evening drumming circle at our house every two weeks for almost twenty years. Sometimes, some of our grandchildren have happened to be staying at our home on drumming-circle day. With the permission—and always delight—of the circle participants, we have invited the children to participate when the circle begins.

This has always been a treat and a joy for the children, and I have been amazed to observe the younger ones, the two- and three-year-olds, who normally could not stay still for more than a few minutes at a time, sit in the circle for as long as forty-five minutes, calm and fully present in the here and now.

Early on, one of the circle members taught the children, as well as our circle, the following simple ritual and song.

Children Call Their Allies

One at a time, people in the circle call aloud the name of one of their allies, such as eagle, deer, or turtle. Then the circle calls the ally, singing together: "Eagle spirit, eagle spirit, we are calling. Come, come and be with us now." Another ally is called and invited to come, and so on.

Children love this ritual and usually want to go on and on with it. Because they can be so enthusiastic in calling their spirit allies, it is helpful for a grown-up to select who in the circle will call their ally next by pointing at them, so everyone has a chance to call out in turn.

I recall an evening when one of our grandsons, then only a year and a half old, was quietly sitting in the circle. He could hardly speak and his vocabulary was still quite limited, so we had not pointed toward him to indicate it was time to call out his ally. But after the other children had already called out several of their allies, my grandson's older sister, then about five, looked reproachfully at Noëlle and me and said, "What about my little brother?" We looked at our little grandson, pointed to him, and the circle was silent for a while as everyone looked and smiled at him. He opened his mouth and, with a little bit of struggle, said, "Baby beluga." We grown-ups marveled that he could understand what the ritual was about, not to mention that he could actually say those two words. But the other children were not surprised, and the ritual continued. The beluga whale has continued to be an important ally for my grandson. Over the years, the children have expanded the ritual on their own, spontaneously calling other spirits to come and join the circle, such as the sun spirit, the moon spirit, the wind spirit, and the rain spirit.

Small children go naturally in and out of a shamanic state of consciousness, are aware of the presence of spirits, and have a relationship with one or more allies, whom they often call their "animal friends." I believe this ability is part of human nature and is true for all children, wherever they are on our planet. For the great majority of children, certainly in the modern Western world, this capacity closes up or goes dormant as they grow older. Often this is a result of the way parents, family, teachers, or peers react to their mention of spirits or animal friends. These reactions at worst can be punitive and judgmental: "Talking like that is bad." At best they may be condescending or mocking: "This is just your imagination—get real." And then as adults, to reenter the state of connection with the spirit world, they have to sign up for workshops on shamanism to relearn what they knew very well as children!

I have learned from children that the best response I can give when they mention a shamanic experience is to respect them, acknowledge their experience, and perhaps recount a similar experience I've had. Most of all, I have learned to react in a casual, "no big deal" way. Shamanic experiences and spirits are part of their daily life and nothing to make a fuss about.

One of my grandsons is particularly sensitive to and aware of spirits. I love to hike with my grandchildren, and when I hike alone with him he will suddenly stop, point, and say, "Grandfather, you see the spirit there?" I reply, "Great! I can't see it, but I can feel it now that you point it out to me," as this has usually been the case. One day when this boy and his family were visiting and we were sitting in the living room with some friends who had stopped by, he walked into the middle of the group and said, "You know, I have three sets of eyes. One set is my normal pair of eyes, one set is to see at night, and one set is to see spirits." Following this declaration, he simply walked out of the room to go and play.

Family Rituals

Rituals have been an important part of my family life for many years. I am convinced that whether they involve only the nuclear family or the broader, multigenerational family, rituals are an essential element of family wellbeing, togetherness, and a sense of belonging to a larger whole. Rituals involve the totality of the participants—spirit, mind, emotions, and the physical body—and they help embody and manifest in the ordinary world the knowledge and power that come from the spiritual dimension. They are a powerful link between nonordinary and ordinary reality.

A group ritual manifests and enhances the interconnectedness between participants. In discussing rituals, Joseph Campbell said, "All a ritual does is concentrate your mind on the implications of what you are doing," and, "Ritual introduces you to the meaning of what's going on."[3] Sandra Ingerman, who in her teaching has highlighted the importance of rituals, has said, "The nature of ritual is that it creates change."[4] Rituals are transformative. They feed every aspect of the human being: the soul, the mind, the emotions, and the body.

Occasions for family rituals are many and varied. The cycles of nature provide opportunities, and in my extended family we have focused on the summer and winter solstices and, at times, the equinoxes. These seasonal rituals are important because they strengthen our awareness of our connection with nature. Then there are formal feasts and holidays; we have had a predilection for Thanksgiving, perhaps because it is a U.S. national holiday that is by and large devoid of commercialization and because giving thanks is so important and makes us feel good.

We also perform family rituals on significant days for family members, such as birthdays and anniversaries, and at events that occur only once, such as engagements and marriages; we did a ritual for my own retirement party. Some of these rituals included friends and colleagues, and in every case, nonfamily members, regardless of their familiarity or level of ease with ritual or their religious persuasion, have expressed great joy and heartfelt gratitude for being able to participate in the ritual.

Following the birth of each of our grandchildren, we have had a naming ritual to welcome the child into the family and onto this earth, with all our children, their spouses, and other grandchildren present. And there are the simple and mundane, yet so important, rituals such as the one at the beginning of a family meal. In our family, it consists of holding hands—we call it the "cosmic handshake"—and being silent for a minute as each of us expresses thanks for the plants and animals who feed us; thanks those who have planted, harvested, transported, and sold us the food; and then voices aloud the names of absent family members and puts them in the middle of the circle. When we perform a family ritual for a special occasion, it is always new and may be created by one or several family members.

Shamanic Journeying to Create a Family Ritual

Do a shamanic journey, or more than one journey if necessary, to ask spirits if they will teach or show you a ritual appropriate to the occasion. The spirits could be your own helping spirits, such as allies or spiritual teachers; the spirit of the family; the spirit of the house where the ritual will be held; a spirit related to the occasion, such as the spirit of the winter solstice; or a combination of these and other spirits. Describe the ritual to the family as they gather to take part.

Established rituals that come from indigenous or spiritual traditions have power because of their sacred and often mysterious origin, their longevity, and the fact that they connect us with all the other people in space and time who have performed the same ritual. Like all religious or spiritual rituals, traditional rituals are vulnerable to rigidity or ossification, where performing them correctly takes preeminence over their meaning or essence. Details such as the direction a circle turns or the color associated with a cardinal direction become an obligatory "must do it right," when, in fact, such details vary from culture to culture.

When a group ritual comes down directly from spirits related to members of the group, the place, and/or the occasion for the ritual, it takes on a special form of power that is immediate and very nurturing. We have found this way of receiving a ritual to be most meaningful for our family rituals, as it makes the ritual come alive in a dynamic, sacred, and magical way. I have always been touched by my grandchildren's excitement and sense of wonder when a new ritual evolves and manifests naturally and with pure grace. Some of the rituals we have performed as a family have been very simple, while others have been elaborate and complex. I suggest being flexible and open to what comes.

Performing a Family Ritual

Turn off the phones and light a candle in a prominent place to denote that this is a sacred time and place. If possible, have drums and rattles available. Start the ritual by forming a circle. Everyone drums or rattles to call their spirit helpers; the spirit of the room, the house, the family, and the cardinal directions; or the spirits of nature nearby. If drums or rattles are not available, use any other percussion instruments. The individual or individuals in charge of the ritual can then lead the family into the ritual as necessary.

A ritual does not need to be elaborate to have power. What is important is for participants to be fully present in body, mind, and spirit, in the here and now, and to have a clear, common intention for the ritual. Leave it to the spirits who bring the ritual to decide how simple or complex it will be.

An Engagement Ritual

I remember a simple ritual we performed at an engagement party for one of our children that included family and friends. We formed a large circle, and one by one, when they felt they were ready, people around the circle went to the middle, picked out a flower from a large bunch of them laid on a table there, faced the couple while holding the flower, and expressed a wish for them as they journeyed through life together. Then they placed the flower in a large vase set next to a candle. When everyone had come into the circle and spoken and a large, beautiful bouquet had been created in the vase, someone in the circle (usually in a ritual such as this it would be the youngest or oldest person in the circle) picked up the vase of flowers and offered it to the couple. Then we all clapped, drummed, rattled, and shouted with joy to celebrate the engagement. A simple ritual such as this has a powerful and lasting impact on the couple and all in attendance. In this case, I recall that the flowers in the vase lasted an inordinately long time; three weeks later they were still blooming!

A Thanksgiving Ritual

Another example of a simple family ritual we performed more recently was for Thanksgiving. The person who had journeyed to obtain a ritual from spirits had also gathered a bunch of stones, each a couple of inches in diameter, and put them inside a basket. One by one, people in the circle stood up from their chairs, took a stone from the basket, went back to their place, and voiced aloud something they were particularly thankful for over the past year. Then they blew their gratitude into the stone and deposited it on an altar set up in the middle of the circle. Thus, a sacred pile of stones was created on the altar and left in place during the remainder of the Thanksgiving celebration.

The power and beauty of ritual was evident that day, as a small incident revealed. One of our grandsons, then about six, had been in a bad mood since early morning, complaining and aggressive. He had made it clear he did not want to participate in our ritual. As we began, he sat sullenly next to his mother, and we assumed he would not participate; we just hoped he would behave so we could celebrate in peace. But then, as we were nearing the end of the ritual, he got up, picked up a stone, and went back to his seat. We all watched, wondering what would happen. He opened his mouth and said, "I am thankful for ceremony," blew into the stone, and deposited it softly on the altar. He had spoken for us all.

A Winter Solstice Ritual

Children have an innate sense of ritual and an uncanny knowledge of right action and right speech in ritual. We once performed an elaborate family ritual at my oldest daughter's home to celebrate the winter solstice. It consisted of several parts, during which the four basic elements—earth, water, air, and fire—were combined in various ways. One of my daughters-in-law had obtained this ritual through a shamanic journey, and this particular ritual had struck me because it called to mind ancient philosophies from India whereby the primordial elements are combined.[5]

Small stones symbolized earth, a bowl of water symbolized water, our breath signified air, and a lighted candle represented fire. At one point, each of us was to take a stone and put it in the bowl of water. Our youngest grandchild, then not quite two years old, had been playing by himself in another part of the house as my daughter-in-law explained the ritual to the rest of the family in the living room. We did not expect him to participate, given his young age and the complexity of the ritual. Yet as we were about to start, he walked into the living room, went straight to the basket of stones, picked one, took it over to the bowl of water, and deposited it inside. Then he left, content, and went back to play.

A Retirement Ritual

Another ritual we performed included children, spouses, grandchildren, close friends, and professional colleagues—about seventy-five people in all. It was for my retirement party. Noëlle and I had journeyed to spirits to obtain an appropriate ritual to do at some point during the party, which we hosted at the local community center.

We divided the participants into three groups. We asked the first to focus on the past, starting with a short, silent meditation during which they were invited, if they wished—as were all the groups—to call upon the spirits of surrounding trees and bushes, the spirit of the building, and the spirit of life, and to come up with three themes that illuminated the professional life I was now leaving. We also asked them to create a short public manifestation of these themes through song, sound, movement, or playacting.

The second group would focus on the present, coming up with three pieces of advice to help me as I went through this transition and creating a short public manifestation of these. The third group was asked to focus on the future, contribute three themes for my post-retirement work, and create a short public manifestation of those themes.

Each group performed enthusiastically, with much energy and fun and laughter. And while many in the party rarely, if ever, engaged in spiritual practice or ritual, the comments we received about their experience were uniformly positive. And the ritual helped me make my transition into retirement harmonious and joyful.

A Ritual for the Death of a Pet

Not only are family and community rituals important when celebrating special occasions or events; they can also be a source of healing, solace, resolution, and fortitude in unexpected, difficult, or unusual situations. One such occasion happened when Noëlle and I were visiting grandchildren and their parents who were living in the mountains. We arrived to hear from our eight-year-old granddaughter, who was in tears, that her three fish had died; she had found them that morning in their fishbowl, whose newly changed water had been too cold. There was much grief and a big dilemma. How to dispose of the three fish?

Outside there was snow, and the ground was frozen; there was no way to bury the fish. The kitchen garbage was out of the question. The parents suggested the toilet bowl.

Noëlle proposed, "Let's do a ritual and ask our spirit allies to help." Our granddaughter revealed that she had otter as an ally. Noëlle said, "We can ask otter to take the fish all the way to the ocean as a resting place." We set up a ritual space in the living room, a candle in the middle, and the fish in a plastic bag next to the candle. All family members present sat in a circle, and we began singing the song I described earlier to call our allies. The children got to call as many spirits as they wanted. Then, going around the circle, each one of us told what we had enjoyed about these fish, all the good memories. We all thanked the fish for their presence among us over the past months.

Then we all went into the bathroom, with our granddaughter carrying the fish in their plastic bag. We crowded around the toilet bowl in the small bathroom, and she put the fish inside. She called upon otter spirit to please take the fish down all the way to the ocean to a good resting place. And she flushed the toilet.

The children went back to play, and life went on. Our granddaughter had been asking to go to the pet shop to replace the fish immediately, but she let go of that idea. She continued to grieve appropriately, and after a while she considered not having fish as pets anymore. They are very sensitive to temperature change, she had discovered, and it was too hard to lose them.

SHAMANISM IN DAILY LIFE

A shamanic practice that is aware of and evokes the sacred in everything, even in the more routine and ordinary aspects of daily life, gives me joy and support. It is, I am convinced, one way to reconsecrate life, to live in harmony with all that is. Modern Western culture tends to compartmentalize everything, keeping the various parts of ourselves and our lives separate. For many in the West, the religious experience is associated with specific times and days of the week and with special events in the religious calendar, and the rest of life is somehow disconnected from religion. Even many well-meaning shamanic practitioners I have encountered seem to adhere to this cultural trait in their own shamanic practice. They practice shamanism when they are in a drumming circle, workshop, or formal ritual or shamanic session, but shamanism is out of sight, out of mind, so to speak, in their professional, family, and social lives.

Tom Cowan and Evelyn Rysdyk speak to the importance of making our shamanic practice relevant to daily life while emphasizing the classic shamanic journey to spirits of the natural world and to our own spirit guides.[6] As I noted earlier in the chapter, the mundane objects of daily life are all made of earth stuff and have a spiritual dimension. They are entirely compatible with shamanic journeying, and combining the two lends deeper meaning to the ordinary world around us. This is why I routinely journey to the spirits of the man-made objects that surround me and that I interact with during the course of my day. In this way I can acknowledge their natural origins and sacred nature and make them part of the reconsecration of my own life.

Contacting the Spirit of a Man-Made Object

In your daily life at home, the man-made objects whose spirits you may want to contact are often right beside you, such as your personal computer, cell phone, house, or car. I recommend meeting the spirits in the Middle World, and the journey is very straightforward.

Stand or sit next to the object, or if it is a structure, such as a house, get comfortable somewhere inside it. Close your eyes and with your intention enter the Middle World right there where you are; there is no need to go anywhere. Call the spirit of the object or structure. You may see, hear, sense, or feel it, or perhaps a combination of these. Honor the spirit, and ask if it would be willing to provide help and guidance for the greater harmony of the Whole. If you have a request, make it. Thank the spirit and return to ordinary reality.

I try to contact the spirit of my PC whenever I use it, although I do at times forget. At first the spirit showed itself in the form of a young child. Then, many months later, it changed and showed itself in the form of an animal. Its latest form was a picture of a sun, rather like a child would draw it, with a stalk like a sunflower's. As I mentioned, spirits are formless, and the form in which a spirit shows itself is usually part of a message. I understood the message from this last form to be to always approach my PC with a smile as I get ready to use it. The guidance I have received from the spirit of my PC has been diverse, from help in composing a difficult email, to a suggestion to call my sister on Skype, to a recommendation that I play a specific piece of music as I work on the computer.

As part of my brief daily morning ritual, I communicate with and honor the spirit of my house and the spirits of nature in my immediate surroundings. If I am going to spend time in my office and use my computer, I communicate with and honor the spirits of both. I also quickly communicate with spirits of organizations, places, and buildings I will interact with or visit during the day. I always acknowledge and honor the spirits. At times, I ask for counsel or the most appropriate outcome in light of the greater harmony of the Whole, now and into the future, for any meeting, project, or event I will be involved in during the day. As always, I strive for detachment from desired or anticipated outcomes that come from personal ego.

As I sat down to write this book, I called for counsel and support. In addition to calling on my own spirit helpers, I also called upon the spirit of the book, the spirit of shamanism, and other spirits related to the subject matter I was writing about. As I get into my car to run an errand, I contact the spirit of the car. As I sit down to work on my tax returns, I even communicate with, honor, and bless the spirit of the U.S. Internal Revenue Service! The opportunities are endless. Spirits are everywhere, and as we acknowledge their presence and honor and bless them—seeking counsel, support, and appropriate outcomes—we become more fully human; we help manifest the interconnectedness of everything; and we contribute to harmony, true being, and right action.

8

Shamanism in Professional Life

o O o

To many of us, the term *modern world* connotes to a large degree the economic, technological, political, and institutional systems in which we carry out our daily activities, including our professional work. And because our professional work, whatever that may be, consumes a major portion of our lives, adapting shamanic practice for our professional work environment is an essential element of reconsecrating the world we live in.

In traditional shamanic cultures, the shaman often practiced in the mainstream of society, helping his or her community with its daily activities, such as hunting, gathering, fishing, farming, launching expeditions, and constructing buildings.[1] The shaman did all of these things in addition to his or her primary soul work, which included healing, divination, and working with the dying and the dead. In modern societies, mainstream activities include engaging in commerce, finance, and manufacturing; governing; educating; providing health care; and doing research and development, to name just a few. How can today's shamanic practitioners work to support the mainstream activities of modern society?

I believe that it is important to *work with spirits within this mainstream*—the spirits related to the businesses, governments, and other institutions (such as community, educational, research, and nonprofit institutions) that perform these mainstream functions. By bringing spirit into these realms, evoking the sacred there, and manifesting the interconnectedness of everything, we can help heal ourselves and our communities. We can help our society live in harmony with the planet and all its inhabitants, face the social and ecological crises society has wrought, and prevent further strife. To manifest spirit within the mainstream, we must evoke *the shaman within* in our work life.

For much of my professional career, I worked for large corporations, specifically in the energy field. As a physicist, I was initially involved in the development of energy technologies and systems, including nuclear energy. Later I worked in environmental protection, also on behalf of a large energy corporation. I spent part of my career teaching and doing research in a major university, and I have worked closely with federal and state governments as well.

Since my early youth, I have been concerned with issues such as environmental protection, social justice, human relations, and social action. I have long been aware that the business world—particularly as represented by large corporations—has a bad reputation among spiritual, environmental, social justice, and nontraditional communities, and that reputation is at times well deserved. My conscious choice to work in the corporate world was based on a deeply felt conviction that doing so was the most effective way to bring about change in the areas I deeply cared about. While those outside the mainstream can and do accomplish important work by challenging institutions and stimulating change, I believe that substantial change must ultimately come from within the mainstream.

Most people I have worked with in corporations are good, decent human beings; they are not better or worse than those I've met in spiritual, environmental, and social justice communities. I've experienced the presence of greed, a lust for power, and arrogance among individuals in corporations and in all those communities. I've also experienced firsthand the defects of a system of commerce, economics, and finance that was developed without concern for the environment, social justice, or the public good.

In the preface, I described my introduction to shamanism in the early 1980s and my interest over the years in bringing traditional shamanism into modern life. In particular, I had a strong desire to bring my shamanic practice more fully into my professional life—in ways that went beyond seeking guidance from my spirits in traditional shamanic journeys—and to do so while maintaining the full integrity and essence of shamanic tradition. Through working with spirits, I came to understand that the way

I could do this was not by teaching shamanism to business people (I had thought of developing a special workshop for them), but rather by bringing spirit into my daily professional life.

To accomplish this, I needed new shamanic practices, adapted to the corporate work environment. I quickly realized I could find no one to teach me such practices, nor could I find any writings on the matter. So I turned to spirits—my own spirit guides and others—for direction, and as I practiced shamanism in work environments over many years, I learned much from these spirits.

SHAMANIC PRACTICES FOR THE WORK ENVIRONMENT

When working shamanically inside modern groups and institutions, it is critical to maintain the integrity of and respect for traditional shamanic knowledge, in terms of the nature of nonordinary reality and how to communicate and work with spirits. It is also essential to focus on the ethics principles outlined in chapter 1 and to always strive for impeccability. At the same time, our working environments today are vastly different from traditional shamanic societies, and we must find new ways to work shamanically in them.

Practicing shamanically in today's work environments requires daily—sometimes hourly—work, awareness, and attention. It is very difficult and requires much practice. We tend to be "asleep" and forget to do our shamanic practice when we are at work; we *forget* that spirits are all around us and that everything is sacred and interrelated. Remembering the spiritual dimension in everything is perhaps the real challenge in bringing shamanism into professional life, not the practices themselves; it certainly was for me.

The professional-life practices I learned from spirits are based on shamanic principles that will be familiar to you by now. An important one is that everything that has form in this world has a spiritual dimension. This includes man-made objects, such as buildings, cars, and computers, as we saw in the last chapter. It also includes people and our organizations, from small groups to corporations and nations. Because we have prejudices about ordinary reality, it is sometimes difficult for us to admit or recognize the spiritual dimension of modern objects, people, or groups.

We may not want to believe that a big, ugly truck speeding on the highway has a spirit, or that the U.S. Department of Defense or a political party or a big multinational oil company has a spirit, just as we tend to resist the idea that Adolf Hitler, Saddam Hussein, or Osama bin Laden had a soul or spirit, just like anyone else.

Another principle that applies here is that everything in this world is connected—that everything we do to bring harmony, anywhere and at any time, has repercussions elsewhere. The same holds true if our intention is to bring about disharmony.

Many of the shamanic practices I use in my work take place in the Middle World, the nonordinary aspect of the physical world of space, time, and matter. This is the world where we work with the souls of the dead and where we do long-distance healing and divination. Just as we can meet and work with spirits of nature in the Middle World, we can meet and work with the spirits of the workplace there. This is how I have effectively worked shamanically in the corporate world.

Obviously when I participate in a business meeting, work with a client, make a presentation to a group, fix a car, or, for that matter, cook a meal or climb a snowy mountain peak, it is not possible or appropriate to take my drum, lie down with a bandana over my eyes, and journey. While I have done such classic shamanic journeying in professional work, I have also learned other ways to shift into nonordinary reality and connect with spirits, often in a very limited amount of time, when I am in professional settings.

The teachings about professional life that I have received from spirits and put into practice over many years can be organized into three categories:

- Working with nontraditional spirits through the traditional journey
- Shifting quickly from ordinary reality to nonordinary reality and back while in the work environment
- Using special practices adapted for the work environment

The Traditional Journey and Nontraditional Spirits

While working with corporations and governments, I have often made traditional shamanic journeys to communicate with what I call nontraditional spirits, such as the spirits of organizations, cities, buildings, rooms, and technological objects, seeking counsel, personal guidance, or support from these spirits.

The journey to contact the spirits of organizations and work environments is similar to the journey to contact the spirits of man-made objects, which I described in chapter 7. While you can meet the spirits anywhere in nonordinary reality, I recommend you meet them in the Middle World at the location where the physical object is or where the organization is principally found. Doing so honors the ordinary-reality aspect of the object or organization.

Journeying to Spirits of Organizations and Work Environments

With one or more of your spirit helpers, journey in the Middle World to the location of the object or organization. With your intention, call its spirit. Honor and bless it, and ask if it is willing to provide help and guidance for the greater harmony of the Whole. Make your request and ask your questions. When it is time to return, thank the spirit, journey back to where you started from, and then return to ordinary reality.

As a general matter of ethics, whenever I do journeys of this type, I ask for permission to do the work from spirits, usually my own spirit guides and the spirit I'm journeying to, and if I make a request of the spirit, I always start with something like, "If it is appropriate in light of the greater harmony of the Whole, I would like to request . . ."

I undertook one such journey in 1990 when I took a job with a major energy corporation in California to manage its environmental programs. I had worked for that company in a different capacity before, but I wanted to better understand it so I could advance its environmental commitment and performance quickly and take it as far as I could. I journeyed to the organization's spirit, which taught me essential things about its fundamental nature, helping me see the bigger picture. What I learned helped me shed my prejudices and beliefs concerning the organization and be more in harmony with spirit in my work. I worked closely and regularly with that spirit and still communicate with it now that I am retired.

As another example, I served for many years in the 1990s as chief staff liaison on the President's Council on Sustainable Development (PCSD), supporting my company's CEO, who was a member of the council. This body reported directly to President Clinton and consisted of ten company CEOs, ten heads of environmental and social justice organizations, and five cabinet secretaries. It was headed by Vice President Al Gore, and its objective was to develop a blueprint for a sustainable America, integrating economic, environmental, and social-equity concerns.

Clearly the task before the council was a formidable one, requiring that participants work in harmony for the greater good, a need that was perhaps not obvious in a group with such diverse membership. In preparing for council meetings, I journeyed to the spirits of the council, the White House, and the nation, and to other relevant spirits, seeking guidance for myself and asking that the meeting lead to the most appropriate outcomes in accordance with the greater harmony of the Whole, now and into the future. When I got to my hotel room, usually in Washington, DC, I also journeyed to the spirit of the city and of the meeting place, including the building and specific room. My intention here was the same: to seek guidance and ask for the most appropriate outcomes.

Although it is never possible to link this kind of shamanic work and results as cause and effect—the point of doing shamanic practices is the doing of them, not results—I confess to having been amazed by some of the developments that took place within the council.

Following are descriptions of two specific journeys I did while working for the President's Council on Sustainable Development. One was to the spirit of the council; the other was to the spirit of a room where the council was to meet.

For the first journey, I was at home in my office, packing and preparing for the coming quarterly meeting in Washington. My plane was to leave early the next morning. I took out my drum and journeyed to the spirit of the PCSD.

Along with a few of my allies, I journey in the Middle World
to the East Coast. I fly quickly and can see the landscape

below me—the Sierras, then the Rocky Mountains, the Great Plains—and I arrive in DC. I fly to the Jefferson Memorial, to the Lincoln Memorial, and then to the Department of Commerce, where the meeting will take place. From there I go to the Capitol, then to the White House.

I call the spirit of the PCSD. As in previous journeys, it shows itself as a large gray-green dragon with sharp scales. It is standing in the middle of a street, perhaps Pennsylvania Avenue, spitting fire while people and cars move about apparently undisturbed. It is impressive, and I am somewhat subdued.

I honor the spirit and ask that the coming PCSD meeting be the most appropriate possible for the welfare of the country and of the Whole. Then I ask if the spirit would be willing to provide support and guidance for the meeting. It tells me to prepare for the meeting by visualizing the great spirit, the authentic being, of all PCSD members and staff, and honoring them. I am not to judge. The spirit tells me that when I travel there, I need to be aware of and honor the authentic beings of all the people I meet—airline employees, passengers, taxi drivers—so I can remain in that state of honoring for the meeting. The spirit says that the spirit and energy of water will be important in this meeting. As I drink water from the glass provided in the room, I need to contact the spirit of water and ask for the most appropriate outcome from and support for the meeting.

I then find myself on the lawn in front of the White House. I see the dragon on its hind legs, looking calm; I think I almost see a smile. I ask if there is any more advice I can receive. The spirit reminds me that the PCSD members are still debating what sustainability means. It says that sustainability is nothing more than a win-win for everyone—not only for all living humans, but also for other species, for the earth, and for all descendants.

Then the dragon lies down, but not on the ground—it appears to float just above the lawn. It tells me to understand and remember that I do not know much, that there is yet a great deal for me to learn. I need to carefully listen to what everyone in the meeting is saying, including those I do not usually agree with, and learn without judgment. I also need to contribute my own wisdom, my current thoughts and understanding. The spirit says that this group is trying to make a good, hearty soup. Many different ingredients, added by everyone, will be needed, and in the right mix. This is our task.

Now I clearly see a smile on the dragon's face. I thank the dragon and quickly return in the Middle World to my home.

For the second journey, I was in my hotel room in Washington in late afternoon. I had just flown in from the West Coast and the PCSD meeting was to start the next morning at nine. I had a half hour before dinner with PCSD colleagues, and I decided to journey to the spirit of the room we would be meeting in at the Department of Commerce. It was a large, marble-lined space that a colleague at the department had shown me on a previous trip.

I journey with some of my allies in the Middle World to the Department of Commerce building, enter, and go to the meeting room. I call the spirit of the room. It shows itself as a prairie dog, or perhaps a squirrel, brown in color. It is large, however— twice my size—and seems to be smiling. I honor the spirit and ask if it would help the PCSD reach the most appropriate outcome for the greater welfare of the Whole. The large prairie dog spirit asks me to help it, and my allies put "decorations" around the meeting room, garlands of flowers and leaves, cords strung with nuts. We all work together, and the collaboration is beautiful, as are the results.

When we are finished, I ask the spirit for personal guidance for the meeting. The spirit says that when I enter the room I am to think about and honor all the people who have been in meetings here before and who have manifested harmony and Oneness. The spirit says to also include those who built the room and who have manifested harmony and Oneness. It says to have no judgments and adds that during the meeting, I need to repeat my intention to manifest harmony and Oneness and dedicate my intention to those who will meet in this room in years to come. They are my descendants. The spirit also says not to focus on achievements, but to be in the present moment and trust.

I thank the spirit and ask if it has any more advice. It smiles and tells me to be aware of what direction I face during the meeting and to use the energy of that direction. The spirit also tells me to remember that it is here, always, and to call on it. If I need inspiration or encouragement, I need only close my eyes briefly and see the garlands we have strewn around. It flashes a big smile. I thank the spirit and return to my hotel room.

These two journeys involved the spirits of a group and a place. Another effective practice is to journey to the spirit of an individual colleague, client, or associate. Again, as a fundamental matter of ethics, it is not right to do anything shamanically to another person without that person's permission. But it is appropriate and sometimes useful to connect with the authentic being of an individual, acknowledge and honor it, and express respect, love, and good wishes for that person. This can be a useful practice with anyone with whom we are going to have an interaction in ordinary reality. It can be particularly useful if we harbor negative or uneasy feelings toward that person or if we have fears, concerns, or misgivings about the interaction.

Journeying to the Authentic Being of a Colleague

In this practice, journey in the Middle World with the intention to meet the soul or authentic being of the person, wherever he or she may be. When you do so, say hello, acknowledge the high spirit of the person, honor it, and express positive sentiments to the person's authentic being. You do not have to agree with that person about anything as far as ordinary-reality matters go in order to do this.

> When you offer good wishes, do not have in mind any specific outcomes, but only what is the most appropriate for the greater harmony of the Universe. When you are finished, say farewell, and return from the journey.

This is not an easy practice, particularly if we harbor judgments or other negative feelings toward the person. But acknowledging the divinity and purity of their *spirit* is all that is necessary. A journey like this can change the way you interact with that person in the future.

Rapid Shifts between Ordinary and Nonordinary Reality

The second type of shamanic practice that is highly useful in professional settings consists of shifting repeatedly and quickly from ordinary reality to nonordinary reality and back. A subset of this practice is the ability to be in ordinary and shamanic states of consciousness simultaneously—that is, to sense and communicate with spirits while also sensing what surrounds us in the ordinary world and performing ordinary tasks.

This practice can actually be useful in any shamanic work and in any ordinary-world situation. It has been a major source of learning for me.

As with all shamanic work, you achieve this rapid shift in consciousness through clear intention. It requires what I call "Buddha awareness": being sufficiently "awake" and attentive so that you do not forget to do the practice. I have done it while in meetings, in discussions with colleagues, when carrying out tasks such as writing or planning, and in multiple other situations and locations. My purpose is usually to get information from spirit, to receive personal counsel or guidance concerning my own thoughts and actions at that moment.

The spirits I call upon are my own allies and spiritual teachers, spirits of places—such as that of the room or office I'm in or of the airplane I'm in—or spirits of organizations, such as that of the corporation I happen to be dealing with. I can do this with my eyes open, and getting an answer usually takes no more than a few seconds. When I briefly shift my state of consciousness and call them, the spirits are right there, and I can see, feel, and hear them. I have found them to be very receptive to this way of communicating.

Just as important as quickly communicating with spirit is the ability to shift back rapidly and impeccably into our ordinary state of consciousness, so we can be fully present to the situation at hand. Shifting back and forth in this manner is a fundamental skill of the shaman. It is only through practice, and more practice, and yet more practice over a period of years that we can become adept at this.

One way to learn this approach and become more skilled with it is to practice in our daily personal lives—in nonprofessional settings. For example, I love to hike and trek, and while I am walking, I repeatedly make contact with either my allies or the spirits around me while remaining aware of the natural world through which I am moving. This not only helps me improve the use of the practice, but it also makes for a much richer hiking experience!

Special Practices

When working shamanically in the mainstream, I have found that certain special practices given to me by spirits are highly useful. Some of these serve general purposes, such as bringing forth harmony, while others are for specific purposes, such as solving a particular problem or assisting a group in finding clarity during a discussion.

A practice I learned from spirits many years ago involves a form of *word doctoring*. Its purpose is to help bring harmony to a situation, a group of people, a place, or an event. The term refers to using the power of sacred words or vocalized sounds in healing, divination, and other shamanic and spiritual practices. While I learned to do this in the twentieth century, word doctoring, particularly in its poetic form, was an important practice among my Celtic ancestors of Western Europe.[2]

Word Doctoring

Before you do this practice, check with spirits that this is an appropriate time and place to do so, and ask their permission.

To do the practice, quickly acknowledge the spirits of the four directions and make contact with the spirits of the four elements of water, air, fire, and earth. You may use whatever is at hand—a glass of water, your breath for air, the lights in the room for fire, and your body to represent the earth element. Then ask for a single word, which will emerge spontaneously. This whole process takes less than thirty seconds.

Now use this word when you speak, incorporating it into ordinary sentences. You will not impose the power of the word on people you converse with; it is an offering that they can accept or not.

The word you receive is usually unrelated to the subject or situation at hand. Instead, it is an ordinary word that takes on a sacred aspect. I have at times found it a challenge to insert the word into my ordinary speech; it calls for creativity and brings some lightheartedness to the practice.

I have often been astounded by the impact of this practice. I recall a time in the Foundation for Shamanic Studies' three-year "Masters Class," an experiment Michael Harner did in the late 1980s that combined graduates from the first West Coast advanced shamanism program with graduates from the first East Coast program. In our first meeting, at Westerbeke Ranch in Sonoma, California, bringing the two groups together was not working. The dynamics were awkward, and there were many conflicts, both open and hidden.

I had told Michael about my shamanic work in corporations, and on the third day of the meeting, as we all sat in a circle, he asked me if I would describe to the group what I was doing in that work—the word-doctoring practice in particular. As I finished explaining the practice, Michael asked me to use it to help with group harmony. Unbeknownst to him or anyone else in the group, I had actually done so while I was describing the practice. The word I had been given was *kitchen*. Though it was challenging, I had inserted it into my explanation. The change in the group dynamics during that session, and for the rest of the five-day meeting, was remarkable. Again, as is the case with all shamanic practices, whether this shift was linked to the practice is irrelevant; the point was for me to do it and for all the credit to go to spirits—although in this case, Michael also deserves a bit of the credit for asking for the practice!

Another example goes back to my work with the President's Council on Sustainable Development. We had been meeting for about two years, and an issue that appeared intractable was threatening to break the group apart and unravel its hard-won consensus work. The issue was growth versus no-growth: Environmental and community leaders, as well as some of the cabinet secretaries, argued that continued growth in the rate of resource use and in the economy made it impossible to reach a sustainable society. The corporate leaders and the rest of the cabinet secretaries argued that continued growth was essential if we wanted to provide economic wellbeing for everyone, eliminate poverty, and have the financial resources to protect the environment.

A critical two-day meeting took place in the same ornate conference room in the Department of Commerce building in Washington I have previously described. The future of the council appeared to be at stake.

I used everything in my bag of practices to implore spirit to help. I worked with the spirits of the room, the building, the Department of Commerce, the council, and the city. During the meeting's first session, I used my word-doctoring practice to help bring harmony to the situation. I did not take sides—growth or no-growth—in making my plea to spirits; I only asked for harmony and the most appropriate outcome. The word I received was *rainbow*—not an easy word to introduce among such an august group! I remember saying something like, "Sometimes I have the feeling that sustainability is like looking for the treasure at the end of the rainbow," which led to some approving laughter. By the end of the meeting, a breakthrough—as surprising as it was welcome—saved the day and the future of the council. The group realized and agreed that the growth/no-growth debate was a false and ill-defined one—that to reach a sustainable and just society, some things must grow while others must not. For example, it is important that pollution, toxic contamination, poverty, and natural-resource depletion do not grow. And it is important that quality of life, environmental health, open space, savings, and profits grow. Once this resolution was reached, the council was able to productively concentrate on developing policy recommendations that would lead to these outcomes simultaneously.

I encourage you to seek other special practices from your spirit guides for use in your own professional work.

PRINCIPLES, ETHICS, AND GUIDELINES FOR
SHAMANIC PRACTICE IN PROFESSIONAL LIFE

In addition to the general principles of ethics that are applicable to any shamanic work (see chapter 1), there are several other important items to consider when doing shamanic work in your professional world.

First, it is essential to let go of judgments and beliefs—about people, organizations, places, man-made objects, and outcomes—for these practices to be effective; that is, for spirits to help or intervene. We all know that letting go of judgments and desired outcomes is not easy, particularly if you know a great deal about the matter at hand. Yet doing so is essential for bringing a heavy dose of humility to these practices and for keeping us from attempting to manipulate or impose a solution. For example, when I chaired meetings and sought help from spirits, I learned to always ask for the most appropriate outcome for the meeting despite also having a well-defined objective as part of my meeting agenda.

I will share an example. I taught a workshop many years ago in a beautiful old monastery in the Ardennes region of Belgium. The cook for the center, a wonderful man, was a native of India and an illegal immigrant. He had asked the Ministry of the Interior for a "green card," giving him permission to stay and work in the country, but had not received it and was to be deported. He asked if we could help.

The participants in the workshop asked me if there was anything we could do for him shamanically. I suggested we journey as a group in the Middle World to the Ministry of the Interior building in Brussels, communicate with the spirit of the ministry, and ask for the most appropriate outcome in this matter.

Well, I almost had a mutiny on my hands! You see, the Ministry of the Interior is universally despised. The group told me that there was no way *that* ministry could have a spirit. And they didn't want to ask for the most appropriate outcome; they wanted to ask that this man be granted permission to stay in Belgium and work. After some discussion, the group finally let go of their beliefs and expectations, and we journeyed as a group to the spirit of the ministry without demands. There was no way for any of us to know what was best for this man, but we took it as our responsibility as shamanic practitioners to seek the support of the spirits on his behalf. He eventually received his green card, and he did not stay on as a cook!

Another matter of ethics dictates that we not take credit for any outcome in shamanic work. Our job is to ask spirit for help, and if there is credit to be assigned, it goes to spirit.

The principle of refraining from shamanic work unless you have permission applies to an organization as well as an individual; we need the permission of one or more of its members. That said, if you are yourself a member of an organization, it is ethical and appropriate to do shamanic work for that organization without consulting anyone else. It is also ethical, desirable, and often very effective to use shamanic practices to work on *ourselves* in relationship to the organization. This can lead to significant changes in how we interact with the group and the people within it.

As with any type of shamanic work, before attempting shamanic work in the workplace, we need to have knowledge in both the ordinary and nonordinary world. I once heard Tom Harmer, author of *Going Native,* speak of his experience living with American Indians. He observed that Indians know nature—nature lore and animal behavior—while most nonindigenous people, including shamanic practitioners who work with nature spirits, do not. Such knowledge is necessary for practitioners to be most effective in their shamanic work. The same applies to working with spirits of corporations, buildings, institutions, or machines. The more we know and understand these things in ordinary reality, without judgment or prejudice, the better our shamanic practice.

I have also learned that when working with spirits it is important to follow through concerning a future event, meeting, task, or other professional activity. Make sure to communicate with the spirits as you prepare for the activity, as you begin the activity, and as you move through the activity. Then, afterward, thank the spirits for their support.

My shamanic work in the corporate world has been subtle and discreet, as I learned from spirits it should be. There is no need to shock people or act in strange ways that could be interpreted as antagonistic or lacking respect. Still, over the years there have been occasions when people have come to me, driven solely by intuition or some other inner insight, to ask whether I was doing anything unusual. If I am asked directly, I usually answer honestly. One of my bosses, a man I respected greatly, told me one day with a smile, "You're some kind of a wizard, aren't you? It's okay—just go on wizarding!"

Working shamanically in the corporate world can be a lonely path. Businesspeople often regard shamanism, and spiritual practices generally, with fear and suspicion. At the same time, the spiritual community often regards the business world with prejudice and hostility. Yet occasionally, openness can be found within both camps, and for me, this has been enough to feed my heart and allow me to continue to pursue the path.

Even absent open and explicit support for shamanism in the workplace, I have always known that there were others in the business world doing this work, even if I had not met them yet. This hunch was born out once on the PCSD, when we hired some consultants to help us do long-range planning and strategizing. Several months later, a member of the drumming circle that meets at our home said she knew a man who was a shamanic practitioner and was interested in joining our drumming circle. Imagine my surprise and delight when the doorbell rang and I opened the door to find one of those consultants standing there, holding his drum and rattle!

SHAMANISM IN OTHER KINDS OF PROFESSIONAL WORK

It is possible and desirable to bring spirit to any workplace. There is no job that is not appropriate for shamanic work—construction work, medicine, agriculture, art, or food- and hospitality-service professions. In all of these environments, we can ask spirit to do whatever is most appropriate to bring harmony, love, connectedness, and unity to our world. It has been a blessing for me to hear people I have taught tell me how they brought the practices I described into their own professional settings. There is no end to the possibilities.

Noëlle, a psychologist and long-time psychotherapist with a private practice, has been a pioneer in integrating shamanism into her professional life, and she has done so while respecting her clients and the ethics that underlie both the shamanic and psychotherapeutic practices.[3] Her approach has the great merit of inviting the totality of her client's being into the therapeutic and healing process.

While I have been retired for a number of years, I still use the practices I describe in this chapter in the several types of work I continue to engage in. I have served on boards of directors for organizations, including an academic institution and nonprofit policy and advocacy groups. I have routinely worked with the spirits of these organizations, of the boards, of the meeting rooms, buildings, and cities in which they are located, and of various organizational offices, as well as spirits related to organizational missions and activities.

And I continue to seek spirit help and support for my shamanic teaching in Europe, the United States, and Canada. When I prepare for a workshop, I journey in the Middle World to the location where I will be teaching, whether I have been there before or not, and contact the spirits of the room and building and other local spirits, such as those of the town or city or of neighboring mountains or trees. I ask for counsel and for the most appropriate outcomes. I also journey to the spirit of any workshop sponsors and to the spirit of the group of workshop participants. I work with spirits related to the contents of what I will teach. I always work with my own spirit helpers too. I work with them all, before and during the workshop and on the trip back home. And when I arrive home, I again contact those spirits to thank them for their support and ask for any further guidance. In this way, I find that my travel and teaching activities acquire a completely different character that is way beyond and larger than my little individual self. A sense of the sacred and of the communion with all permeates me and nurtures my soul.

It is my hope that more shamanic practitioners will bring their practices into their workplaces, wherever they may be. I hope more of us will let go of beliefs, judgments, and expectations and know deeply that everything is sacred and interconnected, and that it is our job to help manifest that sacredness by working with spirit. In this way, we can do our small part to bring harmony and truth to our modern world.

9

Shamanism and Modern Scientific Discovery

◦ ◉ ◦

SCIENCE IS A MAGNIFICENT CREATION OF THE HUMAN MIND

Modern science is one of the greatest achievements of the human species, to the extent that it describes and explains the incredible beauty of the universe and helps us develop technological tools that are in harmony with the Whole. As I noted in chapter 3, it is a magnificent creation of the human mind. It is also a double-edged sword, an amazing and powerful tool that can illuminate and inspire, as well as denigrate and destroy. As we explore the relationship between modern science and shamanism, I will focus on the positive, beneficial aspects of science—the aspects that the large majority of scientists are pursuing.

Science attempts to unravel and describe the intricate workings of what in shamanic parlance we denote as ordinary reality. For the past century, science has done wonders in revealing to us the incredible world in which we live and the astonishing ways in which it functions. It is important to understand, however, that science is not an absolute. With every discovery and new understanding come new questions, new unknowns, new inquiries. For those who regularly follow scientific advances—and I am one of them—it is difficult not to marvel and be elated and inspired by what we are learning about this wonderful world.

Science probes into the very small, delving into the weird quantum world of the elementary particles that make up ordinary matter. It also explores the very large, investigating the multitude of astounding cosmic objects that populate the immense universe we live in. Science has not only traveled far into space, but also far back in time to reconstruct the very birth of our universe, as we will see in chapter 11. Back on Earth, science is unraveling the physical forces and geological processes that have shaped and continue to shape this rocky and watery planet we call home. Science is also delving into the very core of life, learning about the living cell and the unimaginable chemistry at the basis of life. And science, in a deep introspection, is inquiring into the very instrument that created it in the first place: the brain and its mysterious workings. The list of scientific inquiries and discoveries goes on and on. Its endless nature is one of the things that make science such an exquisite human endeavor.

THE RECIPROCITY AND SYNCHRONICITY BETWEEN SCIENTIFIC AND SHAMANIC KNOWLEDGE

As I said in the introduction, I see no inconsistency between science and shamanic knowledge. In fact, I have been intrigued for many years by what I call the reciprocity and synchronicity between ordinary-reality and nonordinary-reality knowledge and practice, between scientific and shamanic or spiritual knowledge. I am not saying that science can *explain* nonordinary-reality or shamanic experiences or that shamanic knowledge can *explain* ordinary-reality phenomena. I am saying that there are metaphors, idea connections, between one reality and the other, which can lead to insights and deeper understanding in both.

Modern science—and in particular quantum physics, cosmology, relativity theory, and neuroscience—can help us understand, formulate, and deepen shamanic knowledge and practice. On the other hand, it is well established in the history of science that many scientific discoveries and achievements—major and minor—were initiated by insights or intuition unrelated to deductive reasoning. I propose that some of these insights or intuitions were the result of scientists connecting, consciously or unconsciously, with the spiritual dimension of reality—nonordinary reality.

It is not possible here to cover all the areas where the reciprocity and synchronicity between scientific and shamanic knowledge can enrich the shamanic practice, so I offer some examples that have been particularly useful to me. They occur in the fields of time; the void; interconnectedness, nonduality, and the power of intention; and the nature of ordinary and nonordinary reality.

Time

Time is one of humanity's most important concepts, yet most of us do not understand it well. Until the fourteenth century, we related to the natural cycles—the rhythm of day following day, the phases of the moon, and the apparent movement of the sun through the year. With the advent of the mechanical clock in the fourteenth century, time gradually became an abstract concept, divorced from natural cycles, and now time for most of us is "clock time," the regular ticking of seconds, minutes, and hours, embedded within calendar time.

It is fair to say that much of modern life is controlled by time. We are nearly enslaved by time and its passing, and enormously influenced by the past and future in our notions of who we are and what we must do.

Various cultures perceive time differently. While in the Judeo-Christian and European traditions time is a linear phenomenon, in many Asian and Mesoamerican traditions it is a cyclical phenomenon. When Isaac Newton formally introduced time in scientific theory, he defined time as an absolute, linear, independent variable. At the beginning of the twentieth century, Albert Einstein showed that depending on the relative velocity of objects and the influence of matter on time through gravity, time was not absolute or linear, but could be stretched, contracted, or made to bend and turn upon itself and move backward, thus opening the possibility of travel into the future and the past.[1]

What Einstein's theories of relativity tell us about the malleability of time resonates with an ancient belief or concept held by many people around the world; Mircea Eliade refers to this idea as the *myth of the eternal return*.[2] People believed that, through rites and the use of intention, it was possible to go back in time to the very beginning, *in illo tempore*, and start anew. For example, when ancient people enacted a cosmogony ritual manifesting the creation of the world and human beings, they went back to the beginning and the creation of the universe truly happened again, through the ritual. Another example is a marriage ritual in which the man and the woman went back to the very beginning and enacted, for the first time, the original union of masculine and feminine.

This belief about the malleability of time and humans' ability to navigate it through both ritual and intention is very powerful. As we go back to the beginning, we return to the Source, to authentic being; we are no longer father or mother, son or daughter, husband or wife, or the many masks or facets of the ego that we wear. We are no longer controlled or defined by the stories that have been told over time. We do not forgo responsibilities toward anyone or anything; however, as we start from the beginning, children, parents, and others are no longer just a responsibility—they are authentic beings. A spouse is no longer just a responsibility; he or she is our companion, authentic being.

I have used Einstein's malleability of time and the myth of the eternal return to propose to workshop participants two powerful shamanic journeys. In one journey, the intention is to die to the world and come to birth from within. In the other, the intention is to learn more about the fundamental nature of shamanism.

In the first journey, we go back to our early childhood and become again our inner child, our sacred child, our divine child. We came into this world as authentic being, and our inner child is our true nature, pure authentic being. Much has changed throughout our lives because the ordinary world is impermanent and subject to continuous change. Only authentic being is permanent, eternal, and immutable. We begin again as the inner child although we are now in an adult body, with experience and knowledge. In the context of the myth of the eternal return, we start a new life that fully integrates the innocence, purity, and authenticity of the child with the experience of the adult.

This practice is, in a sense, an initiation. We are on a "dismemberment journey" with very specific intention. The dismemberment initiation is an ancient and widespread shamanic practice: in this journey, we are dismembered by spirits and put back together, or "re-membered" as a new body, a new being.[3]

Beginning Again as Inner Child

To do this journey, go to the Lower World and ask spirits, with your intention, if they would be willing to dismember you so you can die to the world and let go of the past, with its truths, its goals, its dogmas of meaning, its stories and gifts. Ask to be re-membered at the beginning of your life so as to come to birth from within, from the Source, as authentic being, as your inner divine child. After you have been re-membered, ask for the poem or song of your inner child.

When you return from the journey, go outside in nature and perform your own ritual, whatever strikes you as appropriate, to fully manifest and embody this initiation to the inner child and your start of a new life. Acknowledge your courage to let go of the past. Incorporate the poem or song into your ritual.

In the second journey, we recover the story, or myth, of the first shaman. This myth is very ancient and widespread and plays an important role in shamanic traditions. It has been documented and summarized by Mircea Eliade in shamanic cultures of Siberia, Central Asia, Tibet, the Pacific Islands, and South America.[4] In the journey, we go back in illo tempore to the time when the first shaman came into being, and we become the first shaman.

Becoming the First Shaman

To do the journey, go to one of your spirit teachers and ask if he or she would be willing to take you to the first shaman. Introduce yourself to the first shaman and ask that person to tell you the story of how he or she became a shaman. Ask permission to relate the story to others, because, when working with a group, it is good to follow this journey with a storytelling ritual.

Storytelling is both ancient and classic shamanic practice and sacred play. In the circle, each person tells the story of the first shaman—and tells it using "I," starting with, "This is how I became the first shaman." Each participant uses gesture, dance, or song, and the audience reacts and participates as well. By recovering the story of the first shaman, we deepen our understanding of the fundamental principles of shamanism, the sacredness and interconnectedness of everything. By telling and enacting the story, manifesting it in ordinary reality, we heighten the awareness of these fundamental principles in ourselves and the audience, which contributes to universal harmony.

The Void

The void, nothingness, is an important concept, both in spiritual traditions and in modern science. Many years ago Sandra Ingerman introduced me to a wonderful shamanic journey during which I was invited to jump into the void. While this idea was frightening at first, the journey proved a profound experience for me. I have done this journey a number of times since then, and its teachings have been many.

The void is not a vacuum, empty of anything. Ordinary-reality knowledge—in this case, from quantum physics and cosmology—can give us insights into the void and help us prepare for this journey. According to quantum physics' understanding of ordinary reality, the vacuum is filled with *potential energy:* negative energy compared to the positive energy of motion or the energy inherent in matter. This vacuum energy permeates the universe of space and time. It is the lowest-energy state of our space-time universe. The vacuum can be described as made up of a very large number of energy fields, each field representing in potential all the forces and matter particles of the universe. Each field has a superposition of energy states, analogous to the many notes that can be obtained from a single plucked guitar string. This vacuum energy has been observed experimentally and shown to have a tangible physical presence and influence.

According to Heisenberg's uncertainty principle of quantum physics, the vacuum energy field is subject to constant fluctuations, which, as a result of the equivalence of mass and energy, lead to the continuous appearance of virtual particles. Virtual particles are pairs of matter and antimatter particles that interact and vanish almost as soon as they are produced. Thus, a vacuum seethes with a multitude of virtual particles. The big bang theory of the creation of the universe, a theory that has been confirmed by many experimental observations in recent years, describes the creation of matter, space, and time from the vacuum energy. The vacuum is thus the source of all ordinary-reality existence—galaxies, stars, planets, and life on the planets.

There is no violation of the law of conservation of energy when we consider the apparent creation of our universe from "nothing." Modern cosmology has shown that the total energy of the universe is zero. The positive energy of matter and motion exactly balances the negative, potential energy of the vacuum. Thus, form is indeed an illusion, as spiritual traditions, particularly in the East, have said for millennia. The universe, with all its forms, has zero energy and zero mass. Only when it is experienced as duality—mass and motion energy (positive energy) and potential energy (negative energy)—does the universe or form have existence. One could say that pure consciousness, or awareness, must be present to recognize this form and its existence and nonexistence.

Cosmology has also shown that the vacuum energy is responsible not only for the creation of the universe and its early inflation, but also for its accelerating expansion, as demonstrated experimentally in very recent years. The vacuum energy is the so-called dark energy that pervades the cosmos and creates an antigravity force, accelerating its expansion. In one scenario, as the universe expands, seemingly forever, the vacuum energy comes to dominate all other forces. As the temperature of the universe falls faster and faster, as stars exhaust their nuclear fuels and implode, and as the reduced influence of gravity prevents the creation of new stars, the universe will become a lifeless, structureless collection of particles and radiation. It will lose all memory of how it began—a complete loss of information.

The vacuum is the potential of all that is or can be. It is formless. The universe and its forms can only be observed from a state of duality. Again, the universe's total energy is zero. Modern physics' concept of the void is very similar to the concept of the void in ancient Asian spiritual traditions, particularly the Indian concept of *sunya,* the pregnant void, the nonbeing, the potential and source of all being.

Jumping into the Void

In doing a shamanic journey to jump into the void, it is important to work with the allies or spirit teachers who are particularly close to you at this time. Ask your spirit helpers if they would be willing to take you to the edge of the void in nonordinary reality. It could be anywhere in the Upper or Lower World.

Jumping into the void is crossing the threshold, entering and following your own true adventure. It requires courage. It's a journey from the realm of conscious, rational thought into the zones of energies of the body that are moving from another center, from authentic being. It is a shamanic initiation. It is good to go into this journey as the inner child, with the innocence and trust of the child and the attention of the mature adult.

When you come to the edge of the void, ask your spirit helpers to step back; they do not come into the void with you. Take the time to be in a full state of attention, and jump.

When I first did this journey, my allies took me to the twelfth level in the Upper World, a level and a region I had never been to before. I visit it only when I do this practice of jumping into the void. When I came to the edge of the void, I called upon all the courage and trust I could muster—and jumped.

The experience of jumping into the void cannot be readily described with everyday language. There was nothing to do; I could only be. I experienced pure consciousness, the Source, and here the word *experience* is too limited. I was my true authentic nature. I experienced nonbeing, formlessness, and complete interconnectedness. I was the One.

Nonduality, Interconnectedness, and the Power of Intention

Nonduality, the interconnectedness of everything, and the power of intention are fundamental concepts of shamanic knowledge and practice. Quantum mechanics, the scientific theory that successfully describes the microscopic realm of elementary particles that make up our ordinary reality, can shed insights into these important concepts.

Nonduality

Quantum theory, on which all modern electronic gadgetry is built, accurately predicts the behavior of the microscopic world. It tells us that elementary particles (such as electrons and protons) and photons (such as visible light, radio waves, or X-rays) behave both as waves and as particles.

This is a concept that our logical mind has a hard time comprehending. It is not that these basic constituents of the universe are at times either a particle or a wave. They are both, simultaneously. Particles or photons only exhibit either wavelike or particlelike properties when there is an experiment and an observer. And in a different experiment, the same particles or photons may exhibit the opposite behavior.

This wave/particle behavior is a good metaphor for the concept of nonduality. Nonduality is nonseparation; it is the absence of "either-or." Only when we attempt to observe or measure Reality with ordinary-reality means will Reality display dualistic or separate features.

Quantum physics is a theory of probabilities. It does not predict precisely where a particle or photon is, what its properties are, or what will happen to it. It only provides the *probability* of its location, its properties, and what will happen to it. Quantum physics tells us that elementary particles or photons are actually probability wave functions, giving, for example, the probability that a particle will be at any given place in the cosmos. The amplitude of the wave is a measure of the probability of finding the particle at any given location. It takes an observation or measurement of the particle—that is, an observer, or knowledge of the particle on the part of an observer—for the wave to collapse to one particular probability and location in space, so we observe or know the particle to be in that particular location.

A related quantum-theory concept that also provides insight into nonduality is the so-called superposition of states. A particle or photon can be in a number of different states—that is, have different physical characteristics at the same time, a superposition of possible particular states of existence. Only in the presence of an observer will the particle or photon assume one of the possible states of existence. This is also true for groups of particles and photons. Thus, a particle or photon can be at different places, have different values of energy, and be in different spin states at the same time. As Amir Aczel says in his book *Entanglement: The Greatest Mysteries of Physics,* "No longer do we speak about 'here or there'; in the quantum world we speak about 'here *and* there'."[5]

This is nonduality in physics. Similarly, the shamanic experience of nonordinary reality, such as the shamanic journey, is an experience of being here *and* there, of witnessing multiple forms and formlessness; it is an experience of nonduality.

Interconnectedness

The wave function that describes the probability of finding a particle at any given location is relatively large at locations where the particle is most likely to be found and becomes smaller at locations where it is less likely to be found. The wave function extends throughout space, although its values become negligibly small as we move away from the more likely locations. Every person or ordinary-reality being or object is entirely made of a very large number of elementary particles. The probability wave functions extend throughout the entire cosmos, so that all elementary-particle wave functions overlap or interact with all other particle wave functions in the world. This is a wonderful metaphor or reflection of the shamanic concept of the interconnectedness of everything.

Another quantum phenomenon that can give us insights into interconnectedness is a strange one called *entanglement.* Two particles that have become linked temporarily through some physical interaction, such as two elementary particles colliding with one another or two photons emitted from the same atom, are said to be entangled. Quantum theory says that after they separate, no matter how far apart they may be, as one particle undergoes a change in properties the other particle will also instantaneously change. Experiments performed since the early 1980s have verified the phenomenon of entanglement and confirmed that a particle in one place can indeed be affected by what is done somewhere else. Entanglement is directly related to the concept of superposition of states mentioned earlier, when the superposition is applied to a system of two or more particles.[6]

Entanglement can provide insights into the enhanced interconnectedness that arises when a group of shamanic practitioners work together. Many have experienced this when performing a healing with a larger community present, or in a group, or when a group or community does world work. When shamanic practitioners act as a group, this enhanced interconnectedness remains afterward, no matter how far apart the members of the group find themselves. This has been my experience with the groups Noëlle and I have led in North America and Europe in multiyear advanced shamanism programs. It is as if the fibers that connect us in the web of interconnectedness, the Anglo-Saxon concept of Wyrd I spoke about in chapter 3, become more alive, more vibrant, as we become entangled.

The Power of Intention

Throughout this book I have mentioned the important role and power of intention in shamanic work. In shamanic practice, intention is transformation. It is through intention that we transform, cross the boundary, and interact with and impact nonordinary reality. Clarity, integrity, and authenticity of intention help us be impeccable in nonordinary reality. Quantum physics provides us with metaphors that can help us understand, visualize, and appropriately use the power of intention.

The concept of particles being probability wave functions that extend throughout space and the phenomenon of entanglement have been useful to me in grasping more fully the power of intention. We and all other beings in this universe are collections of possibilities. Because we are connected to everything, our intention impacts everything, even if only to the slightest degree. And since our actions, thoughts, and intentions do indeed affect the rest of the world, we understand that we must take responsibility for them; this is what impeccability is all about. Understanding interconnectedness also tells us that we have the ability and the power to influence the world for good, to do effective world work.

It is often said that to create peace in the world, the first and perhaps most important step is to have peace inside. As chapter 12 will discuss, this principle is the foundation of world work: to help bring harmony to the world, we must first bring harmony to ourselves. We do world work when we use the power of intention and of interconnectedness to create as much inner harmony as we can and intend harmony for the world.

The Nature of Ordinary and Nonordinary Reality

This last example of the reciprocity and synchronicity between scientific and shamanic knowledge comes from my shapeshifting practice. Say that I am in my living room, and I journey in nonordinary reality to the Upper World to visit my shapeshifting teacher. I shapeshift into an ally while in the Upper World. I then journey back to my living room, as the ally, in the Middle World. Next, with my intention, I come back to ordinary reality, still shapeshifted as the ally. I move about the room, go outside, and walk in nature, still as the ally. What reality am I in when I walk shapeshifted as the ally? Am I fully in ordinary reality, or in nonordinary reality in the Middle World, or in both realities?

I inquired about this matter over a period of time, exploring the nature of ordinary and nonordinary reality and the relationship between the two. I repeated the exercise I have just described, varying where I did the shapeshifting (Upper World, Middle World, or Lower World), varying the journey, and at times doing multiple shapeshifting. I asked my shapeshifting teacher and other spirits to teach me about these two realities. It was subtle work that required much clarity and impeccability.

Adyashanti, in talking about meditation, says that any meditation that uses a method leads to different states of consciousness, but these states are impermanent, limited, and conditioned.[7] Attachment to these states of consciousness creates dependency and keeps us from true, pure consciousness. As I inquired, spirits confirmed this principle, teaching me that the shamanic state of consciousness is a limited one, arrived at by a method. It expands our consciousness and it allows us to connect with the world of spirit, yet it is limited.

I have learned by experience that in shapeshifting—particularly deep shapeshifting into allies or other entities, as well as multiple shapeshifting—we go beyond the shamanic state of consciousness into pure consciousness by becoming the consciousness of the animal or entity we shapeshift into. As a result, we are in neither ordinary nor nonordinary reality; we are in Reality, pure reality, which corresponds to pure consciousness. Indeed, the concept of ordinary reality and nonordinary reality is only a model, a description of Reality, like the chakra model that describes the energy body or, for that matter, the model of the Lower, Middle, and Upper worlds that describes nonordinary reality. These models are very useful, but they are not what they describe.

Understanding the nature of ordinary and nonordinary reality is akin to understanding the nature of forces in physics. I believe the latter is a good metaphor, and it helped me understand and formulate what I learned in my shapeshifting practice. In physics, it is understood that four fundamental forces in the universe together comprise all the known forces. The four forces are gravity; electromagnetism; the weak nuclear force, which is responsible for radioactivity; and the strong nuclear force, which holds the elementary particles of the atomic nucleus together. The four forces are thought to be manifestations of a single unified force and are undifferentiated from one another at extremely high energies and temperatures, such as during the very short time at the birth of our universe following the big bang, and also very likely at the center of a black hole.

As the energy and temperature decrease, as happened when the cosmos expanded following the big bang, the unified force goes progressively through what we could call phase changes, like steam turning into water and ice, and the four forces are progressively perceived as differentiated, separate forces. Physicists have developed and tested a model that combines the electromagnetic and weak nuclear forces, and recently proposed models combine the electromagnetic and the weak and strong nuclear forces. The development of a model that combines all four forces, including gravity, is the current holy grail of physicists, and superstring theory is at the forefront of becoming this model.

In a similar way, in pure consciousness, there is one Reality, but at a low level of consciousness, awareness, or perception (a "low energy"), Reality has gone through a phase change and is perceived as split into two realities, ordinary reality and nonordinary reality. By awakening to pure consciousness, which shapeshifting and other spiritual disciplines can help us do, we perceive and experience just one Reality.

Most people in the modern world know only ordinary reality. Although many have spontaneous experiences of nonordinary reality, they often do not understand these experiences, or they ignore them or fear them. As we learn shamanic practice, we learn to perceive nonordinary reality. The next step in this spiritual path is to perceive only the one Reality.

I cannot conceal the enthusiasm with which I approach, and the inspiration I gain from, my simultaneous pursuit of scientific knowledge and shamanic practice. It is as if, for me, science and shamanism have become entangled in space and time throughout my life. I am awed by the contributions modern science, the brainchild of our mental capacity, can make to greater harmony in our world. And I am awed by the contributions shamanism can make to the same end. Perhaps the merging of the wondrous capacity of modern science with the wisdom of the shamanic perspective will teach the human species to use its amazing toolmaking ability for the purpose of creating greater harmony and wellbeing for all beings on Earth. And perhaps through this merging, the human species will learn to cooperate with other species and the natural environment, as I propose in chapter 13.

10

Journeys to the Spirits of the Cosmos

○ ◐ ○

THE COSMOS AS OUR NATURAL ENVIRONMENT

For thousands of years, shamans and shamanic practitioners have communicated with spirits in their environment. Until very recently this environment has been limited to the natural world on planet Earth and what we could see in the heavens with the naked eye. Thus, in the shamanic tradition there is much emphasis on working with spirits of nature and with spirits of celestial objects such as the sun, the moon, the planets, and the visible constellations.

Today, we have come to learn through science that our natural environment is much more than nature on the earth and what we can see in the heavens from our place on the earth. The twentieth century saw a great blossoming of *astronomy*, the scientific study of celestial objects that inhabit the universe; *astrophysics*, a branch of astronomy that studies the physical constitution and properties of celestial objects; and *cosmology*, the study of the origin, evolution, and large-scale structure of the universe.

With the expansion of these scientific fields have come dramatic improvements in observational technologies such as telescopes, and new designs that enhance our ability to observe the universe are continually being introduced. Astronomical telescopes are now found on many high places around the planet and in orbits high above the earth's atmosphere. While early telescopes collected, focused, and magnified only visible light, today's telescopes capture waves from the entire electromagnetic spectrum, from X-rays to infrared light to radio waves. With great advances in spectroscopy—the study of individual wavelengths of the observed spectra—we have an amazing window into the nature and detailed workings of the universe, extending in an almost unbelievable way our ability to perceive our environment through our ordinary human senses.

A BRIEF HISTORY OF OUR AWARENESS OF THE HEAVENS

The recent explosion in our knowledge of the cosmos has led to a staggering and accelerating evolution in our understanding of our place in the universe. An earth-centered consciousness dominated our species for millions of years, and we have, in just a few centuries, completely uprooted this way of perceiving our world.

Until the middle of the sixteenth century, Western cultures (and many others) considered the earth to be the center of a celestial sphere upon which moved the sun, the moon, other planets, and the visible stars. This was only about 450 years ago—a mere snippet of time. Then in 1543, Copernicus showed that the earth actually rotated around the sun, and he introduced the concept of the sun-centered universe. Kepler and Galileo then expanded upon his work.

Later we came to understand that the sun was a star just like the other visible stars, and the astronomers among us demonstrated the existence of many other stars that were invisible to the naked eye. Over time, they estimated that there could be as many as a billion stars in a large grouping called the Milky Way galaxy.

In the late eighteenth century, William Herschel introduced the galactocentric theory, the theory that the sun was at the center of our galaxy, which filled the universe. It is interesting how the human species has considered for so long that we, or the earth, or our sun, must be at the center of the universe! The galactocentric theory held until 1918, and it was only during the 1920s that scientists realized our Milky Way was just one of many galaxies. Then, in 1929, Edwin Hubble found that the galaxies were receding from one another at great speed—that in other words, the universe was expanding.

In the decades since Hubble's discovery, others have observed and studied numerous strange objects in our universe, such as quasars, pulsars, and black holes. Today we know that there are about one hundred billion stars in the Milky Way and upward of one hundred billion galaxies in the visible universe, some containing up to a *trillion* stars.

Moreover, scientists are concluding that visible matter—all the stars, galaxies, and other visible objects—makes up only about 5 percent of the total mass and energy content of the cosmos. About 30 percent is made up of invisible "dark matter" that exerts a strong gravitational force, and 65 percent is made up of a mysterious field of "dark energy," which I mentioned in our last chapter and which exerts an antigravitational force at large distances. While scientists have proposed various theories to explain dark matter and dark energy, we have yet to understand their nature and origin.

The immensity of the universe, relative to our own little planet, is difficult to grasp. And as if that were not enough for our minds to grapple with, today at the frontiers of cosmology, physicists are proposing that our universe may be only one among a multitude of universes.[1]

The radical shift in consciousness from earth centered to cosmos centered has not yet been fully assimilated into the consciousness of most people, who still hold on to an earth-centered view. I am convinced that, despite this lag in general understanding, a cosmos-centered consciousness will sooner or later have an immense impact on how we see ourselves as human beings, how we understand life, how we think and act, and how we care for our planet, other people, and the other inhabitants of the planet.

Many books and other resources, such as the NASA website, contain superb photographs and descriptions of the planets, stars, galaxies, and other cosmic objects. Many of these photographs were obtained with the orbiting Hubble Space Telescope, one of the most amazing eyes of our astronomical technology. Perusing these resources is an excellent way to evoke wonder at the beauty and grace of our universe and its inhabitants. And that wonder can inspire us to want to know the spiritual dimension of the universe.

WHY COMMUNICATE WITH SPIRITS OF THE COSMOS?

We have come to know that our natural environment is an incredibly vast cosmos inhabited by countless near and far astronomical objects, such as galaxies, black holes, pulsars, quasars, and supernovae. Now that we know they exist, it is important for shamanic practitioners to expand upon traditional communication with the nature spirits of the earth and communicate with spirits of these objects of the cosmos as well. There are many good reasons to include them in a shamanic practice.

First, as I have pointed out throughout the book, in the shamanic tradition there is a spiritual dimension to reality; everything is sacred and has spirit. Just as our planet Earth has a spirit—called Mother Earth, Gaya, Pachamama, and other sacred names—all cosmic objects, near and far, also have spirits. To visit them, acknowledge their existence, and honor and bless them is part of the consecration of our (newly expanded) environment.

Next, by entering into contact with spirits of the cosmos, we can deepen our personal spiritual path and awareness, strengthen our service path, and bring more harmony to our relationship with the world. When we communicate with these spirits, we expand our consciousness of the interconnectedness of everything: our consciousness of the One, of authentic being.

A spiritual consciousness of the cosmos can also foster impeccability on Earth and as we venture into the heavens. By becoming conscious of how our little planet fits into the immensity of the cosmos, we can dramatically reduce our mistreatment of our home and its inhabitants, including other human beings. We can also help ensure that as our technological tools expand, we do not objectify the cosmos and "conquer" and exploit space the way we have conquered and exploited Earth.

Finally, spirits of the cosmos have their own characteristic knowledge and power, and we can learn from their wisdom and seek their help. And just as when we communicate with spirits on Earth we can become more comfortable with our planet and know we are an integral part of it, communication with the spirits of the cosmos helps us be more at ease with the immensity and strangeness of the cosmos and know that we are part of it as well.

WORKING SHAMANICALLY WITH SPIRITS OF THE COSMOS

Before you undertake any journey deep into the cosmos, it is important to understand the unique nature of these journeys, do some preparatory work that will help you journey safely and effectively, and have an idea of what you might encounter.

Journeys in Space-Time

When I started my exploration of the spiritual dimension of the cosmos many years ago, I worked closely with my familiar spirit guides and helpers and then, as I proceeded further, with the spirits I encountered in the cosmos itself. All of these spirits led me to journey in the Middle World of nonordinary reality. These are not only long journeys in space, but also in time.

As we journey in the Middle World to very distant cosmic objects that are perhaps billions of light years away, we are moving in space-time—that is, we are journeying *backward* in time. Here's why: When we see an object in space, we see it as it was in the past, when the light that is reaching our eyes in the present moment left the object—and the objects of the cosmos are often many light-years away. A light-year is the distance light travels in one year; it travels at 300,000 kilometers a second, or 186,000 miles per second. There are about 32 million seconds in a year, so a light-year is about 6 trillion miles, a very long distance compared to earth-based distances. It takes about eight minutes for light to travel from the sun to the earth, so when we see the sun, we see it as it was eight minutes earlier. For an object 10 billion light-years away, it takes light 10 billion years to travel to Earth, so we see the object as it was 10 billion years ago. Thus, a journey to the spirits of the cosmos also requires a journey into the past.

Preparing to Journey to the Spirits of the Cosmos

In all journey work, but especially for journeys in the Middle World to distant cosmic objects, it is important to be fully in your body and grounded—that is, connected and rooted energetically to the earth—before you start. This means being entirely in the moment. Such preparation will help you focus your intention and journey impeccably in nonordinary reality. It will also enable you to cross impeccably from ordinary to nonordinary reality and back.

It is good to invite your allies and teachers to accompany you and to ask for their support. I have also found it useful to obtain from my allies and teachers a tool in nonordinary reality that I can use to ground myself, both in preparation for a journey and following my return. These tools will differ depending on the journey. For example, in one case, I received a small cylindrical object, made of hard polished wood, which I was asked to squeeze in my hand in order to ground myself. In another case, I received a small crystal ball, representing Earth, and was asked to press it over my chakras for grounding.

It is also important to have some experience in Middle World journeying, beginning with journeys to objects in our own solar system. You might start by journeying in the Middle World to a place that has special power for you, such as a tree, a rock, a meadow, a body of water, or a mountain. Then, from there, journey in the Middle World to an object in the solar system such as the sun, the moon, another planet, or a comet. When you meet the spirit of the object, greet it, honor it, and ask for support and guidance in your journeys into the immense cosmos.

While Middle World journeys are fast in the sense that you go from place to place much faster than you ever could in ordinary reality, it is important not to do so instantaneously, but instead to see or sense the journey itself, observe items along the way, and return to ordinary reality while recognizing the way back. Fully experiencing the journey helps you maintain full attention and a focus on your intention, and it helps you stay attentive to possible interference by your mind.

My workshop participants and I have found that spirits of the cosmos are benevolent, welcoming, and eager to work with us. The energy of the journeys and of the interactions with spirits is quite different from that of earth-based journeys, however, and takes getting used to. In journeying in the cosmos, we can encounter quite a bit of violence in the form of explosive expansions and contractions of energy. This violence is the nature of the cosmos and is expressed in the life cycles of stars, galaxies, and other cosmic objects. This cosmic violence is not the same as the cruel and aggressive violence so sadly common among us humans; rather, it is the source of the matter and energy that gave rise to and nourish life. Encountering it can, nevertheless, be intense. It is important to prepare for it.

Working with spirits of the cosmos also makes us aware that we are not the center of the universe. Given our longtime cultural, psychological, and intellectual fixation with being at the center, this realization can shake us deeply; our belief is engrained in us, even if we do not recognize it. Preparatory journeys such as those I have just mentioned can help you deal effectively and harmoniously with the intensity of the cosmos. Again, journeying with your allies or teachers can also be a great help.

THE LIFE CYCLE OF A STAR

As I talk about journeys to spirits of various objects of the cosmos in the remainder of this chapter, I will describe cosmic objects and phenomena using simple physics. Gaining a little insight into the physical forces at work is good preparation for your journey and will help you gain an appreciation for the power, size, and dynamics of the entities you will be visiting.

To begin, let me introduce you to the life cycle of a star. As you will see, the birth, life, and death of stars are the source of our own lives.

An atom in matter consists of a tiny nucleus, with a positive electric charge, surrounded by a rotating cloud of negatively charged electrons. The nucleus itself is made up of protons, which are positively charged, and neutrons, which are about the same mass as the proton but have no electric charge. The chemical elements are differentiated by the number of protons in their nuclei. The lightest element, hydrogen, has one proton and no neutrons. The next heaviest element, helium, has two protons and two neutrons, and so on. Carbon has six protons, oxygen has eight, and uranium has ninety-two. The universe is primarily made of hydrogen and helium, which were forged during the early moments following the beginning of the universe at the big bang.

In the vast clouds of hydrogen and helium gas found in galaxies, there can be nonuniformities in the amount of gas within the cloud. Regions of a cloud with higher densities of material will gravitationally attract material from their surroundings. As material comes together—usually in a swirling motion—a large, rotating spherical concentration of gas results. As more matter coalesces, gravity increases, the sphere becomes more and more compact, and the pressure and temperature of the gas become so high that the electrons are stripped from the hydrogen and helium nuclei. If there is enough material present, the high pressure and temperature will allow thermonuclear reactions to occur in which two nuclei of hydrogen combine or fuse to produce a heavier helium nucleus.

It turns out that the mass of the resulting nucleus is less than the sum of the masses of the two lighter nuclei. This loss of mass has transformed into energy, as Einstein described in his famous equation on the equivalence of mass and energy.

This is the source of the energy of the sun and other stars. As energy is generated inside the star, this creates a pressure, directed outward, that prevents gravity from collapsing the star any further, just as the pressure of the hard rocks inside the earth prevents gravity from making the earth collapse inward. The star becomes a stable sphere.

An average star will burn its hydrogen fuel and shine for many billions of years. Heavier stars burn their hydrogen fuel much faster and have much shorter lifetimes. Our sun, an average-size star, is about five billion years old and will shine for another five billion years or so.

When a star has burned almost all its hydrogen fuel, it no longer generates enough energy to hold off gravity, and it starts to collapse inward again. As it collapses, pressure and temperature increase further, and elements heavier than hydrogen fuse, creating still heavier elements. The star goes through a turbulent process in which it expands to become a giant sphere, throwing gases and materials into space. Some of this material ends up in interstellar clouds of hydrogen and helium. The heavier elements, including metals, created inside the star by fusion and ejected from the star, are a source of material for the creation of planets—and ultimately living beings like us.

When the star can no longer sustain fusion reactions, gravity takes over again, and the star collapses. A star with the mass of the sun will collapse until it is about the size of the earth. At this point the outward pressure of the compressed material counteracts the force of gravity. This small remnant is called a *white dwarf,* and it emits very little energy or light. In about five billion years our sun will become a white dwarf.

If the star is at least about eight times as massive as the sun, it collapses in a colossal explosion called a *supernova* and ejects its outer layers into space at high speed. If the star is less than about forty times as massive as the sun, there is enough matter to compress what remains of the star to a state in which all the nuclei are broken up into their component protons and neutrons. Protons are then pressed against electrons, forming neutrons, and the star remnant becomes an incredibly compact rotating sphere of neutrons—a *neutron star.* A neutron star has a radius of only about ten kilometers, and it is so compact that a thimbleful of neutron matter would weigh about a billion tons on Earth. As it gets smaller and thinner, the speed of the star's rotation increases, just as a spinning ice skater's speed of rotation increases when she brings her arms closer to her body. A neutron star has an intense magnetic field. It will slowly radiate away its rotational energy, transforming its kinetic energy of rotation into beams of electromagnetic energy, including radio waves. Like the rotating lamp of a lighthouse that emits light pulses, a rotating neutron star emits radio-wave beams, which are picked up on Earth as radio pulses.

A rotating neutron star is called a *pulsar.* After a million years or so, the pulsar will have slowed down enough that it no longer emits radio waves, and it becomes a silent neutron star.

If the star starts out at least forty times as massive as the sun, the compressed neutrons cannot overcome the force of gravity, and the star continues to collapse. It becomes smaller and smaller, denser and denser, and there is nothing to stop this continuing collapse. Ultimately the star reaches an infinitesimally small size—essentially zero—and infinite density. Such a strange state is called a *singularity,* and the star is now a *black hole.*

JOURNEYS TO THE SPIRITS OF THE COSMOS

Let me give you examples of the wide variety of cosmic objects to which you can journey and the many different intentions you can hold during those journeys. In doing so, I hope to convey a sense of wonder and excitement for the incredible beauty of the universe and the power and beauty of the journeys themselves. Here is a place where modern science and shamanism can truly become entangled.

All the journeys described here, as well as the intentions underlying them, were given to me by spirits over a period of several years. There are, however, countless other possible journeys and intentions you can have when working with spirits of the cosmos; what follows is only a small window into an immense and exciting new world.

To immerse us right away in the vastness and strangeness of the universe, I will start with a journey to a quasar. Quasars are among the brightest and most distant objects in the universe, and likely among the lesser known. We will then journey to a pulsar, a cosmic object we can find in our own galaxy.

Next we will make a powerful and beautiful journey inside the huge black hole at the center of our galaxy. We will then contact the spirit of our home galaxy, the Milky Way, and the spirit of our largest galactic neighbor, the Andromeda galaxy. We will journey to the spirit of a young, newly born star and work with the spirit of a supernova, a massive star in its explosive dying process. Finally, as an example of world work, we will journey to the spirit of a *galaxy cluster*, one of the larger structures of the cosmos.

Quasars

Quasars, as I mentioned, are among the brightest and most distant objects in the cosmos. They shine hundreds of times more brightly than a typical galaxy, and some are as far away as 10 to 12 billion light-years from Earth. Since the universe is estimated to be about 13.7 billion years old, when we see a quasar, we are seeing an object in the very early life of the universe.

Quasars are large galaxies formed from the collision or merging of two or more galaxies. The intense brightness comes from a region at the center of the quasar not much larger than our own solar system. The quasars are powered by massive black holes at their center.

A black hole's gravity is so powerful that anything that comes close enough is pulled in and all its matter is compressed to a point of practically infinite density. A black hole's gravitational field is so strong that even light cannot escape it, which is why a black hole cannot be seen directly.

In a quasar, gas, dust, and stars concentrated near the center are pulled in by the black hole, and as they spiral around and into it, they accelerate to extremely high speeds, close to the speed of light. In doing so, they heat up and emit intense energy in the form of radiation, including visible light. This is what gives quasars their brightness.

Journeying to a Quasar

In journeying to a distant quasar, a particularly useful and appropriate mission or intention is to ask the quasar spirit for help in healing our planet Earth. This is a form of world work, which I will describe in chapter 12.

When you start this journey, accompanied by your allies or teachers, part of your intention is to be led to a quasar; the intention to be led to a cosmic object is necessary in all such journeying. As you leave the earth in the Middle World, be conscious and observant of the solar system, then of other stars in our galaxy. As you leave our galaxy and move swiftly through space, observe around yourself a wondrous world of galaxies and galaxy clusters. As you near the quasar, notice its brilliance and vibrancy.

First, call the spirit of the quasar. As it manifests itself, it is important to greet it, honor it, and bless it, as you will probably be the first human ever to have visited and contacted the spirit of that particular quasar. You may then ask the spirit if it would be willing to give you a *vision* of a healthy, healed, and ecologically whole planet Earth. This vision could take various forms, including figurative or symbolic ones, but it is important to ask that this be a vision that you will be able to manifest—for example, a painting, drawing, sculpture, or poem.

After observing the vision well, thank the spirit of the quasar, honor it again, and start back to Earth. As you travel very fast in the Middle World again, be conscious of the journey home.

When you have returned, be sure to manifest the vision you have brought with you. Since the vision comes from spirit, this physical manifestation of it will be a sacred power object. The manifestation of a spirit vision or message in ordinary reality, in space and time and through ordinary matter, is one way the shaman brings back the power of the spiritual dimension and links ordinary and nonordinary reality. The manifestation of your vision will contribute in a powerful way to the healing of our planet. Put this sacred object in a special place of honor in your house or apartment.

To give you an example of a sacred power object, here is a vision of planet Earth, in the form of a poem, that a quasar spirit gave me during one of my journeys.

> I saw your planet in a dream
> Like a jewel
> With blues, and browns, and whites
> And greens and oranges
> All reflecting beauty and joy.
> I plucked that planet from my dream
> And put it on a bracelet
> For your ankle
> So when you walk you will see
> Who your Mother really is,
> And it will remind you
> To be her loving child again.

In journeys such as these, we contribute to greater harmony in our world in ways beyond the simple manifestation of the spirit vision. The cosmic objects we have visited, in this case a quasar, become communicating presences. Interacting with them changes our consciousness, and consciousness changes behavior. Our sense of connection with and respect for the cosmic object internalizes a respectful behavior toward the earth as part of the cosmos. This new behavior, along with the manifested quasar spirit vision, has a direct impact on the wellbeing of the planet and all its inhabitants, because everything is related and interconnected. Any reckless disregard for the earth or denial of the impact of our behavior becomes less possible, less comfortable, and less culturally endorsed.

Pulsars

A journey to the spirit of a pulsar is a wonderful way to complement the journey to a quasar. Here, you seek an incantation to empower and help bring about the vision of a healthy planet Earth that you received from the quasar spirit. As you saw in the description of a star's life cycle, pulsars are remnants of relatively heavy stars that have burned all their fuel and can no longer shine. They are very dense, compact objects that rotate at very high speed, some as fast as a thousand revolutions per second. As they spin, they emit rapid pulses of radio waves that can be picked up on Earth. Pulsars, like driftwood washed upon the ocean shore, still carry the wisdom and energy of a long life.

Journeying to a Pulsar

With your intention and the help of your allies, journey in the Middle World to a pulsar in our galaxy. Call the spirit of the pulsar, greet it, honor it, and bless it. Ask the spirit if it would be willing to give you an *incantation* to empower the *vision* of a healthy planet Earth that you have received from the quasar spirit and have manifested.

Incantations are sacred words or songs. They have an important role in many shamanic traditions, and they have the power to heal, to summon one's spirit helpers, and to divine, among other powers. Sacred words or sacred songs played a particularly important role in ancient European Celtic shamanism.[2] Incantations have power when they come directly from spirit.

The incantation you receive from the pulsar spirit could be a word, a few words, or a few lines, in English or another tongue. It could also be a few sounds or a brief melody, with or without words. It is important to understand the incantation well, so ask the spirit to repeat it if you are not certain you have it or will be able to remember it when you return to Earth. As always, it is important to thank the spirit before you come back.

After you have returned, you can say or sing the incantation while looking at the manifestation you created of the quasar spirit's vision. The purpose is to focus your intention and empower the vision so it becomes a reality for the planet. To continue to empower it, say or sing the incantation whenever you pass by the manifestation of the vision.

Black Holes

When I first decided to journey inside a black hole to meet its spirit, I felt a mixture of intense fear and raw excitement, the way you might feel if you were about to intentionally plunge into a complete unknown. I had no idea what to expect. I remember telling Noëlle I was going to journey inside a black hole and asking her to watch over and check on me. As it turned out, it was one of the most profound and—perhaps oddly—soothing journeys I have experienced.

Black holes are very strange cosmic objects: the force of gravity within them is so strong that nothing can escape. Any material coming close enough will be pulled in by this irresistible force. As I described earlier, very massive stars reaching the end of their lives explode as supernovas, leaving behind a black hole. At the center of the black hole is an infinitely small, infinitely dense state of matter called a *singularity.*

Around the singularity is a spherical boundary called the Schwarzschild radius or event horizon—a virtual boundary that forms the periphery of the black hole and where gravity becomes infinite. Any material that falls within that boundary can never escape, being itself brought to nothing at the singularity and adding mass to the black hole. Even light cannot escape if it falls within this boundary, which is why black holes are black and, as I mentioned earlier, cannot be seen directly. As a black hole absorbs material, or sometimes merges with another black hole, its mass and radius increase.

Massive black holes have been detected at the center of many galaxies, including our own. The reason we know there is a massive black hole at the center of our galaxy is that stars and gas have been observed moving at incredibly high speed around the galactic center and emitting strong X-rays. This indicates that there must be a very strong source of gravity at the center. Based on the speed of the stars, such a gravitational field must be produced by an object with a mass of two to three million times that of the sun—a very massive black hole.

The black hole at the center of our Milky Way galaxy is a wonderful place to journey. I have found it to be particularly appropriate for working on and learning about oneself and how to be more impeccable in both ordinary and nonordinary reality.

Journeying to a Black Hole

With your intention and the help of your allies, go in the Middle World toward the center of our galaxy. The Milky Way's black hole is in the constellation Sagittarius. When you reach the black hole, journey into it through the event horizon and ask to meet its spirit. When you meet the spirit, greet it, honor it, and bless it. Then ask if it would be willing to teach you something about, and provide you with information on, *your fundamental essence,* your true nature—who you truly are. When the journey is over, thank the spirit and come back to wherever you are in ordinary reality.

Following is an example of such a journey.

On my first journey inside the black hole in the center of our galaxy, I am accompanied by some of my allies and carry with me various power objects I have received from spirits. As I enter the black hole, I find myself in a space, an energy that I find nearly impossible to describe. I see myself floating in various places in this space, as if there were more than one of me. I see things—the best word I can use is *energies*—falling into the black hole.

I call the spirit of the black hole. I see and sense the spirit as a large presence, crystal-like, a beautiful material, like a pillar. Yet it is unlike anything I have encountered before. I experience an intense sense of wellbeing. It is like being home, returning home, having never left home. There is complete acceptance—of who I am, of what is. I sense living compassion, truth, love, joy, and yet utter simplicity. I experience in a deep way what it is to be in the now, where nothing is everything. I know the experience is in itself a message from the spirit.

The black hole spirit tells me that in my essence are Truth and Love and that these are the same. The spirit says that I have the power to speak the truth in a way that is love, and it reminds me of times when I have done so. The spirit encourages me to be aware of and manifest this power. I thank the spirit and reluctantly leave the black hole and return to my home.

In a later journey to the spirit of our galaxy's black hole, the spirit shows itself to me in various forms—animal forms, plant forms, and human forms—changing from one to the other. I ask the spirit the meaning of what I am observing. The spirit says that it can show itself to me in any form I desire and in particular any form from our planet Earth. I remember a Native American spiritual leader who took my workshop "Shamanism and Spirits of the Cosmos" and said that the spirits of the quasar and the pulsar were his grandparents. I ask to see the spirit of the black hole as my four grandparents, who all died many years ago. The spirit shows itself as my two paternal grandparents and my two maternal grandparents. It is beautiful and loving!

I have done this journey many times and so have participants in my workshops. It can sometimes be very intense. The issue is often not that you have difficulty getting out of the black hole, but rather that the feeling or sensation while there can be one of such wellbeing that you would rather stay. So it is important to be impeccable and return when it is time or, if you are journeying to the sounds of a drum, when it calls you back. It is good to have other people present when you do this journey, both to make sure you return fully and to share your thoughts and feelings with afterward.

The Milky Way Galaxy and the Andromeda Galaxy

Galaxies are in many ways the major inhabitants of our cosmos. They are homes for stars and other cosmic objects related to the life cycle of stars, such as pulsars, black holes, supernovae, and, of course, planets, which are all held together through gravity. Galaxies are also home to *nebulae,* which are large clouds of molecular gas. Some of these nebulae have very striking shapes, and they are the nurseries where new stars are born. Galaxies come in different sizes and shapes, the more common shapes being elliptical or spiral.

The Milky Way galaxy comprises about a hundred billion stars, and interstellar gas and dust. It is spiral shaped and lies more or less on a horizontal plane, like a disk; it has a central bulge and several spiral arms, like a pinwheel. The disk has a diameter of about a hundred thousand light-years and rotates about its center like a giant carousel. As we discussed earlier, a massive black hole resides in the center.

The galaxy also has a spherical halo, about two hundred thousand light-years in diameter, that consists of low-density gas, widely separated stars, and about 120 globular clusters, which are compact groupings of hundreds of thousands of stars. Our star, the sun, is located on one of the spiral arms, about thirty thousand light-years from the center. On a clear night, without light pollution, we can see the galaxy's edge as a streak or band of white light against the sky. There are striking photographs of similar spiral galaxies made with some of our large telescopes.

For me, the Milky Way galaxy has now become my home. After spending my early years on one continent and now living on another, traveling around the planet, and focusing much of my professional work on protecting the earth's environment, I internalized a deep sense that this entire planet was my home. Then, as I started doing shamanic journeys to contact spirits of objects throughout our cosmos, I realized that this was a limited, parochial view, and my deep, embodied sense now is that the Milky Way galaxy is where I dwell. Perhaps as my consciousness further matures, I will also see this view as too limited and deeply sense that our universe, our cosmos, is my home. Meanwhile, the journey to the spirit of our home galaxy is the one I most often carry out as I travel to spirits of the cosmos. The spirit of the Milky Way galaxy is for me a very nurturing and healing connection, a source of repeated wisdom, counsel, and advice.

Another galaxy I journey to is a nearby galaxy called Andromeda. Andromeda and the Milky Way are part of a small congregation of galaxies called the Local Group. The Local Group contains about 30 galaxies and is a loose structure centered on the Milky Way and Andromeda galaxies, with a diameter of about 5 million light-years. All the galaxies in the Local Group interact with one another through gravity. Their motions are like a dance. Andromeda is the largest galaxy in the Local

Group; the Milky Way is the second largest. Andromeda is visible from Earth with the naked eye—the farthest object visible with the naked eye, in fact. Like the Milky Way, it is a spiral galaxy. Its disk has a diameter of about 200,000 light-years, and it hosts about 400 billion stars, which whirl around its large central black hole. Andromeda lies about 2.4 million light-years from our galaxy and is about 60 percent larger and brighter than the Milky Way. Beautiful photographs have been taken of Andromeda; you can see examples in books such as Ken Croswell's *Magnificent Universe* and David Devorkin and Robert Smith's *Hubble: Imaging Space and Time*.

The Andromeda and Milky Way galaxies are moving toward each other at a speed of several hundred kilometers per second, and they may well collide and combine one day—several billion years from now. In a sense, Andromeda is betrothed to our own Milky Way. As a member of our Local Group, Andromeda knows about relationships, in particular its relationship to the Milky Way. For this reason, I have found that a good mission or intention when journeying to Andromeda is to learn about *relationships*.

Journeying to Andromeda

With your intention and the help of your allies, journey in the Middle World to the Andromeda galaxy. As you approach it, call its spirit. Greet the spirit and honor and bless it. Ask the spirit of the galaxy if it would be willing to offer counsel on how you can improve the way you relate to other people, so as to be in greater harmony with the Universe. As you are ready to leave, thank the spirit and come back.

The following was my first journey to Andromeda with this mission in mind.

I journey in the Middle World to the Andromeda galaxy and am accompanied by two of my allies. We leave the solar system, then our galaxy, and travel through beautiful space, with bright objects passing by. The sight of Andromeda is awesome, and I feel my heart filling up with emotion. I reach the outskirts of the galaxy and call the spirit of Andromeda. Something forms in the center of the galaxy and comes up, as if growing out of the center. I think at first it is a huge flower, but then see it as a large sphere with multiple layers, soft and substantial, in rather darker hues. I greet the spirit, honor and bless it, and bring greetings from planet Earth.

The spirit shows it is glad to see me, and it appears as if it has prepared a grand welcome for me. I feel grateful. I ask the spirit if it would be willing to counsel me on how I could improve the way I relate to other people so as to be in greater harmony with the Universe.

The spirit says I need to focus on my part of the relationship, which is my responsibility. I need to have a clear and positive intention, relate from that, and not be driven by the other person's intention, behavior, or way of relating. The spirit says that doing this clearly will create an energy that invites my partner to relate that way.

The spirit then suddenly transforms into a young, healthy woman—strong, with braided hair. She tells me to go and be in one of the spiral arms, similar to the one in which our sun sits in the Milky Way. Then she approaches me quickly and kisses me. I feel a strong connection with her. She tells me that to relate, whether it is in a new or a continuing relationship, I need to act consciously, to make a "gesture" toward the other, with all my intention. She says that being passive, just waiting or reacting, is not relating. She smiles. I thank the spirit and come back.

In chapter 3, I spoke about relationships and impeccability in relationships. The spirit of Andromeda taught me that I have complete responsibility for my part of my relationships with other people, nature, society, and spirits. I am not responsible for their part. Andromeda also taught me that in relating, I needed to have a clear intention, be fully conscious of my intention, and manifest that intention through my behavior. That is the nature of a true relationship.

Young Stars

So far I have described journeys to cosmic objects that are rather old, such as quasars, pulsars, black holes, and galaxies. We can also journey to objects that are among the youngest in the cosmos: stars that were very recently born. Our own galaxy turns out to be a major creator of new stars, and about ten stars are born every year. Many star nurseries can be found in the spiral arms of the Milky Way.

It is not easy to observe newborn and young stars because they tend to be shrouded in the gas clouds, or nebulae, in which they are born. If you would like to see photographs of nebulae with young stars shining through at the edges, some beautiful ones are available in the books *Magnificent Universe* and *Hubble: Imaging Space and Time*. Recent technological advances in telescopes have allowed us to observe very young stars in our neighborhood of the galaxy. These stars are born as part of what is called a young-star group, association, or cluster. Some of these groups are less than two hundred light-years from Earth (recall that our galaxy is about a hundred thousand light years in diameter). They range in age from a few million years to about thirty million years. For an average sunlike star, ten million years old is 0.1 percent of its expected life, which is ten billion years. Transposing to the life expectancy for a human being, a ten-million-year-old sunlike star is equivalent to a human infant of about two to three months old. These stars are indeed babies.

Journeying to a Young Star

With your intention and the help of your allies, journey in the Middle World to a nearby very young star cluster, approach a young star, and call its spirit. Greet the spirit, honor and bless it, and welcome it to the universe. Ask the spirit if it would be willing to teach you about the inner, or sacred, child in you. In the last chapter, in talking about time and the myth of the eternal return, I spoke about the inner child, the essential innocence and wholeness with which we come into this world—authentic being—and which, as we age and move into adulthood, we tend to hide, repress, or deny. Ask the spirit of the young star what aspect of the inner child would be most appropriate for you to let reemerge or reestablish. As you are ready to leave, thank the spirit and come back.

Supernovae

Supernovae are among the brightest and most energetic objects in the cosmos. As we have seen earlier in this chapter when exploring the life cycle of stars, a supernova is a massive star in its death throes, exploding violently. (There is another kind of supernova, which arises when a white dwarf accumulates gas drawn from a companion star in a binary system, but that type is not our destination here.) A journey to a supernova is a powerful and wonderful way to learn about violence, death and birth, and interconnections. It is also a way to deepen our understanding of the three fundamental and interrelated forces of the universe that are spoken about in many spiritual traditions: creation, maintenance, and destruction.

I have found that merging with a supernova is a particularly powerful way to work with it and learn from it and its spirit. I spoke about merging in chapters 4 and 6. Merging is an ancient and widespread shamanic practice whereby one unites or merges with the spirit and the entity with which one is working. It is a common and useful practice in journeying to merge with one's allies and spirit teachers, as well as with spirits of nature, such as those of water, air, or fire. In merging, the teachings we receive from spirits are well embodied, in the sense that they are not registered primarily or solely by the mind, but are also imprinted on our physical, emotional, and energy bodies and, indeed, on our entire being.

A supernova is a wondrous cosmic phenomenon. Let's look in a little more detail at how a heavy star ends its life after it has burned its fuel on its way to becoming a neutron star or a black hole. As we have seen, when a star is heavy, at least about eight times the mass of our sun, it burns its hydrogen fuel much more quickly than the sun. Massive stars deplete their central core of hydrogen in a few hundred million years, compared to about ten billion years for the sun. When the central core of a massive star stops producing energy through nuclear fusion of hydrogen, the core, which is now made of helium, contracts under gravity. This increases the temperature and pressure, allowing the hydrogen that remains in the outer shell surrounding the core to burn. The energy released by the contracting core and hydrogen burning in the outer shell causes the outer parts of the star to expand out to very large distances, and the star is now called a *red giant*.

As the star's helium core continues to contract under gravity, the temperature becomes high enough for helium to fuse, creating carbon and oxygen and releasing energy. With the release of this energy, large quantities of gas from the outer shells of the red giant are ejected into space at high speed. The helium in the core burns rapidly, and the core contracts further, increasing the temperature and allowing carbon and oxygen to fuse into heavier elements. In turn, these heavier elements fuse as the core contracts even more, creating new elements, the heaviest of these being iron. Iron cannot be fused, and ultimately, as nuclear reactions and energy production in the core diminish, the star contracts rapidly under gravity to immense density, creating a neutron star or a black hole, releasing enormous energy and creating a massive explosion that ejects the remaining outer layers of the star into space at very high speed. The brightness of the explosion is enormous, shining as much as all the stars of a galaxy put together. The star has now become a supernova.

After the brief, intense explosion, the supernova now consists of an inner core (either a neutron star or a black hole, depending on the mass of the star) surrounded by an expanding shell of material, which is called a supernova remnant. One supernova remnant that was discovered in the 1980s was determined to have exploded centuries earlier and was traced to an extremely bright object that Chinese astronomers observed and documented in the tenth century. The shock wave from the explosion pushes the outer layers out at tremendous speeds that approach the speed of light. The nuclei in these layers create, by nuclear reactions, all the elements heavier than iron, all the way to uranium, the heaviest naturally occurring element on Earth.

All these elements, from carbon to uranium, created either in the star itself or in the expanding layers of the supernova, spread into interstellar space. They will at some point mix with interstellar clouds of hydrogen and helium. When one of these clouds collapses under gravity to produce a new star, these heavy elements make possible the formation of planets like Earth, containing the elements necessary for life. Hence, we are indeed made up of stardust, and the elements that make up our bodies, except for hydrogen, were created in other stars and in exploding supernovae. In addition, oftentimes the shock wave from the supernova explosion creates the initial compression of the interstellar gas, leading to star formation. The deaths of stars and supernovae explosions are necessary for life as we know it.

There are beautiful photographs of supernova remnants in the previously mentioned books by Ken Croswell and by David Devorkin and Robert Smith. Supernovae are awesome and essential phenomena, among the most violent in the cosmos, and the last stage in the death of massive stars. And yet they are the source of life through their creation of the elements necessary for life and their stimulation of more star and planet formation. Because we are made of stuff made by stars and supernovae from long ago, supernovae connect us in a very real sense with the rest of the cosmos. We are indeed One.

A journey to merge with a supernova is a powerful way to learn who we are and what life is about.

Journeying to a Supernova

With your intention, journey in the Middle World to a massive star that is about to undergo a supernova explosion. Call the spirit, greet it, bless it, and honor it. Then ask the spirit if you can merge with it and the supernova. As you merge, with your intention, experience the various stages of the supernova: the swelling as a red giant, the inward crushing of the core, the violent explosion and release of the outer layers, the creation of heavy elements, and the spread of the material into neighboring hydrogen gas clouds.

Because you are in nonordinary reality, outside of time, you will experience the various stages in accelerated time. As you experience the merging, ask the spirit if it would be willing to teach you about *violence, death and birth,* and *interconnections.* Go as far as you can in the supernova process. In doing this journey, it is particularly important to be well grounded, so you may use the grounding tool I mentioned earlier in this chapter and a traditional drumming callback to fully gather yourself and come back impeccably as the journey ends.

I have made this journey several times, letting the supernova spirit guide me as I become either a single atom in the supernova layers or a full layer itself. These journeys have been intense, powerful, and beautiful. In one particularly intense journey, I longed to stay in the journey even though it was jarring. I have learned about violence, death and birth, and interconnections in new ways, gaining new insights, a deeper understanding of what I already knew, and a more fully embodied way of knowing.

In particular, I have learned that violence, as an intense concentration and explosion of energy, is relative to where it happens, how big it is, how it happens, and for what purpose. I understand that violence is needed for creativity and is a natural phenomenon that needs to be experienced naturally. I understand that our bodies "remember" the supernova's violence that gave birth to us, and we long for it. Unfortunately, in our daily lives we tend to forget what violence was meant to do; we yearn for it and return to it with no aim or direction.

As a result of my journeys, I learned that the explosive energy of the supernova is in me and exists as the energy that drives love, laughter, and right action. I now understand more completely that death and birth are the same thing. They are both merely change; one leads to the other. I am conscious that all humans are made of material from the same supernova. All of us, along with the earth, are connected to our supernova, which itself is connected to other supernovae. And we all are made up of hydrogen, which came from the biggest explosion of them all, the big bang.

Galaxy Clusters

Galaxies are not uniformly distributed in the cosmos, and they congregate in clusters of various shapes and sizes. Some clusters, such as our own Local Group that hosts the Milky Way, are small, harboring only a few dozen galaxies. Other clusters are very large, containing thousands of galaxies. The closest of these is the Virgo cluster, about fifty million light-years from Earth. A few clusters are spherical and are called regular globular clusters. Most galaxy clusters are irregular, and the clusters can take various shapes, from clumps to concave or convex walls. Galaxy clusters tend to join and form *superclusters,* which are immense chains of groups of galaxies, looking somewhat like immense spider webs. In between superclusters is mainly empty space.

Galaxy clusters are held together by gravity, and their galaxies interact and move about at speeds of hundreds of kilometers per second. Clusters are communities of galaxies that have existed for a long time. Over time, galaxies in a cluster may combine to form larger galaxies. While such events are often described as "galactic collisions," or a form of "galactic cannibalism," with one galaxy devouring another, they are much closer to a union or merging of two galaxies.

As galaxies merge, few if any stars collide or vanish; stars in galaxies are relatively large distances apart. The motion of the stars shifts, pressure within interstellar gas spawns the creation of new stars, and a new, larger galaxy emerges with a different shape, usually elliptical. As with a merging of communities, new elements and creativity arise in a now united, different, and bigger community.

Spirits suggested I journey to the spirit of a galaxy cluster to provide an opportunity for communities in conflict on Earth to heal. This is world work, and it uses the approach of obtaining from spirits a power object in nonordinary reality. I will describe this approach in more detail in chapter 12.

Journeying to a Galaxy Cluster

Think about communities in conflict for which you would like to offer healing. With your intention and the help of your allies, journey in the Middle World to a galaxy cluster somewhere in the cosmos. Call the spirit of the cluster, greet it, honor and bless it, and ask its permission to do world work. Ask the spirit if it is willing to give you a *sacred object in nonordinary reality* that will help bring about peace,

reconciliation, and harmony for the communities you have
selected. Ask the spirit if it has any specific instructions as
to where and how to place the object. Take the object, thank
the spirit, journey in the Middle World back to Earth, and
go directly in the Middle World to the area you have selected.
Place the object at the appropriate location and do what is
necessary to follow the instructions of the cluster's spirit.

It is up to the communities to use the energy from
this object if they so choose—there is no imposition here.
When you are finished, come back to where you are in
ordinary reality.

Here is an account of a journey I did once for communities in Northern Ireland.

Joined by one of my allies, I leave with the intention of meeting
a galaxy cluster. I travel through the solar system and then swiftly
into space and back in time. I see the cluster, and I am moved. It
is huge, in the shape of a curved wall, with galaxies spread upon it
as though on a curving tapestry. I see it from its concave side.

I call the spirit of the cluster, and right away a large male head
bursts forth. The spirit says, "Hi, Claude." I ask if he is the spirit
of the cluster, and he acknowledges with a nod. The head is bushy,
with much gray hair and a gray beard. I honor, bless, and greet
the spirit.

I ask the spirit if he is willing to give me an object to bring more
peace and harmony to Northern Ireland's communities. He immediately gives me a sphere about a foot in diameter, which looks
like it is made of glass or crystal, with small flowing items like
baby fish inside. He tells me to go put it on top of a mountain
in Northern Ireland. I thank the cluster spirit and journey back
swiftly through space, fly over my home, and go to Northern
Ireland. My ally leads me to a high, craggy peak, like a spire. I

can see the sea in the distance. I place the sphere on the top and fly around it several times while singing. I hear the cluster spirit say that the multicolored little fishlike objects, which are now streaming out of the sphere in all directions, will only be received by those who are open to and want peace and reconciliation, and who are ready for it. The objects will reaffirm their openness to peace and reconciliation, strengthen them by clearing out irrelevant issues, and give guidance on how to act. I thank the spirit and come back home.

Other Possible Journeys to Spirits of the Cosmos

The journeys I have described are just a small sampling of the many journeys and types of shamanic work we can do with spirits of the cosmos. There are many other cosmic objects we can journey to. Some are relatively nearby and members of our home galaxy, such as brown dwarfs, white dwarfs, nebulae, and small black-hole remnants of supernovae explosions. Others are vast cosmic entities not yet fully understood by science, such as dark matter and dark energy, which together make up about 95 percent of the total energy-matter content of the universe. (The visible objects that we have worked with so far make up only about 5 percent. Our ordinary-reality knowledge of the cosmos, which has exploded in recent decades, still has a way to go.)

The more often we acknowledge, communicate with, learn from, and work with spirits of the cosmos, the more our human consciousness will expand. We will become aware of and understand who we are as one species among countless others on this tiny sphere of rock and water we call Earth, a speck in the immense galaxy we call the Milky Way, which itself is one among countless other galaxies in this immense and beautiful universe we call the cosmos. And we will know we are all related, not separate; we are One.

11

The Big Bang

Cosmic Background Radiation and the Creation Myth

○ ● ○

ne of the great discoveries and successes of modern cosmology is the big bang—the birth of the universe—and the ensuing story of the evolution of the universe. This story, as told by science, is a wondrous one that can inspire us and teach us about our place in and relationship to the universe.

Every indigenous tribe, culture, and civilization has its own creation story, part of the collection of myths that underlie every culture. While these stories are beautiful and poetic, few if any can rival the power and awesomeness of the universe story modern science tells. And in this story, science is reaffirming what indigenous myths and wisdom and ancient spiritual traditions have always taught: that we are not separate; that all elements of creation, including human beings, are interconnected; that we all come from the same source; and that we are One.

CREATION MYTHS AND THE UNIVERSE STORY

Modern cosmology and its story of the universe provide us with a great opportunity to work shamanically with creation myths, which are part and parcel of ancient shamanic traditions. In former cultures and civilizations, people knew from oral or written history how they came to be, up to a point in the distant past. There was no ordinary knowledge of what came before that, and this is where creation myths came in—starting where the people's rational knowledge ended. These stories usually told how the universe came to be and how the first people emerged.

Today, we not only know much about the evolution of life and our own species on Earth, but we also know a surprisingly large amount about the growth and evolution of the whole universe. Our expanding universe was born in a huge explosion called the big bang, in which space, time, and all the matter and energy in the cosmos were created. Science has been able to reconstruct the birth and evolution of the universe in astonishing detail, down to a minuscule fraction of a second after the beginning.

The big bang theory has been confirmed repeatedly by multiple observations of widely different phenomena, particularly in the last few years. While speculative theories have been proposed, science does not know at this time, and for that matter may never know, what happened at the very beginning, or before the beginning—although the use of the term *before* is meaningless here since it implies time, and time did not exist "before" the big bang. Thus, it seems important to seek creation myths to fill in this gap and tell us what happened at and before the big bang. How did it all start? The old creation myths, although they are beautiful and still have much to teach us, no longer fill our need for understanding creation.

Myths speak to us in symbolic and poetic language and have always been an important element of all cultures. Joseph Campbell has written about the essential importance of myth in calling forth and awakening the human potential in each of us. He has also explored the need for Western civilization to re-create myths that speak to us in the modern age. He quotes a distinguished professor of psychiatry at the University of California, Dr. John W. Perry, who has characterized the living mythological symbol as an "affect image." Campbell says: "It is an image that hits where it counts. It is not addressed first to the brain, to be interpreted and appreciated. On the contrary, if that is where it has to be read, the symbol is already dead. An 'affect image' talks directly to the feeling system and immediately elicits a response, after which the brain may come along with its interesting comments. There is some kind of throb of resonance within, responding to the image shown without, like the answer of a musical string to another equally tuned."[1] This description of the impact of mythological symbols is very similar to the experience of a shamanic journey, with its multiple visions, happenings, and messages.

Seeking and obtaining a creation myth is a classic shamanic practice whereby the shaman journeys to recover a creation myth to share with his or her people. Creation myths are distinctive; in a given culture or tribal community, there are usually several different versions of them. Michael Harner tells the story of a tribe in Colorado whose elder shamans journeyed during a ceremony to recover a creation myth. They shared their journeys, each telling a different myth. When the younger shamans in the circle became upset and complained that the stories were all different, and hence none could be the real creation myth, an elder shaman explained that the creation story was so immense, complex, and sacred that no single shaman could possibly know and hold it all. Thus, what each shaman brought back was one small piece, one particular perception of the entire story, viewed through a very narrow lens. All the stories together aided in a more complete understanding of creation.[2]

In working with spirits of the cosmos, we can recover a creation myth that will tell us what happened at the big bang and how it came about: it will pick up where science leaves off, give us teachings, and deepen our understanding of our place in the universe and the meaning of it all. Before we do so, however, it is important to know a little bit about what happened after the big bang according to science. While the following section is fairly dense with scientific information, it is a fascinating story, and I invite you to read and absorb as much of it as you can. An important actor in the story of the universe, as we shall see, is *cosmic background radiation*. And while it is possible to recover a creation myth by contacting any of a large number of spirits of the cosmos, it is particularly useful to do so by contacting the spirit of the cosmic background radiation.

THE BIG BANG AND ITS AFTERMATH

First let's review some fundamentals about matter and energy in the universe. Ordinary matter is made up of atoms of the different elements. The atoms consist of small nuclei surrounded by clouds of electrons. The nuclei are made up of protons and neutrons. The protons and neutrons themselves are made up of smaller elementary particles called quarks. Quarks and electrons thus make up ordinary matter.

The universe is also made up of energy in the form of electromagnetic radiation or waves. Electromagnetic waves carry various amounts of energy depending on their frequency, or rate of oscillation. Low-frequency waves have long wavelengths and low energy density. At higher frequencies, wavelengths shorten and energy density increases. The lowest-frequency electromagnetic radiation is radio waves, which are emitted by pulsars and which also carry the signals for our radios and TVs. As the frequency increases, we find microwaves, associated with cooking and radar. Further up the frequency scale are infrared light, visible light from reds to purples, then ultraviolet rays, a well-known threat to human skin. As we go to higher frequencies yet, we find X-rays, of interest to dentists and doctors. At the highest frequencies, we find gamma radiation, the most energetic electromagnetic radiation of all.

As we saw in chapter 9, quantum mechanics shows that electromagnetic radiation, which behaves like waves, also behaves like particles. This has been confirmed experimentally. Thus, electromagnetic radiation can be likened to tiny massless particles called photons. The higher the frequency, the more energetic the photon. This wave-particle nature of light and other forms of electromagnetic radiation is a strange aspect of our reality.

Let us now turn to a very brief history of the evolution of the universe, and how current ordinary matter and radiation—including cosmic background radiation and the visible objects of the cosmos—came to be. We have confidence in this story because its predictions have been confirmed by many experimental measurements. We begin at 10^{-43} second after the big bang, which is when physics can start making sense of what happened. 10^{-43} second is an incredibly short time, being a fraction of a second with 43 zeros following the decimal point. We will also talk about the temperature of the universe, in kelvins (K)—0 degrees Celsius or 32 degrees Fahrenheit equals 273 K.

We start with an infinitesimal point that is expanding following the big bang. Many people imagine that the big bang was akin to a chemical explosion, and so this infinitesimal point must have existed somewhere *in space*. It is important to understand that this was not the case, since space itself was *being created*. In some sense, all space was in the point, and the expansion occurred everywhere.

From 10^{-43} second to 10^{-10} second (a tenth of a nanosecond) following the big bang. This is the beginning of space and time. The universe is a tiny vacuum filled with fields of force and energy. As we saw in chapter 9, quantum theory tells us that a vacuum is not empty, but has energy that undergoes tiny, random "quantum fluctuations." The temperature is about 10^{32} K (that is, 1 followed by 32 zeros).

Then we have what is called cosmic inflation. The vacuum is unstable, and it blows apart. In a very short time, a repulsive form of gravity, or antigravity force, blows the universe to enormous size, by a factor of as much as 10^{26}. The vacuum energy transforms into electromagnetic radiation energy. The photons are extremely high energy, and some transform into particles of matter and antimatter, electrons and antielectrons (positrons), and quarks and antiquarks.

This transformation is expressed in Einstein's famous equation $E=Mc^2$, which says that mass and energy are equivalent and can be transformed into one another at very high temperatures and energies. An antimatter particle has the same mass as its cousin the ordinary particle, but has opposite characteristics, such as electric charge and spin. Matter and antimatter in contact mutually annihilate, creating energy in the form of energetic photons. Tiny quantum fluctuations are greatly amplified by cosmic inflation, leading to small nonuniformities in the density of matter and antimatter, which will be the source of star and galaxy formation.

As the universe keeps expanding, it is still extremely dense; photons and matter and antimatter particles undergo rapid collisions. Then normal attractive gravity takes over, tending to somewhat slow down the expansion. Matter and antimatter annihilate each other. However, in the end there is a small excess of matter over antimatter, since today the universe, including ourselves, is made up of matter. Antimatter, while it can be produced in the laboratory, has never been observed. This imbalance at first seems strange, since matter and antimatter were created in equal amounts. Today, theory and experiments are converging on an explanation that arises from a small asymmetry in the behavior of some fundamental particles. In any case, in this time period, we end up with a quark, electron, and photon soup, the temperature of which drops to 10^{15} K.

From 10^{-10} second to 10^{-4} second (a tenth of a millisecond). As the universe further expands, its temperature falls to about 2×10^{12} K, and quarks unite to form protons and neutrons. The protons and neutrons turn back and forth into each other: a proton and an electron unite to form a neutron, and a neutron ejects an electron to become a proton. Photons collide continuously with electrons.

At 1 second. The universe's temperature is now about 10^{10} K, or ten billion K. Neutron-proton reactions stop. The result of the asymmetric matter-antimatter annihilation is a mix in which protons outnumber neutrons by seven to one. This is the reason the universe is made up mostly of hydrogen: hydrogen has a single proton in its nucleus, while the heavier elements all require neutrons in their nuclei. The universe keeps expanding, and photons keep colliding with electrons, thus being kept within the soup of elementary matter.

At 100 seconds. The temperature is now about one billion K. Nucleosynthesis starts: neutrons and protons stick together, creating nuclei. All existing neutrons join with protons, primarily forming nuclei of helium (two protons and two neutrons), a small amount of deuterium (an isotope or form of hydrogen called heavy hydrogen, with one proton and one neutron), and a smaller amount yet of lithium (three protons and three neutrons). Thus, within a few minutes after the big bang, the universe is composed primarily of hydrogen and helium nuclei (in proportions of about three quarters and one quarter), with small amounts of deuterium and lithium nuclei. Electrons in this primordial matter keep colliding with photons.

At 300,000 years. The universe has kept expanding and cooling, reaching a temperature of about 3,000 K. At this point, electrons attach themselves to protons, forming hydrogen atoms, and to nuclei of helium and lithium, forming helium and lithium atoms. The universe is now filled with a gas made essentially of hydrogen and helium. Electrons, which are now tied to nuclei in atoms, stop interacting and colliding with photons, and there occurs what is called decoupling of matter and radiation. The universe has become transparent to electromagnetic radiation. The photons, which move at the speed of light, are now free to move unimpeded, and photon radiation expands and cools with the universe, filling it, independent of matter. As the radiation expands and cools, its wavelength increases, and its frequency and energy density decrease.

Up to 1 billion years. Matter in the universe has been expanding and cooling, subject to gravity. The tiny random quantum fluctuations that had appeared in the initial energy vacuum have led to small variations in the density of matter in what is otherwise a very smooth universe. Gravity amplifies these small matter-density variations, and large amorphous structures appear in the gas filling the universe. The temperature has dropped to a mere 20 K, or –253 degrees C.

The nonuniformities in the gas of the universe lead, through the action of gravity, to the formation of stars, galaxies, and quasars. The first stars appear about 400 million years after the big bang. The larger density variations, spatially, lead to the formation of galaxies and clusters of galaxies, while the smaller variations lead to the formation of stars, clusters of stars, and nebulae. The temperature inside stars and in their immediate neighborhood is much higher than the low ambient temperature in interstellar space.

From 1 billion years to now (about 13.7 billion years since the big bang). For the next thirteen billion or so years, heavy elements form in stars through fusion of lighter elements and in supernovae explosions, new stars are born, planets form around stars, stars age and die, and galaxies collide and merge, creating larger galaxies. Gravity creates huge galactic structures called groups of galaxies, clusters, or superclusters, extending from a few million light years to about 100 million light years across. Some of the structures are regular and spherical in shape; others are irregular, including wall-like shapes. In between superclusters are vast voids of empty space.

Today the photon radiation has cooled to about 3 K, which is −270 degrees C. Its frequency has decreased so that it is in the form of radio waves, and it is all around us, filling the universe. This so-called cosmic background radiation was first detected in 1965, and it provides strong evidence for the big bang theory.

JOURNEYING TO THE SPIRIT OF THE COSMIC BACKGROUND RADIATION TO RECOVER A CREATION MYTH

The photons in the cosmic background radiation, which fills the universe, were present right after the big bang, and this is why it makes sense to contact the spirit of the cosmic background radiation in our search for a new creation myth. The journey to this spirit to recover a creation myth—a myth that answers the question, what happened at the big bang, how did it all start?—is very powerful. It can teach us much about ourselves and the universe in a way that science perhaps cannot. It is a wonderful opportunity to combine the marvelous and beautiful achievements of modern science with the power, beauty, and insights of the shamanic journey.

I have made this journey several times, each time retrieving a creation myth with different teachings and insights, and I have led participants in this journey in the workshop "Shamanism and Spirits of the Cosmos" I have taught for many years in Europe and North America.

Journeying to the Cosmic Background Radiation

The cosmic background radiation fills the universe and is all around us, so there is no need to journey far in the Middle World. You can stay right where you are, enter the Middle World, and with your intention call the spirit of the cosmic background radiation. If you prefer, you can journey in the Middle World to some place in nature and call the spirit from there.

When you meet the spirit, greet it, and honor and bless it. Ask the spirit if it is willing to give you a *myth of creation* that says what happened "before" and at the big bang. You may be told the story or shown something, or the myth will be provided to you in some other way. In any case, pay close attention and use your conscious mind to store this information so you will be able to remember and share it later. If anything is unclear, ask the spirit for clarification. Thank the spirit, come back, and write down your creation myth.

During my workshops, usually during evening sessions, I have made time for a ceremony in which participants share through storytelling the creation myths they have received, with audience participation, akin to the storytelling ceremony I described in chapter 9 in the recovery of the myth of the first shaman. I suggest participants begin by saying, "This is the way it all started." These ceremonies have always been lively, creative, and profound in their teachings, and great fun. They are an example of the sacred humor and joy that are very much part of the shamanic tradition and practice.

In my own journeys to the spirit of the cosmic background radiation to recover a creation myth, as well as in many of the creation myths participants in my workshops have recovered, classic, traditional symbols occur, such as animal or plant spirit figures and earth landscapes and features. This is not surprising, since the journey or the myth speaks to us in symbolic language; it is a beautiful link and a manifestation of continuity with the ancient ancestry of our species and the shamanic and mythological traditions.

Here is a creation myth I received from the spirit of the cosmic background radiation. There are many symbolic messages in this story, and I invite you to discern them for yourself.

Before there were space and time, before there was anything, there was an immense ocean. The ocean was neither everywhere nor nowhere, for there was no "where." In the ocean there was just spirit. And spirits were neither here nor there, for there was no "here" nor "there." There was just being, pure being.

And one day—so to speak—Coyote felt a strange feeling, a strong desire, a longing, a kind of curiosity that stirred inside him. So he reflected for a long time and he had a thought: "What is there beyond just being? What is there outside of being?"

As he thought some more about this, desiring an answer, Coyote suddenly saw in front of him an island, and on this island there was a big tree with a large crown of leaves, deep roots, and a long trunk. He suddenly noticed there was someone sitting under the tree. As he closely watched the person sitting there, he had a sudden shock, for the person sitting under the tree was himself! Coyote was confused and at a loss for what to do.

And when the sitting Coyote double saw the expression on Coyote's face, she let out a tremendous laugh. But the laugh had nowhere to go, for there was no "where" and no time to move in. And so space came to be, so the laugh could spread, and time and matter came to be, so the sound wave of the laugh could move. The entire ocean of being was sucked or siphoned in one instant into this point of space and time, with all the spirits, and Coyote was sucked in too, and so were the island and the tree and the Coyote double. Everything exploded in all directions as the laughter spread out in space and time. And this is how the universe came to be.

FREQUENT THEMES IN CREATION MYTH JOURNEYS

When I have taught my "Shamanism and Spirits of the Cosmos" workshops, I have asked participants to send me a copy of their creation myths, if they so wish. Many have done so, and I am very grateful to everyone who has taken the time to send them to me. I have thus been able to gather creation stories in French and English from different places where I have taught the workshop, including Belgium, France, Quebec, and various parts of the United States. Each story is unique, beautiful, and powerful, and teaches us about ourselves and our universe. From these many creation stories, I have culled the prominent themes, elements, insights, and messages that tend to be included:

- It starts with a void, an immensity, a great nothingness, formless and without limits, filled with spirits, filled with divinity.
- This nothingness is sometimes given a name: Supreme Being, Great Mystery, All That Was, the One, the Nothing That Is Everything, Great Blowing.
- Something happens within the Oneness, the Void, the Nothingness, and this in turn leads to the big bang. Some of the recurring themes for what happens are as follows: thoughts, ideas, noticing, observing; a longing, curiosity, desire; love; joy; a dream; boredom; forgetfulness, distraction; dancing and singing. There are many references to huge laughter, a huge sneeze, a huge burp creating the big bang.
- At the big bang, there is a primordial sound, a primordial breath.
- The results of the big bang are duality, multiple parts and creatures, and consciousness.
- What led to the big bang or was present at the big bang continues to be manifested in creation: we can still hear the primordial sound; the primordial breath is still here, manifested as a respiration in death and rebirth, repetition and reproduction; and there is a pervasive longing and desire to feel oneness or wholeness, manifested, for example, in the fusion of the feminine and masculine in sexual procreation and in the coming together of individuals in love.

Each individual story has unique power and beauty and elicits unique responses in those receiving them. I invite you to journey and obtain your own big bang creation myth.

12

Shamanic World Work

Healing the Planet and Its Communities

●　◗　●

One of shamans' main purposes has always been to help maintain the balance of spiritual forces within their communities and the larger community of beings. In today's world, with its many-faceted crises, global communications, and global interdependence and interconnectedness, this function is more essential than ever. Our community now encompasses the entire human family, and our home is the entire planet. What I call "world work" is spirit and healing work done with the intention of bringing the spiritual, material, and biological into harmony around the world and offering opportunities for self-healing in traumatized communities and places. It is important work in our individual shamanic practice as well as in drumming circles and shamanic-practitioner gatherings.

The shamanic tradition, with its rich variety of customs and practices, has always been oriented toward service to others, the community, and nature. As Michael Harner says, "[T]he shaman is a person who, in a sense, is a public servant."[1] Shamanism's orientation toward society and the world had great appeal to me when I was first introduced to it. As an incarnated human being living in a dualistic, physical, ordinary-reality world, it made great sense for me to help manifest the interconnectedness and Oneness that I knew in my shamanic journeys. Thus, the personal spiritual path in my shamanic practice has been inseparable from the service path.

Service means that the shamanic practitioner crosses the boundary between ordinary and nonordinary reality to bring about harmony, or balance, between the physical and spiritual realms. The concept of impeccability, discussed in chapter 3, also applies to the service path, as do the same ethics that inform all shamanic work.

THE NATURE OF WORLD WORK

There are many types of world work. We can do world work for the human family with small or large communities; for organizations, situations, and events; for man-made structures, buildings, or cities; and for the planet's environment and the many other species that inhabit it.

World work in human communities is a critical need. So many of them are in conflict with one another, or even at war, as a result of ethnic, tribal, religious, or resource issues. Others are refugees from war and disaster, struggling to survive far from home in makeshift camps. All of these distressing situations call out for world work.

Many places on the earth have suffered traumas resulting from human destruction, mining, pollution, and wars. Many of us have had the experience of walking out on a piece of land and sensing deeply that the place has lost part of its soul, its spirit. And human activities threaten many species. Because of shamanism's inherent connection with nature, many shamanic practitioners undertake world work specifically for the natural environment. Sandra Ingerman, for example, has developed an excellent and powerful approach to address environmental pollution. She uses the ancient healing arts of transfiguration and transmutation to transform both inner, or personal, and outer, or environmental, toxins. She has developed a workshop called "Medicine for the Earth" to teach this approach, and she has taught many others how to present the workshop, so that this method can be disseminated as widely as possible.[2]

As is the case for shamanic healing for an individual, world work for the natural environment does not replace people's environmental restoration efforts. Rather, it empowers natural restoration processes and complements and facilitates restoration by humans.

When undertaking world work, as in all shamanic practice, we should always seek guidance from spirits about what is appropriate, ask permission to do the work, and work in cooperation with spirits, letting them do the healing as needed. World work can include soul retrieval and shamanic extraction healing, among other approaches. One can bring back the soul of a place, a community, or an organization that has suffered trauma. Throughout history, shamans brought back the souls of crops, so this is in keeping with ancient traditions. Extraction is appropriate for places, communities, or organizations that have acquired spirits or intrusions that do not belong there.

Often our allies and/or spirit teachers carry out healings or blessings appropriate to the situation. Or they may teach us what approach to use in a given situation. For example, I have learned to journey and ask spirits to give me an object in nonordinary reality that has the power to bring harmony to those who wish to take advantage of its presence; you'll find instructions for this journey later in this chapter. Another form of world work is psychopomp work, which I will also discuss later in the chapter.

ETHICS AND IMPECCABILITY IN WORLD WORK

Ethics and impeccability are as essential in doing world work as in other forms of shamanic practice. Impeccability means manifesting authentic being through our body, our ego with all its multiple parts, and our mind as we serve others. Impeccable service requires patience, humility, and staying in the heart chakra, with compassion and without care for achievement, success, or recognition. Obtaining spirits' permission; presenting the healing as an offering, instead of imposing it on others; and working as facilitator rather than healer are all essential.

Asking spirits to do whatever is necessary to achieve a most appropriate outcome, consistent with the greater harmony of the Whole, is particularly important in doing work for human communities in conflict, where parts of our ego may take sides and wish for a certain outcome. We need to approach shamanic world work without judgment; let go of beliefs, desires, and expectations; and work with spirits for harmony. This is not always easy given the political and ideological issues that divide the world community. Our intention must always come from the heart as we let spiritual energy do its work. And, as is the case for individual healing, we need to take care of and protect ourselves appropriately.

In many ways, world work is a manifestation of the dictum that to have harmony outside, we must have harmony inside. The external world reflects the state of our inner life; it all starts with the individual. When we build personal harmony within and strive for impeccability, both in ordinary and nonordinary reality, we powerfully transmit harmony and impeccability around the world through the web of interconnections. It is important to work with our spirit helpers to become conscious—with compassion and humility—of the violence, cruelty, hatred, and terrorism present within ourselves, even as we remain conscious of the presence of their opposites: solidarity, generosity, love, and joy. We need to approach shamanic world work from authentic being. Nothing else will suffice.

EXAMPLES OF WORLD WORK

The following practices were given to me by spirit, and I have done them on my own, taught them in my workshops, and shared them in drumming circles.

Community Healing: Use of a Nonordinary Reality Object

This practice can be used in many regions of the world that are in deep and often violent conflict. It involves journeying to spirits to obtain a power object in nonordinary reality, with the intention of providing an opportunity for healing among these distressed communities.

Select a conflict for which you would like to offer healing. Also select a spirit from whom to receive a power object, or ask your allies to indicate to you which spirit to go to. With your intention, and your allies' help, journey to the spirit. Greet, honor, and bless the spirit, and ask its permission to do the world work you intend. Ask it if it will give you a sacred object in nonordinary reality that you can bring back into the

Middle World and place in the region you have selected to help bring about peace, reconciliation, and harmony. Ask the spirit if it has any specific instructions. Take the object, thank the spirit, and go directly in the Middle World to the area you have selected.

Put the object where the spirit indicates, or, if it has not indicated a place, select one. Do whatever else is necessary to follow the spirit's instructions and the counsel of your allies. Remember, it is up to the communities whether to choose to use the energy from this object; you are not forcing anything on anyone. When you are finished, come back to where you are in ordinary reality.

To give you a sense of how this practice works, following is a journey I once did for communities in Sudan.

I consult my allies, who suggest I go to the spirit of Africa to obtain a power object. With several allies, I journey there in the Middle World. I am somewhere above the center of the continent and call its spirit. The spirit shows itself in the form of a large crocodile with brilliant and kind eyes. I greet and honor the spirit, and ask its permission to do world work in Sudan. The spirit agrees. I ask the spirit if it will give me a sacred object in nonordinary reality that I can bring to Sudan to help bring about peace, harmony, and reconciliation.

The spirit transforms itself into a man and a woman; both look healthy and radiant. The couple is holding hands, and I notice that they also clasp the hands of two children standing on either side of them. The children themselves are holding hands with other children, forming a huge circle of children.

The man comes forward and gives me an object. It is a piece of wood, about ten inches in diameter and three feet long and shaped like a thick spiral. It is dark brown, almost black, and smooth and shiny. On top are attached a number of colored ribbons, and straight, thin sticks come out of the bottom. I take the object, thank the spirit, ask where I need to place the object, and ask for any further instructions. The crocodile reappears and tells me he will accompany me and show me where to place the object.

With the crocodile and my allies, I fly east to Sudan. The crocodile leads us near a river. There are low hills in the distance, and there are large fallow fields around us. The crocodile instructs me to place the power object standing up, about fifty feet from the river, along what looks like a straight dirt road. I wonder how the object will stay up, and at that moment the long thin sticks at the bottom break up into a multitude of beautiful small crystals, deep blue and shiny. I place the piece of wood into the heap of crystals, where it is stable. The ribbons at the top are blowing in the wind. I ask the crocodile for other instructions, and it tells me that the people who feel the object will know what to do. Then the crocodile vanishes.

My allies suggest we form a circle around the object, and I go inside to seek peace and harmony within myself. I notice then that the man, woman, and all the children are forming a very large circle around the power object. I thank the spirit of Africa, and together with my allies, I return home.

I described another example of this type of world work in chapter 10 when journeying to a galaxy cluster.

Shapeshifting and World Work: Sick and Wounded Spirits?

The shapeshifting practice I described in chapter 6 is very useful in world work. Transformed as an ally, you will know how to offer a healing or a blessing or bring forth harmony without thinking or planning: this keeps your spiritual or shamanic ego from taking control. The practice offers a way to be authentic being and let the spiritual energy flow by itself. One example of this type of world work is to do a healing while shapeshifted for a place that has been damaged or traumatized by toxic materials, bombings, or other human destruction. One such world work I did was for a place near Baghdad, Iraq, that had been severely impacted by bombing raids.

I shapeshift into one of my allies and travel in the Middle World to this place, taking time to fully experience the journey. As I arrive, I call the spirit of place and ask permission to perform a healing. The spirit shows itself as a young woman in a long light-blue robe, with long hair. Her face expresses great sadness and her entire body speaks of pain. I know she is telling me there is much sadness and pain here. She smiles and gives me permission to proceed.

As an ally, I sense what to do in a different way from when I am myself. I start circling around the place, running. I call upon other local spirits, which, in animal and other forms, appear and join me in running. Working with several other spirits, we bring together into the middle of our circle some water from a nearby river, some dirt from the ground, a pocket of air, and light rays from the sun.

As we bring the elements together, a huge canvaslike structure appears, covering the entire area about twenty feet above the ground. The area now lies in semidarkness. We place ourselves at the edges of the canvas, surrounding the area as if to hold the structure there. Then, very softly and slowly, the canvas disintegrates into millions of tiny specks that fall onto the ground like tiny, shining raindrops.

Along with the other spirits, I start crisscrossing the area, moving in all directions, until a huge pattern of shiny intersecting lines is woven over it. As we return to the surrounding circle, I see the lines slowly melting and sinking into the ground. There is a sense of peace and tranquility. I can feel the healing energy. I thank the spirit beings around me, thank and honor the spirit of place, and journey back in the Middle World. Back home, I shapeshift back into myself.

This kind of world work can also be done without shapeshifting. If you do so, it is important to do the Middle World journey to the chosen place accompanied by your allies or other helping spirits. Because the healing energy comes from the spirit world, it is important to let the allies and other spirits do the healing work and to cooperate with their instructions.

As I found in my journey to Baghdad, spirits—in this case the spirit of place—sometimes show themselves as sick, wounded, or depressed. But they are not actually so afflicted; these are characteristics of the dualistic, ordinary physical world. The spirit world is nondual, and these states are ordinary-reality phenomena. The spirits' appearance simply contains a message for us. You may feel a strong desire to heal these spirits as the spiritual or shamanic ego attempts to take over and to blissfully—though inappropriately—work to heal the spirit. This is a case of anthropomorphic projection onto the spirit world. *Remember: what needs healing is the place, not the spirit.*

Multiple Shapeshifting and Group World Work

Another application of shapeshifting in doing world work is to use multiple shapeshifting coupled with the concept of building internal harmony within so as to transmit harmony externally through the web of interconnections. One example of this type of world work is to support our fellow human beings in places where there is disharmony, such as regions of conflict or war, with much pain on all sides. The work can be particularly powerful if done with a group of shamanic practitioners; this is group world work.

Shapeshifting as a Group

The group decides on a particular region, and everyone journeys there together in the Middle World, asking their allies to guide them to the appropriate place. Once there, people sit in a circle in the Middle World and ask the spirit of place for permission to do the work. Then, with the help of their helping spirits, everyone selects three allies and multiple-shapeshifts into those three animals. At that point there is nothing else to do except to be and to feel harmony rising within. The intention is for this profound inner harmony to spread to the region and the people there. It is an offering. There are no judgments, desires, or expectations. When the work is completed, perhaps at the callback if there is drumming, everyone returns and shapeshifts back into themselves.

Acknowledging and Honoring the Authentic Being of a Societal Leader

In chapter 8 on shamanic practice in professional life, I described the practice of journeying in the Middle World to meet the soul or authentic being of a colleague, client, or associate. The intention is solely to acknowledge and honor the authentic being or divinity of the person. The same practice can be used for world work. In this case the person could be someone with influence on the national or international scene: a government leader, a politician, a terrorist leader.

This is not easy work to do, particularly with people we greatly dislike. The intention must be to acknowledge and honor their authentic being, nothing else: no judgment, manipulation, beliefs, desires, or expectations. When people in my workshops ask what they can do shamanically concerning a situation with a government leader they strongly dislike and disagree with, I propose this practice of journeying to that person's authentic being. This suggestion is often initially met with resistance or disbelief: how can we stand to journey to and honor the authentic being of such a terrible person?

The key is to understand that we need not agree with the person or their behavior. And such a journey does not preclude taking action in ordinary reality to try to remedy any harmful acts the person may have committed. But we have a choice. Either we acknowledge and honor the authentic being of the person, which is pure and divine, or we send negative and hostile energy. I submit that in the latter case, we merely contribute further to the disharmony, violence, or negativity of the situation.

Group World Work Using an Ancient Celtic Practice

One of my spirit guides, an ancient Celtic shaman from southern Belgium, gave me the following practice, which is done in a group. Working with spirits, we set the intention to bring peace, compassion, and harmony to our planet and its inhabitants. The practice can be used for a region of the planet, several regions, or the entire planet. Here, as for all world work, it is important for group participants to empty themselves of judgments, beliefs, and expectations.

A Celtic World Work Practice

Group participants sit in a circle. With the help of spirits and in the Middle World, the leader or someone else the group has designated places a big empty cauldron in nonordinary reality in the middle of the room. In the first phase, participants drum together, journey in the Middle World, and ask spirits to come into the room and put "nuggets" of energy into the cauldron that will bring peace, compassion, and harmony. They each call upon their own spirits, then spirits from nature, the place, the room, the cosmos, ancestors, little people such as fairies, and so on as they choose. All can see the cauldron filling up as a multitude of spirits gathers around it.

After a while, the drumming stops and the work of filling up the cauldron ceases. Then, at a signal from a participant, the drumming resumes. Everyone journeys in the Middle World, gathering as a group around the cauldron, taking hold of it together, and flying with it in a pre-agreed-upon direction. As they fly with the cauldron, they tip it so the "nuggets" can spill out and rain over the earth.

For example, the group can travel around the planet, moving in a zigzag fashion, staying longer over areas that need more healing. It is important to perceive the others in the group flying and holding the cauldron together. Being a nonordinary-reality cauldron, it will not empty of "nuggets" until the group has returned. All return as a group and, at a participant's signal, the drumming stops.

It is important here again to emphasize that participants are not doing anything to anyone without their permission, which would be unethical. This is an offering of nuggets. It is up to nature and people to choose to work with them or not. In my experience of doing this practice with various groups, I have seen that the work leads to a strong sense of inner harmony and interconnectedness among the group, which by itself is a powerful healing.

Psychopomp World Work

The last example of world work I will describe involves the psychopomp practice in areas that have seen war, terrorist attacks, and major natural disasters. In the psychopomp I described in chapter 4, one helps souls of deceased people who are stuck in the Middle World cross over and move to the light. For individuals who have been trained in the psychopomp practice, it is important to carry out this type of world work because there is so much violence, tragedy, and disaster on the planet. Let me share two episodes from my own experience.

Many years ago when I traveled regularly to Washington, DC, for my work, whenever I had some free time, I would go out and jog for an hour or more. My favorite circuit was to run past the Lincoln Memorial, West Potomac Park, the District of Columbia War Memorial, and around the Tidal Basin past the Jefferson Memorial. Near the Lincoln Memorial was the Vietnam Veterans Memorial.

I had been an active opponent of the Vietnam War and had joined antiwar demonstrations with my family. I usually paid little attention to the memorial, but once, as I was jogging past it, a first and last name suddenly came to me. Then an ally of mine appeared and asked that I perform a psychopomp for the person whose name I had been given: a soldier who had died on the battlefield in Vietnam. I was surprised and puzzled, and after a few minutes, while running, I called upon several allies. I did a Middle World journey to Vietnam, was led to the place where the soldier had died, and did a psychopomp.

In the following years, whenever I ran past the Vietnam Memorial, I was given a name and carried out the psychopomp. I learned through this experience that it was possible—with the right intention, attention, and trust—to be in ordinary and nonordinary reality at the same time in such a circumstance. I was able to perform the psychopomp work, being vividly present in the Middle World in Vietnam, while jogging safely through Washington, DC.

The work was emotionally intense. As often happens to me when I do psychopomp work, when I was led to the place where the death occurred, I had a vision of how it happened—and of course it was usually violent. I was then led to the dead soldier's soul to start the work. Usually, after the soul had departed to the light and with the help of my allies and the permission of the spirit of the place, I carried out some form of healing, cleansing, or blessing. A number of times, I was approached by souls of deceased Vietnamese soldiers, who were also stuck in the Middle World and asking for help. Under the guidance of my allies, I performed a psychopomp for these souls as well. The whole experience over a period of years was very healing for me, and I thank spirits for guiding me into this specific work.

During the war in Bosnia in the early 1990s, many civilians, including children, were killed, often brutally. I felt deeply for these children, imagining my own children and grandchildren in a similar situation, and it brought back memories of growing up in Europe during World War II. So I started doing psychopomp work for children who had died and were dying in Bosnia.

I journeyed in the Middle World, and my allies led me to the soul of a child stuck in the Middle World for whom it was appropriate that I do this kind of world work. As had happened in my work with Vietnam casualties, I typically had a vision of how the child had died. I found this deeply disturbing, and after several months of repeatedly doing this work I felt stressed and overwhelmed. Seeing so many children die was too much. This was a great teaching for me regarding the importance of self-care when doing world work. Driven by the desire to help those children, I was doing too much and not heeding my allies' and spirit guides' warnings. They told me to stop for a while; I did so and regained my balance. Humility, knowing that one is not alone in doing this type of work, and taking care of oneself regardless of the magnitude of the situation are essential to carrying out world work impeccably.

Remember, to help bring harmony to the world "out there," we must first work to bring harmony within ourselves. Any judgments, beliefs, expectations, or attachments that we bring with us when we do world work will significantly diminish or even obliterate the effectiveness of the work we do. Loving ourselves, taking care of ourselves, and being at the still point, authentic being—these are what we need to do to help change the world. Then we can naturally and effortlessly love others and the world, and allow everything to move beyond its self-imposed limitations in its own way. Purity and clarity of intention are essential.

13

Healing Our Relationship with Nature
Creating a New Mythos for the Modern World

● ◗ ●

Humans are part of nature, intimately connected with it and dependent on it for existence. Before modern culture disconnected many of us from the environment upon which we depend, we had an instinctive, inherent closeness with nature. The survival and wellbeing of early hunter-gatherer societies depended on an intimate and detailed knowledge of their surroundings, writes Hugh Brody in his book *The Other Side of Eden: Hunters, Farmers, and the Shaping of the World*. Hunter-gatherers relied on specific observations as well as what we could call intuitive knowledge, often obtained through a shamanic dialogue with spirits in nature. They readily crossed the boundaries between the human and nonhuman worlds in order to acquire knowledge about the natural environment—knowledge they could use to help them navigate ordinary reality.

Thus, the shamanic tradition emphasizes contact and communication with the spirits of nature, manifesting our interconnectedness and helping to bring the spiritual and physical realms of nature into harmony. This is a *work of reciprocity.*

One of the saddest and most terrifying aspects of the modern world is the devastating impact the human species—in particular Western society—has had on the natural environment and on the nonhuman species of our planet. This impact has accelerated alarmingly since the industrial revolution of the nineteenth century. The current state of our environment and the challenges we face in reversing the devastating human impact have been well documented in scientific literature and in popular media. Many have proposed that a key event in our history initiated environmentally destructive patterns: the shift from hunting and gathering to agriculture and herding, beginning about ten thousand years ago. This event brought about a fundamental shift away from knowing the natural environment to controlling and changing it. An excellent treatise on the subject can be found in anthropologist Brody's *The Other Side of Eden.* Other excellent accounts are geneticist and anthropologist Spencer Wells's book *Pandora's Seed: The Unforeseen Cost of Civilization* and Robert Lawlor's *Voices of the First Day: Awakening in the Aboriginal Dreamtime.*

As I mentioned in the preface, part of my career has involved collaborating with others to help inform and set policy. Laws, regulations, and policies are necessary to slow down and prevent further destruction of the natural environment. The past few decades have seen a growing awareness of the need to protect it, leading to the birth and expansion of the so-called environmental movement. Major laws to protect the air, water, land, and threatened species have been passed, primarily in the West, and government agencies are in place to enforce environmental laws and regulations. Public-opinion surveys have recently shown majorities concerned about the state of the environment and seeing environmental protection as a priority for their governments. The scientific community has become increasingly vocal concerning the major threats to our planet and its biosphere, and the protection of the environment has become a major activity of governments.

It is my deep conviction that laws and regulations are not sufficient. Alone, they cannot address our current environmental problems. *There needs to be a fundamental shift in the way humans perceive the natural environment.* Shamanism is one way to bring about such a shift. By awakening within us an awareness of the sacredness and interconnectedness of everything, shamanism provides us with a new mythos, a way of perceiving the world, that can heal humanity's fractured relationship with nature.

TRANSFORMING THE MODERN WORLD'S ATTITUDE TOWARD NATURE: SCIENCE AND SHAMANISM COME TOGETHER

There are five beliefs that I think underlie much of the modern world's attitude toward the natural environment and that have led humans to be so destructive in their relationship with it. It is my sense that the combination and mutual reinforcement of these five fundamental beliefs is responsible for our disastrous impact on the natural world. Knowing myself and from observing others, I know that even environmentalists, conservationists, and others who are working to preserve nature, and even shamanic and other spiritual practitioners who have developed an intimate relationship with the sacred in nature, may still harbor some of these beliefs. Many of us may still think and act out of an anthropocentric sentiment, even if unconsciously. Anyone interested in helping to change our fundamental attitude toward nature must acknowledge and come to terms with these cultural beliefs and look closely to see how they are at work in our everyday lives.

A shamanic perspective and practice, evoking the shaman within, offers a fundamentally different relationship with nature, and modern science is increasingly resonating with the shamanic understanding. Together, science and shamanism are offering us alternative beliefs that, if taken to heart, can help shift the way humanity as a whole perceives nature.

Belief 1: Nature Is an Object

Today we tend to treat nature as a thing, an object. The I-Thou, I-It relationship concept developed by Martin Buber that I discussed in chapter 3 is useful to us here. Recall that an I-Thou relationship is the essence of an authentic, genuine relationship and dialogue. It is between the divine in me and the divine in the other; it is subject-to-subject, a connection. An I-It relationship is a subject-to-object relationship, a separation. In I-It, the other becomes an object, a thing.

Many of us in the modern world often treat nature as an It. We control, manipulate, and dominate it and use it for our own needs and wants. If nature is an object, we can treat it as a commodity and draw on it indiscriminately. We can dispose of our wastes in it and pollute it; we can cut down forests and change the shape of the land as we wish. Nature is assigned an economic value based on its benefits to mankind; as an It, it has no intrinsic value. Kim Heacox, who wrote about his experience as a national park ranger in Alaska, encapsulates well the I-It attitude when he says, referring to a then senator from Alaska, "Landscapes I saw as full (with rivers, ridges, birds and bears) he saw as empty (in need of development and more people)."[1]

As a mammalian species that is part of nature, we humans need to kill plants and animals in order to feed ourselves. In an I-It relationship, we treat these other species on which our survival depends—wild or domesticated—as mere objects, with a monetary value solely based on their being a foodstuff commodity.

While the purchase of a neatly packaged piece of meat at the supermarket naturally leads us to an I-It relationship with the creature that gave its life for us, Noëlle and I recently witnessed a similar attitude in a much earlier part of the food-industry cycle. During a kayaking expedition in the Strait of Magellan in southern Chile, we were invited to visit a large hacienda where thousands of sheep were raised. The owner and his assistants proudly showed us a routine aspect of their work, where young sheep were brutally separated from their mothers and forced into a separate corral. They then had their ears cut and a tag implanted to denote ownership by the hacienda master. Each young sheep had a dollar value—no more, no less.

It is important to emphasize that a sentimental attachment to nature is not of itself an I-Thou relationship. Feeling sad at seeing a deer killed because we find the species elegant, or at seeing trees cut down because they provide such nice scenery and absorb the carbon dioxide we emit in our daily activities, is still I-It. I propose that the environmental movement, while it has been hugely beneficial in protecting the environment and slowing down the human-caused destruction of the planet, is still by and large in an I-It mode. The industrialist or developer looks upon nature as an It, and therefore feels free and justified to destroy it. The environmentalist is dedicated to protecting nature, yet often also sees it as an It; while the protection of nature is vastly preferable to its destruction, a protective stance alone is not enough.

A shamanic practice raises our consciousness and teaches us that everything in this world is sacred. When I contact the spiritual dimension—the spirits of animals, trees, plants, rocks, mountains, rivers—I have a direct experience of the sacred in nature. And this experience impacts my behavior differently than hearing or reading that everything in nature is sacred.

If we deeply *know* that every animal, every tree, every plant, every rock, the water, the air, the earth, are sacred, we will not wantonly hurt, pollute, or destroy them. A shamanic practice teaches us to be with nature in an I-Thou relationship and to see and treat it accordingly. *And seeing nature as a Thou, as sacred, is the fundamental reason we need to respect and care for nature, not because our survival or wellbeing depends on it.*

Hunter-gatherers and indigenous people integrate the principles of shamanism into their daily lives and treat nature in an I-Thou relationship; as Hugh Brody noted in *The Other Side of Eden,* the Inuit have no word for "it" in their language.[2] And the hunter-gatherer attitude toward the animals they kill for sustenance is also I-Thou: "The hunt is something other than mere hunting; rather, it is part of a vitally important relationship. The people depend on the animals, and the animals allow themselves to be killed. An animal's agreement to become food is secured through the respect that hunters and their families show to the land in general and to the animals in particular," says Brody.[3]

In the 1970s, I paid a visit to the author Frank Waters in his home in Tucson, Arizona. I had been much taken by his books on Southwest American Indians, and I wrote him saying that I sometimes traveled to Arizona for scientific meetings and would love to meet and speak with him. He very kindly invited me to spend a day with him. I bought a plant in a flower shop in Tucson as a gift, and when his wife asked me what the name of the plant was, I answered that I did not know; the plant had just appealed to me, as if calling me, and I usually did not pay attention to the names of plants. Waters laughed and said he agreed, adding that botanists give names to plants, but do we ever ask the plants what their real names are? We all laughed, and the day was wonderful from then on.

Waters told me a little story that has stayed with me all these years. It is all about what a true I-Thou relationship with nature is. He said an American Indian elder had recently told him the following:

> You white people are confused, or you have lost your way. On the one side you have your city builders, and when they need to build homes, they come with their big machines and raze a whole hill-top, cutting down all the trees. On the other side, you have your hippies and tree huggers. They will not allow a single tree to be cut down; sometimes they chain themselves to a tree to protect it.

My people, it's different; when we need to build a house, or we need a tree, we walk in the forest and we talk to the trees, and when a good tree calls us, we go over and we ask its spirit permission to cut it down, and we do a short ceremony to honor the tree and express our gratitude. Then when the ceremony is over, we take our axes and happily cut down the tree.

Belief 2: Humans Are Separate from Nature

Today we see ourselves as separate from nature: we are *us*, and nature is *something else*. This, too, enables us to feel justified to use it as we wish, to take dominion and ride roughshod over it. Whatever we do to the natural environment and its creatures can only benefit us and cannot hurt us. This sense of separation from the world, which has deep cultural roots and is reinforced daily by our materialistic way of living, is unnatural. As Robert Bringhurst succinctly says in his book *The Tree of Meaning*, "When you take the world away from a human being, something less than a human being is left."[4]

One of the consequences of feeling separate from nature is feeling separate from nature's inherent rhythms and rates of change. In a shamanic journey to the spirit of the earth, I was given a vision:

I am flying close to the earth and see tops of mountains that have been cut off or damaged and destroyed, and I see people laying large pieces of colored cloth over the tops, as if putting on bandages to heal the wounds. The mountaintops have been razed by coal mining. The earth spirit says that as a result of breaking the relationship to natural time rhythms, the human species is having huge, unnatural impacts on the natural environment.

Natural forces such as wind, water, heat, cold, erosion, and earthquakes modify mountaintops; humans do the same thing, but at a rate that is unnatural. Natural erosion and the breakdown of mountains occur over thousands or millions of years, but we may do it in a matter of months, and the results are major impacts on the land, water resources, and flora and fauna. There are many other examples of humanity's broken connection with the rhythms of nature and our lack of respect for them. One such example is deforestation. Forests naturally lose trees from natural deaths, storms, or the occasional forest fire. The rate at which we remove trees is much faster, leading to destruction or decline of the forests and the loss of habitat for animal and plant species. Another example is greenhouse gas emissions. There is a natural, long-term—over centuries and millennia—variation in greenhouse gas concentrations in the atmosphere, due to natural changes in the carbon cycle and geologic events such as earthquakes. The rate at which we dump greenhouse gases into the atmosphere is much faster, leading to rapid global warming and climate disruptions.

And most humans today have separated themselves from what could be termed "natural time"—the cycles of day and night, the lunar month, and the solar year—and have replaced it with the abstract and mechanical time of clocks and calendars. This separation from natural time manifests and reinforces daily our separation from nature.

Shamanism recognizes that interconnectedness is the fundamental nature of the universe. When I journey to one of my allies or contact the spirit of a tree, a stream, or the earth, I have a direct experience of this interconnectedness. I know that there is a link between us; we are all part of a greater Whole, a greater One. The shaman's relationship with the natural environment is not a dichotomy. The well-known Lakota Sioux greeting "All my relations" expresses well this feeling and knowing of interconnectedness. In discussing native North American sacred plant medicine, herbalist Stephen Buhner has pointed to "the recognition that there is a central unifying force within all things in the Universe, that all life on Earth is related, and is, in fact, kin."[5]

In a shamanic journey some time ago, I was given information about how our interconnectedness with nature affects our behavior toward the natural environment. I had seen an image in a magazine that depicted an American Indian walking in a forest. The caption read, "The right way to live means leave no tracks behind." I had not felt quite right reading that, but did not know why. I did a journey to my spirit guides to find out more.

> In my journey one of my spirit teachers says, "It is impossible to
> leave no tracks behind." I then see a deer walking in a forest, and
> he is leaving tracks and broken twigs behind. Next I see a herd
> of seven or eight elephants walking on a plain and coming to a

stream, about thirty feet wide and fairly shallow. They get into the stream, lie down, and roll over, as if thoroughly washing themselves in the water. They get up and leave, and I see large mud holes in the streambed and changes in the stream banks; the river is somewhat different from before. The elephants have left tracks.

My spirit teacher says that the changes they have left will permit new life to grow; such changes are necessary. I am also shown how birds, and even trees and plants and rocks, leave tracks behind.

My spirit teacher says that leaving tracks behind is part of ecology. To want not to leave a track is to be separate from nature. When one is not separate from nature, one naturally leaves tracks, and these can be beneficial. I understand but do not know how this could apply to human beings. I can see how a deer, an elephant, or a bird would naturally leave tracks that are good, but how can we humans, with all our technological baggage, do the same?

My spirit teacher suggests I contact the spirit of the human species to seek an answer. I have never thought about contacting this spirit before.

I use my intention to call the spirit of the human species. It takes awhile; I walk for a long time along a straight path and come into a temple. At the rear is a seated female figure with a child in her arms. She looks like a Madonna but feels more like a universal mother. I ask who she is, and she says she is the spirit of the human species. She says she has another form, and I find myself in the cosmos and see a large circular form that is emitting intense blue light. It looks like the remnant of a supernova. The cosmic form says it is the spirit of the human species. Afterward, I see the supernova remnant and the mother and child next to one another, as one spirit.

I ask my question about how a human could leave natural tracks. The spirit says that what is necessary is to be in conscious connection with all that is around us, feeling and knowing the interconnectedness. One needs to be aware of giving to the surroundings and receiving from them. All one needs to do is to live within the context of this interconnectedness. Then, as part of life, which is constant change, changes will occur as a result of living within that interconnectedness.

Then the spirit tells me that to not want to leave tracks behind is not only separate, but also arrogant. The spirit shows me the elephants again and says that the elephants alone do not leave tracks; they are cooperating with the mud and the water. As humans walk in the forest, or as deer walk, the tracks left behind are a result of our feet pressing down on the ground and the earth opening to leave an imprint. As we walk on a stick and break it, the stick is cooperating with us. To say we leave no tracks is to ignore this cooperation. The spirit smiles and says the same principles apply when we use our technologies in the natural environment. I thank the spirit and come back.

The shamanic experience of the interconnectedness of everything leads to an expanded concept of ecology. Organisms and the elements in the natural environment are interrelated not only in the physical, chemical, and biological realms, but in the spiritual realm too. This has a major significance for us human beings, for it helps define who we are as a species in terms of our connectedness to the world. Bringhurst says, "Humans, like penguins and seals and lichens and rocks, are interesting because of what they are, but what they really are is in large part a set of interrelations with a world in which they live. The more they recede into a world of their own making, the less truly human they become."[6]

The important concept of boundaries, which we explored in chapter 3 in discussing the notion of impeccability, applies to the concept of interconnectedness and our behavior toward the natural environment.[7] Boundaries delineate the manifestation in the ordinary physical world of individual beings and entities within the One. There are boundaries between us human beings and the natural environment, between us and plant and animal species. These boundaries are permeable. And to preserve harmony and wellbeing in nature, we need to cross them with respect, responsibility, and a balanced exchange.

In discussing the relationship of hunter-gatherers to their natural environment, Brody says, "[T]he boundaries around the human world are porous. This porosity is the way of seeing and understanding the world that underlies shamanism."[8] Referring to the shamanic practice of shapeshifting and the knowledge and respect gained from living the interconnectedness with the natural environment, he adds:

> Hunter-gatherer knowledge is dependent on the most intimate possible connection with the world and with the creatures that live in it. The possibility for transformation is a metaphor for complete knowledge: the hunter and his prey move so close to one another as to cross over, the one becoming the other. Here is an intimacy that secures complete understanding. . . . This ever-present possibility of transformation is both the opposite of, and an equivalent to, control. Rather than seeking to change the world, hunter-gatherers know it. They also care for it, showing respect and paying attention to its well-being.[9]

This is not a call to return to the hunter-gatherer's way of life. It is a call to raise our awareness of our interconnectedness with the natural environment, to feel and live it and thereby know and understand nature. It is a call to show respect and care for our beautiful planet and all its beautiful inhabitants.

Science resonates in many ways with the shamanic principle of interconnectedness. Ecology shows the earth as a web whose organisms are connected with, and dependent on, one another and the elements making up their environment. Break the web and most organisms cannot survive. Another way to think about this is to consider the common saying "We are what we eat." Indeed, all the atoms that make up the billions of cells in our body came from the water we drank and the plants and animals we ate, and the atoms in those plants and animals themselves came from other plants and animals, and so on. Deborah Cramer, author of the books *Smithsonian Ocean* and *Great Waters,* writes, "Carbon is the foundation of life. It exists in every living organism, in every cell. While some is stilled, preserved in fossils over long stretches of time, most is continually recycled. . . . Humans are mostly water and, after that, mostly carbon—carbon that has been passed down through the ages, from the flesh of a fish, the ear of an elephant, the leaves of a plant. Somewhere in each of us is a cell whose carbon elements may have nourished the planet's nascent life."[10] We are indeed completely connected.

The rapidly evolving science of genetics goes further, showing us that, on a genetic level, we are related to the other living species on the planet. Genes within living cells provide instructions for the development and functioning of living organisms. The arrangement of genes in a given species is defined as that species' genome. In recent years, scientists have sequenced—or analyzed and laid out—the genome of many plant and animal species, including humans, and research has shown that we humans share genes with other species. Not only are the human genome and the chimpanzee and other ape genomes similar to within a few percent, but a surprisingly large proportion of genes found in other animals, in plants, and even in bacteria are also found in the human species. For example, recent research has discovered that humans share aging-related genes with yeast and worms.[11]

In his book *Your Inner Fish*, paleontologist Neil Shubin discusses genes shared by humans and other species. He also discusses anatomical similarities, showing that the study of fossils points to similarities between animal fossils and the human skeleton.[12] As Robert Bringhurst has written, "So we ought not to think of ourselves as rising up out of nature or leaving it behind on a lengthening thread. Genetically, we are so deeply enmeshed in the fabric of nature that all separation is an illusion."[13]

Quantum physics also tells us that everything is interconnected at the most basic physical level. All living organisms and everything else on the planet—the rocks, soil, air, and water—consist of atoms and the particles that constitute these atoms. As we saw in chapter 9, all the basic constituents of matter are connected through their overlapping probability wave functions, which define the probability of finding a particle at a specific location. And as we saw in chapters 10 and 11, cosmology tells us that all matter in the universe had its birth in the same momentous event called the big bang and that all the heavy atomic elements that make up our planet and are essential elements in all living organisms came from a gigantic supernova—the explosion of a star long ago: further evidence that we are indeed connected with the rest of nature. There is no separation.

Belief 3: Only Humans Have Intelligence and Are Self-Aware

For many centuries, particularly in the Western world, it has been a tenet that only humans have the faculty of intelligence; we alone are self-aware. The rest of nature is brute and devoid of intentional purpose, and the behavior of other animals is automated, entirely driven by reasonless instinct. And while science has in recent years effectively challenged that notion, this belief in the uniqueness of the intelligent human is deeply anchored in the mind and attitude of most of us.

If we are the only intelligent species, the only one with a sense of self, we have permission to use our unique and superior reasoning powers to mold nature to our own needs, regardless of the destructive impact our actions have. This belief puts us above the rest of nature, in the position of master, with the right to control and dominate. Furthermore, if plants and animals have no mind or sense of self, it is easy to conclude that they do not feel and are senseless of how we treat them. As Gregory Bateson, author of *Steps to an Ecology of Mind,* has succinctly said, "And as you arrogate all mind to yourself, you will see the world around you as mindless and therefore not entitled to moral or ethical consideration. The environment will seem to be yours to exploit."[14] It is clear that believing that only humans are intelligent and self-aware directly reinforces the beliefs that nature is an object and that we are separate from it.

Shamans know from experience that nature is intelligent and self-aware. Indigenous plant medicine, for example, is based on knowledge acquired through the practitioners' intimate communication with the plants themselves. When I communicate with my allies or other spirits of nature, I have the direct experience of knowing and interacting with another intelligence, another consciousness. These spirits have provided me with much teaching and guidance, and I know their wisdom and awareness. *I know they are self-aware and conscious of the Whole and the interconnectedness of all.*

I have found that the intelligence—perhaps I should say the wisdom—I encounter differs among the various animals, plants, rocks, and other natural elements I enter into contact with, and it is different from the wisdom I know in the human species. This is not surprising. And I propose that placing human intelligence above other intelligences in nature has no basis. They are merely different kinds of intelligences.

If we are open to it, animal and plant behavior also shows nature's wisdom and its ability to communicate with us. It is a common experience for me, as I know it is for other shamanic practitioners, to observe animals behaving and communicating in ways that are difficult to label as mere coincidence. For example, as I hike in the hills near my home and have a question in my mind, it frequently happens that a coyote, bobcat, or deer will appear close by and behave, sometimes repeatedly or over an unusually long period of time, in a way that provides clear input into my query. In fact, this happened recently. As I was sitting at my desk writing and asking for guidance from one of my allies, which is a bird of prey, that very bird flew slowly past my window—a very unusual occurrence. In the shamanic tradition, such signs, messages, or communications from nature are called omens or auguries. A benefit of a shamanic practice is that it opens us to these messages.

Other experiences have taught me about communication among different aspects of nature. On a recent hike, as I was going up a hill and approaching an outcrop of rocks resembling a wall laid out across it, I saw four hawks with their talons pointing down, hovering just above a part of the outcrop shaped like a whale, a shape I had noticed before. I shape-shifted into my ally whale and, as I observed the rock carefully, noticed that the shape accurately represented the head and body of a whale, down to a small depression in the rock making the whale's eye, exactly where it was supposed to be. I recognized then that there was communication between rocks and whales, and between other parts of nature, different from the human form of communication yet expressing consciousness. I thought of shapes of different animals in trees and bushes, also always accurately portrayed. This occurs so often it could not be accidental.

Later on the hike, as I connected with the spirit of whale, it told me that nature communicated with itself through the web of interconnectedness, something that we humans perhaps have yet to learn—or relearn—how to do. That night I watched a documentary on crop circles, the strange and often extremely intricate, beautiful, and symbolic designs that appear overnight in fields in different places around the world, with few signs, if any, of someone or something creating them. Those who reject as impossible the notion that the designs are the work of humans frequently advance the hypotheses that they are the work of extraterrestrial beings or entities coming from unseen dimensions, or some other esoteric source, sending a message to humanity. I profess little knowledge of crop circles, but if they are not the work of humans, I wonder if they are not simply a manifestation of the plants' own innate intelligence and if the plants rearrange themselves—perhaps indeed to send us a message.

Another insight I gained from communicating with nature through my shamanic practice is that animals, trees, plants, even rocks, are self-aware, yet our human experience of self-awareness is somewhat different, seeming to focus on the ego. As we saw in chapter 3, only when we manifest authentic being, our divinity, does the ego recede and we become aware of the Whole, of the interconnectedness, of who we truly are. Other species do not seem to experience self-awareness from the standpoint of ego. Is this perhaps because we have a large brain and a highly developed mental capacity, which highlights the ego?

If we see that nature in all its forms possesses intelligence and self-awareness, a truth that shamanic practice brings forth, then our relationship with nature dramatically changes.

Using a variety of experiments carried out with a wide array of plants and animals, from single cells to large mammals with complex brains, scientists have recently shown that they all exhibit intelligent behaviors and demonstrate capacities once believed to be uniquely human. This significant development in the biological sciences is effectively described by anthropologist Jeremy Narby in his excellent book *Intelligence in Nature*. Narby visited and interviewed numerous scientists around the world who were testing various plant and animal species. He tells how they are demonstrating that even simple organisms—such as nematode worms, single-celled slime, and small-brained animals such as bees and birds—behave with intelligence, exhibiting the capacities to have intention, learn, make decisions, deal with abstract concepts, and communicate. Scientists have found the same capacities among plant species. "Science now indicates that plants, like animals and humans, can learn about the world around them and use cellular mechanisms similar to those we rely on," Narby tells us. "Plants learn, remember, and decide, *without brains*" [emphasis mine].[15] He also points out how scientists are discovering that individual cells in living organisms, and even individual proteins, display some form of intelligence, which scientists describe as information processing and computing.

Narby brings a distinct quality to his exploration into the intelligence in nature. As an anthropologist, he has spent considerable time with indigenous people, especially in the Amazon region of South America, and has learned firsthand their shamanic traditions. He has explored with the region's shamans their own understanding and knowledge of nature's intelligence. His experience with these shamans and his interviews with scientists have led him to conclude, "Scientists now confirm what shamans have long said about the nature of nature."[16]

A review of the scientific literature of the past few years shows an amazing array of articles describing intelligent or "humanlike" behavior in countless living organisms and species of plants and animals. Scientists have demonstrated in various animal species sophisticated and adaptable cognition; the ability to make tools and use them decisively to solve problems; the ability to teach, coach, and learn from others and remember what has been taught; multiple ways of communicating, including in some cases the use of some form of grammar and the use of sounds to represent something in the environment; self-awareness or the possession of a sense of self or personal being; altruism and sympathetic and empathic behavior; distinct personalities; the ability to engage in pretend games and make-believe play; the ability to remember the past, plan for the future, and show foresight; the ability to imitate others; a sense of fairness and an aversion to inequity; a basic grasp of abstract concepts and in some cases symbolic thinking; cultural diversity and the maintenance of cultural traditions and conformity to cultural norms; and astonishing use of engineering and architecture, incorporating the use of tools, physical principles, and logic. These examples come from the study of small and large mammals, birds, insects, and fish and other marine life. Such stories and findings are slowly starting to reach the general public media, as exemplified by a 2008 feature story in *National Geographic* magazine titled "Minds of Their Own: Animals Are Smarter than You Think."[17]

This science, while illuminating, is still in its infancy. Studying consciousness in ourselves, let alone in other species, is inherently difficult. We tend to project human traits and abilities onto other species; science often uses human-centered criteria and hence could misread behaviors or abilities in other species whose intelligence may be of a different nature from that of humans.

Jeremy Narby has given much thought to the notion of intelligence as it applies to the study of living organisms. Because he finds the word *intelligence* to often be defined in terms that are purely human, he prefers "the Japanese word *chi-sei,* meaning knowing-ness or recognizing-ness."[18]

Seth Lloyd, a quantum computer scientist from the Massachusetts Institute of Technology, makes the remarkable statement that the elementary particles that make up the universe—such as photons, electrons, or atoms—compute and process information. Lloyd writes, "The history of the universe is, in effect, a huge and ongoing quantum computation. The universe is a quantum computer. This begs the question: What does the universe compute? It computes itself. The universe computes its own behavior."[19] Lloyd uses complexity theory—which explains why classical computers can use a few simple, logical operations to carry out extremely complex computations—to show that the universe's complexity, which we observe around us, naturally arises from its computational ability. "The computational universe *necessarily* generates complexity. . . . As it computes, the universe effortlessly spins out intricate and complex structures," he says, adding that how the universe registers and processes information is "the underlying language of nature."[20]

Robert Bringhurst, who understands deeply the indigenous view of our place in nature, speaks powerfully of the language of the world: "I have been listening to the world for barely half a century. I do not have the wisdom even of a young tree of an ordinary kind. Nevertheless, I have been listening—with eyes, ears, mind, feet, fingertips—and what I hear is poetry. What does this poetry say? It says that what-is *is:* that the real is real, and that it is alive. *It speaks the grammar of being.* It sings the polyphonic structure of meaning itself" [emphasis mine].[21] Nature, in its amazing complexity, astonishing diversity, beauty, and almost infinite array of functions, traits, and abilities, is the manifestation of the universe's underlying computation, the great epic story written in this language. In this sense, there is nothing special about the human brain, which is part of nature; it is just one among a multitude of other manifestations of complexity.

So it is plain that we humans are not the only intelligent species on this planet. Other species display various forms of intelligence. Nature itself is intelligent. The universe is intelligent. Scientists are indeed now learning this truth that shamans have long known.

Belief 4: Humans Are at the Peak of the Evolutionary Pyramid

One of the deepest human beliefs (except perhaps among most indigenous cultures) is that our species is at the peak of the evolutionary pyramid; humans occupy the top place, a position of privilege, in the world. Humans have a much higher value than the rest of nature, and what happens to us humans is what really counts. Hugh Brody has posited that since the agricultural revolution, there has been a tendency to see all changes in human society and the human environment as improvements, an almost religious faith in progress and what has come to be called development.[22] And this viewpoint disregards any impact on the natural environment.

This belief in humans' privileged position is also evident among many of the spiritual and esoteric movements that have emerged in the Western world in the past fifty or so years. These movements usually reject materialism and endorse the good stewardship of the natural environment and peace among humans, and many see or herald the coming of a new and higher consciousness on the planet that will bring forth true peace and harmony. It is sometimes said that the planet Earth will acquire this greater consciousness from us humans, not from other species or the earth itself. This belief, I beg to say, still puts humanity at the peak of the evolutionary pyramid.

The shamanic tradition does not place us in a privileged or superior position vis-à-vis other species. Direct contact and communication with animals or plants through shamanic journeys, shapeshifting, or any other shamanic practice help us become more fully aware that all species are different manifestations of the sacred, with equal value and status in the great scheme of the universe. Shamanic learning makes us aware of our place in the universe; we are different, but equal. There is no pecking order. The poet Skaay, from the Haida nation in the Canadian Northwest, refers to humans as "plain, ordinary surface birds."[23] And this expression of equality of all things in nature finds its expression in the longing voiced by writer Kim Heacox in his defense of the Alaskan wilderness: "I wanted the idea of freedom to apply to wild rivers and bears. I wanted a Bill of Rights for the earth and sky. I wanted an Emancipation Proclamation for the land and sea."[24]

It is we humans who place ourselves at the peak of the evolutionary pyramid. Have we ever asked other species? I have. I have journeyed to my allies and to the spirit of a tree I am close to and asked. The answers were all pretty much in the same vein, with some characteristic humor. My allies and the tree all said that the notion of an evolutionary pyramid was strange. Indeed, it was a self-fulfilling notion; if there is a pyramid, of course someone needs to be at the top. The spirits said that the web of life was much more complex and mysterious than we humans take it to be. The web of life needed to be lived, and then we would know.

For all the great and evident accomplishments of the human species in our social culture, art, and science, our huge and pervasive destructive impact on the natural environment and our brutal destruction of each other through violence and wars hardly support the notion that we are the most evolved species. The great biologist Edward O. Wilson puts a powerful perspective on our place in nature when he says, "If all mankind were to disappear, the world would regenerate back to the rich state of equilibrium that existed ten thousand years ago. If insects were to vanish, the environment would collapse into chaos."[25] Jeremy Narby has posited, with appropriate compassion, that we are a young species, only two hundred thousand years old; that the industrial revolution and ensuing developments have occurred very recently relative to our already short life span; and that we need time to adapt and mature.[26]

When I ask myself as objectively as I can what differentiates the human species from other plant and animal species in the broad realm of intelligence, when I look for what is self-evident, I conclude that we have an unusually large brain with a formidable capacity to invent, make, and use sophisticated and complex tools. While there are other species that also make and use tools, as I described earlier, none of their toolmaking abilities even comes close to that of humans. This ability includes making not only manual and technological tools, but also intellectual ones, such as mathematics, language, and science. Perhaps one of the key things that differentiate human intelligence from that of other species is this unique ability to develop very sophisticated and complex tools.

It is clear, however, that our amazing capacity for toolmaking has been a double-edged sword, as noted in chapter 7. Our tools have been the source of great cultural accomplishments and of great destruction. They have given us an enormous power to impact the planet and all its inhabitants, positively and negatively. They have given us the ability to adapt to many different environments, to control and manipulate the natural environment, and to share these abilities with other humans. At the same time, we seem to lack the wisdom or the intelligence to use them appropriately. As we developed increasingly more sophisticated tools, a process that accelerated after the agricultural revolution, we increasingly lost contact with the consciousness of the Whole and the interconnectedness of reality, leading to disastrous consequences in the use of these tools.

It is also clear that while humans have used their sophisticated tools for destructive purposes, increasingly so in the past few centuries, they have also used their brain capacity and their tools for purposes of incredible beauty, harmony, and wisdom. It is extraordinary that we can discover how our immense universe got its start in the big bang 14 billion years ago and how it has evolved since then, as discussed in chapter 11, and that we can recreate in a huge particle accelerator a state of the universe that occurred a trillionth of a second after the big bang.

A great musician performing Bach's suites for unaccompanied cello is an extraordinary accomplishment by the composer, the maker of the instrument, the performer, and the audience capable of enjoying the performance. And the perfection and harmony of the flight of a small flock of birds over the ocean at sunset is also beautiful and extraordinary. Which is best? Which is most evolved?

I believe this is the wrong question; they are all extraordinary. They are simply different. It is encouraging, if perhaps somewhat ironic, that increasingly in the recent past, humans have used their more refined tools, such as science, psychology, spirituality, and art forms, to try to regain their lost consciousness of the Whole, of interconnectedness. And each of us needs to be aware and remember that this consciousness cannot be found "out there," no matter how beautiful our works. The Whole has no separation. It is already inside us.

Our great responsibility as a species today is to learn how to use our amazing tools in a way that harmonizes with the rest of nature, to use the immense capacity of our large brain as we find our proper role in nature. Traditional hunter-gatherers, like most indigenous cultures today, did not set themselves up above the rest of nature, and they used their tools appropriately. Agricultural society, industrial society, and most of us in the modern world are of a different mind. As Brody points out, however, these two ways of thinking and being are present in each of us, regardless of which society we are born in.[27] The hunter-gatherer values are still within us; the shamanic worldview is still within us. It is an innate potential; ours is the responsibility to find the right balance. The shamanic practice is one way we can do so.

Belief 5: God Directed Humans to Subdue the Earth and Have Dominion over All Living Things

Genesis, the first book of the Bible, is the creation myth or story that has shaped Jewish and Christian cultures, and hence much of Western culture. Hugh Brody has written remarkably and powerfully about the influence of Genesis on the Western world's attitude toward and treatment of nature and other people. He says, "With its place at the center of both knowledge and morality, as the wellspring of Judeo-Christian heritage, and with its place at the source of humanity, surely Genesis was a universal story. Not *a* myth but *the* myth. . . . The images, ideas, and ideals of western civilization again and again take their inspiration and metaphors from the creation story of the Jews."[28] Even though today relatively few in the Western world take Genesis as the literal truth of what happened at the beginning, the influence of the myth of Genesis through the centuries on our unconscious beliefs, thinking, attitudes, and behavior is still very much with us.

Genesis is the story of agriculture, told and written by agriculturists. Brody says, "Genesis is the myth of agriculture and pastoralism, the story that sets the character and consequences of farming and herding. . . . [It] is the creation story in which aggressive, restless agriculture is explained, is rendered an inevitability."[29] Indeed, in his creative acts, God creates the cattle, an act that receives special mention, at the same time that he creates the wild animals and birds. Humans are given the task of tilling the ground and herding domesticated animals. God is very explicit in ordering humans to multiply and to conquer and dominate the earth.

While Genesis makes no reference to the long history of hunting and gathering, it reflects in some of its parts older myths and stories, as is often the case in mythology. Joseph Campbell warns against the literal interpretation of myth: "Mythology is misread then as direct history or science, symbol becomes fact, metaphor dogma."[30] Yet Genesis has been interpreted literally for centuries; it is still interpreted thus by fundamentalist Christians, enhancing a message of dominion and expansion.

The message and injunction of Genesis—for humans to conquer, tame, and dominate nature—has been seen as the word of God for much of the history of Western culture. It manifested and strengthened the four beliefs discussed earlier: that nature is an object and should be treated as such, that we see ourselves as separate from it, that we believe that only humans have intelligence and are self-aware, and that we believe we occupy the top of the pyramid. The influence of Genesis has been felt even in official Western government policies until recently. Kim Heacox quotes Gifford Pinchot, the first director of the United States Forest Service, in 1905, for whom trees were crops: "The first duty of the human race is to control the Earth it lives upon."[31] Robert Bringhurst, referring to the residential schools for aboriginal children on the west coast of Canada that were in operation into the twentieth century and whose mission was to destroy native cultures and impose the new culture of the European colonists, says the schools "taught the subjugation of nature as a duty."[32] The message from Genesis of conquest and domination is not what the shamanic tradition and the shamanic practice teach.

However, as explored in chapter 11, a new creation story is gradually reaching the world's consciousness, and it has the power to transform our beliefs. It comes from the modern science of cosmology, and it tells the evolution of the universe from the big bang until today. It is a beautiful and wondrous story that rivals any other creation story in its poetic and inspiring force. And along with what science tells us about the evolution of planet Earth and the evolution of life upon it, it is a story of oneness, diversity in nonseparation, and equality.

THE TRANSFORMATION MUST BEGIN WITHIN US

In its 2007 symposium "Awakening the Dreamer, Changing the Dream," The Pachamama Alliance made a powerful statement: environmental sustainability, social justice, and spiritual fulfillment are intimately related, it said. Before we humans can respect and take care of the natural environment, we need to respect and take care of ourselves.

I propose that the reverse is also true. Resolving the issue of the domination and destruction of humans by humans ultimately depends on changing our attitude toward and relationship with the natural environment, in the ways discussed in this chapter. This is because humans are an integral part of nature; a human being is, after all, an animal. If we have an I-It attitude toward nature and feel separate from it, then this attitude will include, if only unconsciously, other humans. In many ways, the five beliefs discussed in this chapter also apply to relationships between humans.

A shamanic worldview and practice, combined with science's ongoing discoveries, can help raise our awareness that everything in nature is sacred and interconnected, that there are intelligence and wisdom in all of nature, that we are all equal, and that humans are not superior to other parts of nature.

While it is easy to observe how others are contributing to the destruction of the natural environment, I feel it is important to challenge ourselves to examine how the five cultural beliefs I have outlined may still be influencing our lives and whether our actions reflect our beliefs in the sacred reality of nature. In what ways am I not living from a shamanic perspective? If we truly want to help shift the modern world's attitude toward nature, we must start by looking inside ourselves and facing what we find there, without judgment or shame and with the help of our spirit allies.

The following practice is a deep inquiry into the anthropocentric beliefs that may reside within us.

An Inquiry into Cultural Beliefs We May Hold Concerning Nature

For each of the first four beliefs discussed in the previous section, do a separate journey to a nature spirit, followed by a short ritual. You may select a nature spirit, ask your allies to suggest one, or ask for the appropriate nature spirit to come and meet you. Ask one or more allies to accompany and support you in the inquiry. When you meet the nature spirit, honor and bless it, and ask if it would show you the ways in which this belief may still be influencing your actions and decisions in ordinary reality. Embrace the belief without judgment or shame, and notice where in your body this realization is manifesting. Then ask the nature spirit if it would give you a practice that will help reframe this belief. Thank the nature spirit and come back to ordinary reality.

After each journey, at the appropriate time and place, create a small ritual where you will voice your intention to reframe this belief and to do the practice whenever necessary. At the end of the ritual ask yourself the question: "If nature spirits or the earth said that for life to continue on this planet the human species would have to go extinct, am I ready to accept this?" Notice how your body, mind, and emotions react as you ask, and answer, the question. If you are not quite ready, could it be that there still is some anthropocentrism at work inside of you?

I also recommend that we consider how impeccable we are in our ordinary relationship with nature. Are all our actions guided by the shaman within? This is a daily, continuing inquiry. When I kill an insect that is bothering me, am I aware that I have killed a being whose value is equal to mine? When I pick a vegetable or fruit from a live plant, do I ask permission? Do I express gratitude? Do I offer something in return? When I feed the fire with logs, do I honor the trees whose bodies are turned to ash for my benefit? It is in the little everyday things that often we forget to respect and honor nature. *Remember, the external world reflects the state of our inner life; it all starts with the individual.*

Another way in which shamanic practitioners can contribute is by doing spiritual healing work for the environment, what I have called world work (see the preceding chapter). This can help us manifest an authentic relationship with the environment and can contribute to the preservation and restoration of the natural world by complementing physical and biological preservation and restoration work.

COLLABORATING WITH ALL OF NATURE: A VISION FOR A NEW WORLD

Let me propose that what is needed today is *true collaboration with other species, with the natural elements, and with the planet*—collaboration not only in the world of spirits, but also collaboration in the physical, ordinary world. The spirit and practice of collaboration need to infuse everything from our routine interactions with the natural environment in our daily lives to the crafting of policies, laws, regulations, and international treaties. It means holding the awareness and intention of this collaboration as we go about daily life or enact policies. And it means being open to the unexpected and marvelous happenings that such collaboration will bring about. Imagine legislators crafting a law to protect an endangered species, say the caribou or the black swan, and seeking input from the caribou or the swan. Imagine a regional planning committee working to create coastal ocean preserves and seeking counsel from the ocean, coastal geologic features, and fish and other marine species. Imagine a regulatory body developing rules and regulations concerning the proposed extraction of underground resources seeking guidance from the earth, aquifers, and the resources themselves.

As we confront the many-faceted ecological, economic, and social crises that permeate our world, there is much talk about and emphasis placed, rightfully, on community, on human collaboration and cooperation. We need a much broader meaning of the word *community*, one that embraces all beings on our planet: humans collaborating not only among themselves, but also with all other species and the planet itself.

Here is one example of a first step in that direction: In 2008, the Ecuadorian people and government included in their new constitution an article on the rights of nature. The article acknowledges that nature has the rights to exist and persist, and citizens are given the legal authority to enforce these rights on behalf of nature.

Imagine the power and beauty of the decisions and actions that would result if we humans were to collaborate with all other species and the planet itself in our efforts to preserve and restore the natural environment. Imagine a world where humans carry out their activities, their governance, their social and economic lives, by cooperating with nature, seeing the sacred in it, engaging in an I-Thou relationship with it, and feeling completely interconnected with it. Imagine what might follow if we all recognized the deep wisdom in all of nature, saw everything in nature as equals, rejoiced with nature in being part of this incredible journey that started at the big bang, and loved nature as it is instead of dominating it. Imagine a world where humans use their fantastic toolmaking capabilities to foster cooperation with nature and co-create a peaceful, harmonious, and thriving world.

The shamanic tradition holds the promise of such a world.

Epilogue

I am in the ancient spiritual center of Chavín de Huántar, high in the Peruvian Andes. With me in the main plaza of the ancient ruins are my wife, Noëlle, my sister-in-law, and my brother-in-law. We have just performed a ritual to help us assume our roles as elders in the family following the death of my mother-in-law. As we explore the ancient sacred temples, I enter the galleria. A deep underground cluster of chambers, it holds the main Chavín deity, the Chavín oracle.

As I explore the short galleries and contact the spirit of the deity, I enter a deeper, narrow alley, at the end of which stands the deity's statue—a stele. I can feel its power. As I look at it, though I don't mentally register the animal and human features that are carved upon it, the deity speaks to me strongly. I feel it in my whole body, even if I do not consciously put into words what I hear and understand.

I am pulled, as if by a magnet, to the stele, and I walk toward it without knowingly moving my body. I crash into a glass wall that separates me from the statue—a necessity to accommodate modern tourists. I emerge somewhat from my trance and find that I am not hurt, nor is the glass. I look at the stele, and we continue to communicate. I hear clearly, as if the words were coming right through the glass, that my contribution, my task, is to help lift the veil that separates ordinary and nonordinary reality, to help people see the world in its totality, as it truly is, the reality from which our egos and the modern world separate us.

I thank the deity and am humbled by the task I have been given.

○ ◖ ○

I have now spent nearly thirty years engaged in shamanic practice, daily and in every facet of my life—personal and professional, intuitive and scientific, spiritual and mundane. What have shamanism and my shamanic practice taught me?

That I am one small piece in an immense interconnected web, whether it is called Wyrd, the term my European ancestors used, or by another name.

That I am no more or less important than any other entity in this world; I am no more sacred, special, or wise.

That I have a responsibility and a role in maintaining the harmony of this web as it manifests in ordinary reality: the physical world of space, time, matter, and form.

That I can access this web and communicate with it by entering nonordinary reality, the spiritual dimension of the world. In this way, shamanism has taught me that everything has a spiritual dimension; everything is sacred.

My shamanic practice has also taught me the meaning of free will, the choice I have as an incarnated being to fully manifest my divinity in ordinary reality, in everything I am and everything I do. Free will, I have learned, is the freedom of authentic being, freedom from the dominance of the ego, that persona that we put on ourselves and others put on us and that is not who we truly are. It is the freedom to align my ego-mind will with the will of the Whole, with the will of the One. It is the freedom to align the functioning of that marvelous and complex machine called the human body and its brain with pure consciousness, the spirit that has incarnated this body and brain.

I have also learned that the modern scientific story and the shamanic story look increasingly similar in their understandings of reality. Science has deepened my shamanic practice, and shamanism has guided my scientific and professional practice.

Shamanic traditions and practices are not static: they evolve, adapting to the natural, social, cultural, and socioeconomic conditions of the tribe, the community, the people. I have felt the call to help evolve a shamanic practice that serves our world today as we all really live it, with all its trappings and shortcomings, with its miraculous inventions and discoveries, and with its myriad blessings. This modern version of shamanism, while it looks different from the shamanic traditions of the past and those found today among indigenous people, is firmly rooted in basic shamanic principles. I wrote this book to serve as a bridge between our modern world and those time-honored principles. As such, it continues the tradition of adapting shamanism to the totality of the human environments of the time.

We can learn from existing indigenous shamanic traditions and call upon our ancestral roots, whatever they may be, in this process of adapting shamanism to life today. Yet it is only through contact with the spiritual dimension of our present reality—with the sacred in the here and now—that we can evolve and create a shamanic tradition adapted to the realities of modern life.

This book is an offering to that collective task. I hope it will help open doorways to the shaman within.

Notes

CHAPTER 1   What Is Shamanism?

1. Hugh Brody, *The Other Side of Eden: Hunters, Farmers, and the Shaping of the World* (New York: North Point Press, 2001).
2. For example, see Joseph Campbell, *Historical Atlas of World Mythology, Volume I: The Way of the Animal Powers* (New York: Harper & Row, 1988).
3. John Matthews, *The Celtic Shaman* (Rockport, MA: Element, 1992). Tom Cowan, *Fire in the Head: Shamanism and the Celtic Spirit* (San Francisco: HarperSanFrancisco, 1993). Brian Bates, *The Way of Wyrd* (San Francisco: HarperSanFrancisco, 1992).
4. Tom Cowan, *Yearning for the Wind: Celtic Reflections on Nature and the Soul* (Novato, CA: New World Library, 2003).
5. Mircea Eliade, *Shamanism: Archaic Techniques of Ecstasy* (Princeton, NJ: Princeton University Press, 1972), 4.
6. Michael Harner, *The Way of the Shaman* (New York: Harper & Row, 1980).
7. Eliade, *Shamanism,* 4–6.
8. Shirley Nicholson, compiler, *Shamanism: An Expanded View of Reality* (Wheaton, IL: The Theosophical Publishing House, 1987). See also Eliade.
9. Michael Harner, "Science, Spirits, and Core Shamanism," *Shamanism* 12, no. 1 (Spring/Summer 1999).

CHAPTER 2   Shamanism as a Spiritual Path

1. Eliade, *Shamanism,* 508.
2. Ibid., 265.

3. Joseph Campbell, *Myths to Live By* (New York: Bantam, 1988), 266.
4. For examples of their teachings, I recommend Adyashanti's *Emptiness Dancing* (Los Gatos, CA: Open Gate Publishing, 2004) and Gangaji's *The Diamond in Your Pocket: Discovering Your True Radiance* (Boulder, CO: Sounds True, 2005).
5. Meister Eckhart, quoted by Joseph Campbell in Diane Obson, ed., *Reflections on the Art of Living: A Joseph Campbell Companion* (New York: HarperPerennial, 1991), 115.
6. Obson, 114–115.
7. Jeremy Narby and Francis Huxley, eds., *Shamans Through Time: 500 Years on the Path to Knowledge* (New York: Jeremy P. Tarcher/Putnam, 2001).
8. Adyashanti, *My Secret Is Silence* (Los Gatos, CA: Open Gate Publishing, 2003), 1.
9. Joseph Campbell, *The Hero with a Thousand Faces* (Princeton, NJ: Princeton University Press, 1973).
10. See Ward Rutherford, *Celtic Lore: The History of the Druids and Their Timeless Traditions* (London: Thorsons/Aquarian, 1993); Caitlín Matthews, *The Elements of the Celtic Tradition* (Longmead, Shaftesbury, Dorset: Element Books, 1989); Jean Markale, *Les Celtes et la Civilisation Celtique* (Paris: Éditions Payot, 1992); and John Matthews, *The Celtic Shaman,* as well as Cowan, *Fire in the Head,* and Bates, *The Way of Wyrd.*

CHAPTER 3 Impeccability and the Art of Living

1. Obson, 136.
2. Ibid., 136, 279.
3. Ibid., 209.
4. For more on mindfulness practice and its effects on health, see Jon Kabat-Zinn, *Wherever You Go There You Are: Mindfulness Meditation in Everyday Life* (New York: Hyperion, 1994).
5. Byron Katie with Stephen Mitchell, *Loving What Is: Four Questions That Can Change Your Life* (New York: Harmony Books, 2002). See also thework.com.

6. John J. Prendergast, PhD, personal communication to Noëlle Poncelet.

7. Noëlle's methodology is based on works such as Hal Stone and Sidra Stone, *Embracing Our Selves: The Voice Dialogue Manual* (Mill Valley, CA: Nataraj Publishing, 1989); Richard Schwartz, *Internal Family Systems Therapy* (New York: The Guilford Press, 1995); and Maggie Phillips and Claire Frederick, *Healing the Divided Self: Clinical and Ericksonian Hypnotherapy for Post-Traumatic and Dissociative Conditions* (New York: W.W. Norton & Company, 1995).

8. Obson, 199.

9. Ibid., 193.

10. Sean Kane, *Wisdom of the Mythtellers* (Peterborough, Ontario: Broadview Press, 1998), chapter 3.

11. Ibid., 102.

12. Ibid., 103.

13. Ibid., 103.

14. Ibid., 104.

15. Ibid., 103.

16. Ibid., 110.

17. Campbell, *Myths to Live By*, 149.

18. For more on the concept of Wyrd, I recommend Brian Bates's *The Way of Wyrd*.

19. Martin Buber, *I and Thou* (New York: Charles Scribner's Sons, 1958).

20. Lawrence Fagg, *Two Faces of Time* (Wheaton, IL: The Theosophical Publishing House, 1985), 126.

21. Ibid., 126.

22. Conscious Speech, Gay Luce, personal communication.

23. Marshall Rosenberg, *Nonviolent Communication: A Language of Life*, 2nd ed. (Encinitas, CA: PuddleDancer Press, 2003); Thomas d'Ansembourg, *Cessez d'être gentils soyez vrai!: Être avec les autres en restant soi-même* (Montréal: Les Editions de l'Homme, 2001), published in the United States in paperback as *Being Genuine: Stop Being Nice, Start Being Real* (Encinitas, CA: PuddleDancer Press, 2007).

24. See, for example, Adyashanti, *Emptiness Dancing*, chapters 11 and 13.

25. This idea comes from Gangaji, who uses the term *spiritual ego* instead of *shamanic ego*. I have heard her speak of it in at least one of her many recorded talks.
26. Questions from Noëlle Poncelet, based on the work of Byron Katie on projections and judgments. See also Katie's book *Loving What Is.*
27. Robert Bringhurst, *The Tree of Meaning: Language, Mind and Ecology* (Berkeley, CA: Counterpoint, 2008), 175.
28. Campbell, *Myths to Live By,* 89–90.
29. Bringhurst, 273.

CHAPTER 4   The Art of Dying

1. Obson, 98–99.
2. Bringhurst, 300–301.
3. Ibid., 302.
4. Eliade, *Shamanism,* chapter 2.
5. Ibid., chapter 6.

CHAPTER 5   The Art of Healing

1. Eliade, *Shamanism,* 182, 326.
2. Harner, *The Way of the Shaman,* xvii.
3. Eliade, *Shamanism,* 216.

CHAPTER 6   The Art of Shapeshifting

1. J. Krishnamurti, *This Light in Oneself: True Meditation* (Boston: Shambhala, 1999), 6.
2. David Wagoner, *Traveling Light: Collected and New Poems* (Urbana and Chicago: University of Illinois Press, 1999), 124–125.
3. John Matthews, *The Celtic Shaman,* 3.
4. Gay Luce, personal communications. I was introduced to this metaphor as a participant in Gay Luce's Nine Gates Mystery School.

5. See for example *Métamorphoses/Metamorphosis* (Montréal, Québec: Guilde Canadienne des Métiers d'Art/Canadian Guild of Crafts, 2006). This book contains photos of the Inuit art.
6. Obson, 265.
7. Adyashanti, *The Impact of Awakening* (Los Gatos, CA: Open Gate Publishing, 2000), 113.

CHAPTER 7 Shamanism in Family and Daily Life

1. James Gleick, *Faster: The Acceleration of Just About Everything* (New York: Pantheon Books, 1999).
2. Thomas Berry, *The Dream of the Earth* (San Francisco: Sierra Club with the University of California Press, 1988).
3. Obson, 90.
4. Sandra Ingerman, *Soul Retrieval: Mending the Fragmented Self* (San Francisco: HarperSanFrancisco, 1991), 165.
5. Joseph Campbell, *The Mythic Image* (Princeton, NJ: Princeton University Press, 1981), 90.
6. Tom Cowan, *Shamanism as a Spiritual Practice for Daily Life* (Freedom, CA: The Crossing Press, 1996). Evelyn Rysdyk, *Modern Shamanic Living: New Explorations of an Ancient Path* (York Beach, ME: Samuel Weiser, 1999).

CHAPTER 8 Shamanism in Professional Life

1. Gary Doore, ed., *Shaman's Path: Healing, Personal Growth and Empowerment* (Boston: Shambhala, 1988). See also Eliade, *Shamanism,* and Harner, *The Way of the Shaman.*
2. Miranda Green, ed., *The Celtic World* (New York: Routledge, 1995), 423–442. Markale, *Les Celtes et la Civilisation Celtique,* 187–201.
3. Noëlle presented her work under the title "The Client's Inner Guide as Mentor and Co-Therapist" at the Eighth International Congress on Ericksonian Approaches to Hypnosis and Psychotherapy and the Milton H. Erickson Centennial, Phoenix, Arizona, December 5–9. 2001.

CHAPTER 9   Shamanism and Modern Scientific Discovery

1. Richard Wolfson, *Simply Einstein: Relativity Demystified* (New York: W.W. Norton & Company, 2003).
2. Mircea Eliade, *Cosmos and History: The Myth of the Eternal Return* (Princeton, NJ: Princeton University Press, 1954).
3. Eliade, *Shamanism,* chapter 2.
4. Ibid., chapter 3.
5. Amir Aczel, *Entanglement: The Greatest Mystery in Physics* (New York: Four Walls Eight Windows, 2002), xi.
6. Ibid.
7. Adyashanti, "True Meditation," article from the website Adyashanti (adyashanti.org): Teachings: Writings (2011).

CHAPTER 10   Journeys to the Spirits of the Cosmos

1. Martin Rees, *Before the Beginning: Our Universe and Others* (Reading, MA: Addison-Wesley, 1997). Alex Vilenkin, *Many Worlds in One: The Search for Other Universes* (New York: Hill and Wang, 2006).
2. Cowan, *Fire in the Head,* chapter 4.

CHAPTER 11   The Big Bang: Cosmic Background Radiation and the Creation Myth

1. Campbell, *Myths to Live By,* 89–90.
2. Michael Harner, personal communication.

CHAPTER 12   Shamanic World Work: Healing the Planet and Its Communities

1. Doore, 11.
2. Sandra Ingerman, *Medicine for the Earth: How to Transform Personal and Environmental Toxins* (New York: Three Rivers Press, 2001).

CHAPTER 13   Healing Our Relationship with Nature: Creating a New Mythos for the Modern World

1. Kim Heacox, *The Only Kayak: A Journey into the Heart of Alaska* (Guilford, CT: The Lyons Press, 2006), 158.
2. Brody, 14.
3. Ibid., 126–127.
4. Bringhurst, 62.
5. Stephen Buhner, "Sacred Plants: Native American Herbal Medicine," *Native Peoples* (January/February 2007), 68.
6. Bringhurst, 311–312.
7. Kane, chapter 3.
8. Brody, 233.
9. Ibid., 242.
10. Deborah Cramer, "Science Notebook: Scientific Observations," *Science News* 174, no. 11 (November 22, 2008).
11. Ewen Callaway, "Common Age: Worms, Yeast and People Share Genes for Aging," *Science News* 173, no. 11 (March 15, 2008).
12. Neil Shubin, *Your Inner Fish: A Journey into the 3.5-Billion-Year History of the Human Body* (New York: Pantheon Books, 2008).
13. Bringhurst, 266.
14. Gregory Bateson, *Steps to an Ecology of Mind* (San Francisco: Chandler, 1972), 468. Quoted in Bringhurst, 174.
15. Jeremy Narby, *Intelligence in Nature: An Inquiry into Knowledge* (New York: Jeremy P. Tarcher/Penguin, 2006), 91.
16. Ibid., 146.
17. Virginia Morell, "Minds of Their Own: Animals Are Smarter than You Think," *National Geographic* 213, no. 3 (March 2008, 36–61).
18. Narby, *Intelligence in Nature,* 138–139.
19. Seth Lloyd, *Programming the Universe: A Quantum Computer Scientist Takes on the Cosmos* (New York: Alfred A. Knopf, 2006), 3.
20. Ibid., 5, 9.
21. Bringhurst, 43.
22. Brody, 138–139.
23. Skaay, quoted in Bringhurst, 42.

24. Heacox, 197.
25. This quote was distributed to participants at a Pachamama Alliance event in San Francisco, California, in November 2007, and was attributed to the biologist Edward O. Wilson.
26. Narby, *Intelligence in Nature*, 82. Also Jeremy Narby, personal communication, October 2008.
27. Brody, 293–294.
28. Ibid., 69–70.
29. Ibid., 96–97.
30. Joseph Campbell, *Flight of the Wild Gander: Explorations in the Mythological Dimension* (Novato, CA: New World Library, 2002), 53.
31. Heacox, 175.
32. Bringhurst, 58.

Recommended Reading

Amir Aczel, *Entanglement: The Greatest Mystery in Physics* (New York: Four Walls Eight Windows, 2002).

Adyashanti, *Emptiness Dancing* (Los Gatos, CA: Open Gate Publishing, 2004).

Jim Al-Khalili, *Black Holes, Wormholes & Time Machines* (Bristol, UK: Institute of Physics Publishing, 2000).

John Barrow, *The Book of Nothing: Vacuums, Voids, and the Latest Ideas about the Origins of the Universe* (New York: Pantheon Books, 2001).

Brian Bates, *The Way of Wyrd* (San Francisco: HarperSanFrancisco, 1992).

Robert Bringhurst, *The Tree of Meaning: Language, Mind and Ecology* (Berkeley, CA: Counterpoint, 2008).

Hugh Brody, *The Other Side of Eden: Hunters, Farmers, and the Shaping of the World* (New York: North Point Press, 2001).

Tom Cowan, *Fire in the Head: Shamanism and the Celtic Spirit* (San Francisco: HarperSanFrancisco, 1993).

Tom Cowan, *Shamanism As a Spiritual Practice for Daily Life* (Freedom, CA: The Crossing Press, 1996).

Tom Cowan, *Yearning for the Wind: Celtic Reflections on Nature and the Soul* (Novato, CA: New World Library, 2003).

Ken Croswell, *Magnificent Universe* (New York: Simon & Schuster, 1999).

David Devorkin and Robert Smith, *Hubble: Imaging Space and Time* (Washington, DC: Smithsonian National Air and Space Museum in association with National Geographic Society, 2008).

Terence Dickinson, *The Universe and Beyond,* 3rd ed. (Buffalo, NY: Firefly Books, 1999).

Mircea Eliade, *Cosmos and History: The Myth of the Eternal Return* (Princeton, NJ: Princeton University Press, 1954).

Mircea Eliade, *Shamanism: Archaic Techniques of Ecstasy* (Princeton, NJ: Princeton University Press, 1972).

John Fix, *Astronomy: Journey to the Cosmic Frontier,* 2nd ed. (Boston: WCB/McGraw-Hill, 1999).

Adam Frank, "How the Big Bang Forged the First Elements," *Astronomy* (October 2007), 32–37.

Gangaji, *The Diamond in Your Pocket: Discovering Your True Radiance* (Boulder, CO: Sounds True, 2005).

Henning Genz, *Nothingness: The Science of Empty Space* (Reading, MA: Perseus Books, 1998).

Brian Greene, *The Elegant Universe: Superstrings, Hidden Dimensions, and the Quest for the Ultimate Theory* (New York: W.W. Norton & Company, 1999).

John Gribbin, *Q is for Quantum: An Encyclopedia of Particle Physics* (New York: The Free Press, 1999).

Alan Guth, *The Inflationary Universe: The Quest for a New Theory of Cosmic Origins* (Reading, MA: Perseus Books, 1997).

Michael Harner, *The Way of the Shaman* (New York: Harper & Row, 1980).

Edward Harrison, *Cosmology: The Science of the Universe,* 2nd ed. (Cambridge, UK: Cambridge University Press, 2000).

Stephen Hawking, *A Brief History of Time: From the Big Bang to Black Holes* (New York: Bantam Books, 1998).

Craig Hogan, *The Little Book of the Big Bang: A Cosmic Primer* (New York: Copernicus, 1998).

Sandra Ingerman, *Medicine for the Earth: How to Transform Personal and Environmental Toxins* (New York: Three Rivers Press, 2001).

Sandra Ingerman, *Shamanic Journeying: A Beginner's Guide* (Boulder, CO: Sounds True, 2004).

Sandra Ingerman, *Soul Retrieval: Mending the Fragmented Self* (San Francisco: HarperSanFrancisco, 1991).

Sandra Ingerman and Hank Wesselman, *Awakening to the Spirit World: The Shamanic Path of Direct Revelation* (Boulder, CO: Sounds True, 2010).

Sean Kane, *Wisdom of the Mythtellers* (Peterborough, Ontario: Broadview Press, 1998).

Byron Katie with Stephen Mitchell, *Loving What Is: Four Questions That Can Change Your Life* (New York: Harmony Books, 2002). See also thework.com.

Robert Lawlor, *Voices of the First Day: Awakening in the Aboriginal Dreamtime* (Rochester, VT: Inner Traditions, 1991).

Arkan Lushwala, *The Time of the Black Jaguar: An Offering of Indigenous Wisdom for the Continuity of Life on Earth* (Ribera, NM: self-published, 2012).

Steve Nadis, "Tales from the Dark Side," *Astronomy* (September 2006), 30–35.

Jeremy Narby, *Intelligence in Nature: An Inquiry into Knowledge* (New York: Jeremy P. Tarcher/Penguin, 2006).

Iain Nicolson, *Unfolding Our Universe* (Cambridge, UK: Cambridge University Press, 1999).

Martin Rees, *Before the Beginning: Our Universe and Others* (Reading, MA: Addison-Wesley, 1997).

Martin Rees, *Our Cosmic Habitat* (Princeton, NJ: Princeton University Press, 2001).

Michael Rowan-Robinson, *The Nine Numbers of the Cosmos* (Oxford, UK: Oxford University Press, 1999).

Evelyn Rysdyk, *Modern Shamanic Living: New Explorations of an Ancient Path* (York Beach, ME: Samuel Weiser, 1999).

Joseph Silk, *The Big Bang,* 3rd ed. (New York: W.H. Freeman and Company, 2000).

Kathleen Dowling Singh, *The Grace in Dying: How We Are Transformed Spiritually as We Die* (San Francisco: HarperSanFrancisco, 2000).

Brian Swimme and Thomas Berry, *The Universe Story: From the Primordial Flaring Forth to the Ecozoic Era—A Celebration of the Unfolding of the Cosmos* (San Francisco: HarperSanFrancisco, 1992).

Steven Weinberg, *The First Three Minutes: A Modern View of the Origin of the Universe,* 2nd ed. (New York: Basic Books, 1993).

Spencer Wells, *Pandora's Seed: The Unforeseen Cost of Civilization* (New York: Random House, 2010).

Richard Wolfson, *Simply Einstein: Relativity Demystified* (New York: W.W. Norton & Company, 2003).

Following are books that had a major influence during my early adulthood on my increasing awareness of "another" reality. They are timeless and I recommend them.

Carlos Castaneda, *A Separate Reality: Further Conversations with Don Juan* (New York: Simon & Schuster, 1971).

Carlos Castaneda, *The Teachings of Don Juan: A Yaqui Way of Knowledge* (Berkeley, CA: University of California Press, 1968).

Louis Pauwels and Jacques Berger, *Le Matin des Magiciens* (Paris: Editions Gallimard, 1960). Published in the United States as *The Morning of the Magicians* (New York: HarperCollins, 1971).

Frank Waters, *Book of the Hopi* (New York: Ballantine Books, 1969).

Frank Waters, *The Man Who Killed the Deer* (Denver: University of Denver Press, 1942).

Frank Waters, *Masked Gods* (New York: Ballantine Books, 1970).

Colin Wilson, *The Mind Parasites* (New York: Bantam, 1968).

Colin Wilson, *The Philosopher's Stone* (New York: Crown, 1971).

Additional Resources

Association Terre du Ciel: Rue de Chardenoux, 71500 Bruailles, France; terre-du-ciel.org. This organization sponsors shamanic workshops in France.

Tom Cowan: riverdrum.com. Includes Tom's schedule of workshops on Celtic shamanism.

The Foundation for Shamanic Studies: PO Box 1939, Mill Valley, California 94942; shamanism.org. Includes schedule of shamanic workshops by Foundation faculty worldwide, and drumming CDs.

Sandra Ingerman: sandraingerman.com and shamanicteachers.com. Includes Sandra's schedule of shamanic classes, workshops, and trainings; drumming CDs; and schedules of shamanic workshops worldwide by teachers who have trained with Sandra.

The Pachamama Alliance: Presidio Bldg 1009, PO Box 29191, San Francisco, California 94129; pachamama.org. Includes information on the Awakening the Dreamer symposium, workshops and trainings, and journeys to the Ecuadorian Amazon.

The Society for Shamanic Practitioners: shamansociety.org. The society is dedicated to supporting the re-emergence of shamanic wisdom in modern Western culture.

TETRA: Avenue Parmentier 92, 1150 Bruxelles, Belgique; tetra-asbl.be. This organization sponsors shamanic workshops in Belgium.

Acknowledgments

This book, in more than one way, is the product of a lifetime. And I cannot adequately give thanks everywhere it is due.

My first thank you goes to my wife, Noëlle, my life companion for fifty-three years as of this writing. Noëlle has been a constant source of love, inspiration, challenges, and learning throughout the writing and publication of the book. Together we have explored and practiced shamanism for about thirty years, each in our own way, respecting and enriching the other. And we have regularly taught shamanic workshops together in many places around the world.

I want to thank the many men and women I have had the privilege to meet and learn from worldwide, many of them indigenous, for their spiritual teachings and wisdom. I particularly owe much gratitude to my teachers Michael Harner and Sandra Ingerman, who introduced me to the shamanic tradition. I thank them for their emphasis on maintaining the integrity of the shamanic principles and on learning from one's own spirit guides.

I want to thank my high school and university physics teachers of long ago. Early in my life, they instilled in me a love for physics and science and an enthusiasm for discovering, delving into, and getting to know the astoundingly beautiful world we are privileged to live in.

The thousands of students who have taken my shamanic workshops have also been my teachers. I thank them for their love and openness.

I am grateful to those individuals who took the time to read my early manuscripts—Sheryl Cotleur, Tom Cowan, Janique Gascoigne, Gay Luce, David Patten, Maggie Phillips, Ann Poncelet, Eric Poncelet, Ninon Poncelet, Noëlle Poncelet, Steven Poncelet, Augustine Rasquin, Anita Sanchez, and Kit Tennis. Their feedback and suggestions greatly added to the book. And their support, love, and encouragement aided me in my task.

I owe an immense gratitude to Sheridan McCarthy of Meadowlark Publishing Services, without whose competent and careful editing this book would not be what it is. And I owe the same gratitude to my Sounds True editor, Amy Rost, whose creative and insightful suggestions made my messages come through more efficiently and seamlessly. I also want to thank Jennifer Brown at Sounds True for her early support and recommendations.

Many individuals, friends and relatives, have offered loving support and encouragement. I thank them all. Sheryl Cotleur, frontlist buyer, provided valuable information, counsel, and support concerning the complex task of publishing a book. My children, Ann, Eric, Steven, and Janique, and their spouses, were a constant source of support. And I want to offer my deep gratitude to the members of our biweekly drumming circle—Meg Beeler, Christina Bertea, Jeff Brown, Christine Donohue, Cameron McKinley, Linda Milks, Noëlle Poncelet, Sandy Skull, Pat Usner, and Julia Weaver—for their unwavering support and frequent invocations for spirits to help and guide me.

Foremost, I am grateful to my spirit guides and to many other spirits, for their unconditional guidance, teaching, input, and counseling. When I speak with them about the book, I call it our book. It has been a work of heart-full collaboration.

Index

About the Author

Claude Poncelet, PhD, is a physicist who is passionate about astrophysics and cosmology. He has spent his professional life teaching as a university professor and working in the corporate world to protect the environment. He has worked at the state and federal levels on environmental policy and has served as chief liaison on two presidential commissions on sustainable development and environmental quality. He has taught shamanism in Europe, Russia, Ukraine, and North America for about twenty-five years and is driven to help develop a shamanic tradition for the modern world in the twenty-first century. With his wife, Noëlle, he volunteers for the Pachamama Alliance and leads trips to the Ecuadorian Amazon for the alliance. He lives in the San Francisco Bay Area.